A Guide to Publishing User Manuals

User Manuals

KEN WHITAKER

John Wiley & Sons, Inc.
New York / Chichester / Brisbane / Toronto / Singapore

Publisher: Katherine Schowalter

Editor: Theresa Hudson

Managing Editor: Micheline Frederick

Text Design & Composition: Ken Whitaker

Designations used by companies to distinguish their products are often claimed as trademarks. In all instances where John Wiley & Sons, Inc. is aware of a claim, the product names appear in initial capital or all capital letters. Readers, however should contact the appropriate companies for more complete information regarding trademarks and registration.

This text is printed on acid-free paper.

This publication is designed to provide accurate and authoritative information in regard to the subject matter covered. It is sold with the understanding that the publisher is not engaged in rendering legal, accounting, or other professional service. If legal advice or other expert assistance is required, the services of a competent professional person should be sought.

Library of Congress Cataloging-in-Publication Data:

ISBN (pbk) 0471-11846-X

Printed in the United States of America

10 9 8 7 6 5 4 3 2 1

DEDICATION

I dedicate

this book to

to the few people

on this planet

who can only be described as...

Fearless!

TABLE OF
CONTENTS

Dedication   **v**

Table Of Contents   **vii**

Preface   **xv**

1 **Justifying a User Manual**   **1**

Why Even Write a User's Manual? 2

The Impact of Great Documentation. 2

Selecting Hardware and Software 4

    Who's the DTP Market Leader? 4

    Selecting Hardware 6

    Selecting DTP Software 7

    Selecting Complementary Software Tools. 8

The Documentation Process. 9

Fitting into the Development Process 11

    Defining a Set of Milestones. 11

    Role of Documentation Management. 12

    Should You Be Required to Be the Expert? 14

    Is the Writer Really Accountable?. 16

        What if the Product Continually Changes?. 16

        Leaving Time for Research. 17

        Documentation Isn't Informed 17

    Resolving Conflicts in Opinion. 17

    Prioritizing Documentation Tasks. 18

    Translating a Publication to Another Language. 20

    Using Documentation Contractors 20

    How Engineering Can Help Documentation. 21

    How Marketing Can Help Documentation 22

Using the Right Tools for the Job. 23

Make Yourself Printshop-Independent 25
Does Your Printshop Speak Windows? 25
Last-Minute Printer Modifications 26
Ken's Top 10 Guidelines 26

2 Style Design Guidelines   29

About This Chapter 29
Components of a Publication 30
Why Worry about Styles? 31
Defining a Page Design Style 32
Organizing Files In a Publication 33
Using Publication Templates 34
Planning the Publication 35
Binding Your Manual 35
Binding as Copy Protection 38
Determining the Document Size 38
Designing the Page 38
Storyboarding the Publication Style 39
Outlining the Manual 39
Defining a Publication Hierarchy 40
The Page Layout Layer 42
The Paragraph Layer 43
The Graphics and Table Layer 45
The Overrides Layer 46
Writing Style Guidelines 46
Two Different Approaches 47
Using a Reference Approach 47
Using a Task Approach 47
Showing Keywords 49
Showing Out-of-Context Terms 49
Handling Dashes and Spaces 49
Using Hyphenation 50
Showing Keyboard and Display Text 50
Creating Tasks 51
Using Sideheads for Notes 51
Documenting Menu Commands 51
Creating Programming Styles 52
Referencing Files 53

3 Page Layout   55

About This Chapter 55
Planning the Publication 56
Keeping Production Costs Under Control 56
What Size Should the Manual Be? 57

What about Page Count? 58
Laying Out the Page 59
Master Page vs. Body Page 59
Creating a Publication 61
Using FrameMaker 62
Creating a Chapter 62
Saving a Chapter 64
Creating a Publication 65
Using Corel Ventura 66
Creating a Publication 66
Saving the Chapter 70
Adding Chapters to a Publication 70
Opening an Existing Publication 70
Defining Headers and Footers 71
Using FrameMaker 73
Viewing Facing Pages 73
Creating the Header 73
Creating the Footer 74
Creating the Chapter Tab 75
Using Corel Ventura 77
Viewing Facing Pages 77
Creating the Header 78
Creating the Footer 79
Creating the Chapter Tab 81
Managing a Publication 84
Using FrameMaker 85
Keeping Track of Publication Information 85
Adding Chapter Files 85
Rearranging Files 86
Verifying the Page Layout 87
Saving a Template 87
Using a Template to Change the Publication 87
Using Corel Ventura 88
Keeping Track of Publication Information 88
Verifying the Page Layout 88
Rearranging Files 89
Placing Finishing Touches 89
Using FrameMaker 89
Snapping a Page 89
Using Typographic Quotation Marks 90
Typing Key Symbols 90
Planning for Automatic Saves and Backups 90
Redisplaying the Chapter 91
Using Corel Ventura 91
Snapping a Page 91
Using Typographic Quotation Marks 92

Typing Key Symbols 93
Planning for Automatic Saves and Backups 93
Redisplaying the Chapter 93

4 Text 95

Fontography 96
Using Text Characteristics to Advantage 96
Using Font Technologies 97
When to Use Type 1 97
When To Use Truetype 97
Mixing Truetype with Type 1 98
Administrating Fonts 98
Defining Paragraph Tags 99
Basing One Tag on Another 99
Defining a Paragraph Tag 101
Using FrameMaker 102
Using Corel Ventura 109
Body Text Paragraph Tags 116
Serif Font Paragraph Tags 116
Sans Serif Font Tags 118
Using FrameMaker 118
Using Corel Ventura 119
Special Paragraph Tags 120
Using FrameMaker 121
Using Corel Ventura 122
Defining Lists and Run-in Paragraphs 124
Serif Font Paragraph Tags 124
Sans Serif Font Tags 124
Using FrameMaker 125
Using Corel Ventura 126
Configuring for Automatic Numbering 127
Headings 128
Examples of Great Headings 128
Choosing Tags for Headings 129
Using Color and Capitalization 132
Using Rules in Headings 133
Paginating Headings 134
Defining Heading Tags 135
Using FrameMaker 137
Using Corel Ventura 139
Setting Header and Footer Paragraph Tags 141
Sans Serif Font Paragraph Tags 141
Using FrameMaker 142
Using Corel Ventura 142
Rules for Indexing and Referencing 143

Referencing within Documents 143
Using FrameMaker. 148
   Creating an Index Entry 148
   Creating a Reference Marker 148
   Referencing a Marker. 149
   Updating all Markers 149
   How to Handle Unresolved References 150
   More Reference Formats 150
Using Corel Ventura. 151
   Creating an Index Entry 151
   Creating a Reference Marker 152
   Referencing a Marker. 153
   Updating All References 153
   Handling Unresolved References. 154

5   Graphics and Tables   155

Organizing Graphics 156
   Structuring File Directories. 157
   Albums. 157
      What an Album Tracks 158
   Choosing File-naming Conventions 160
Making Artistic Drawings 161
   Drawing. 162
      Using DTP Drawing Tools 163
   How Visio Works. 163
Creating and Working with Images. 165
   Brief Overview of Image Files. .165
Taking Screen Captures 167
   Screen Capturing Options 168
   In Summary 169
Inserting Graphics into Your Application 169
   The Wrong Way to Copy Graphics to Your Publication 170
   The Right Way to Copy Drawings to Your Publication 171
   Placing Graphics as Repeatable Objects. 171
      Using FrameMaker 171
      Using Corel Ventura 174
   Anchoring Graphics. 179
   Captions 179
   Bad Design Examples 179
   Good Design Example. 181
   Using FrameMaker 182
   Inserting In-Line Graphics 189
   In Case You Didn't Know. 190
   Using Corel Ventura 190
Adding Shadows to Graphics 196

Using FrameMaker 197
Using Corel Ventura 198
Adding a Shadow to a Screen Capture 198
Using Photoshop to Create a Shadow 198
Using ImagePals to Create a Shadow 203
Final Note on Image Shadows 204
Adding a Shadow to a Drawing 204
Using the ImagePals Image Editor 208
Preparing Your Drawing. 209
Examples 209
Using FrameMaker 209
Do Shadows Have to Be This Difficult? 211
Using Painter to Add a Shadow 211
Using Alien Skin's Drop Shadow Plug-In 212
Handling Overlapped Image Objects 213
A Quick Overview of Color Separation 214
Choosing the Right Printer 215
Printing the Spot Color Plate First. 215
Printing the Black Plate Last. 216
Color Separating Drawings. 216
The Sample Graphics. 217
Viewing the Color Plates 218
Printers Can Produce Different Results. 220
Color Separating Images. 222
Using FrameMaker. 222
Creating a Spot Color. 222
Creating the Drawing. 224
Setting Overprint and Knockouts 225
Using Corel Ventura. 226
Generating "Killer" Tables 227
Necessary Table Features. 228
New Paragraph Tags 228
Using FrameMaker. 229
Creating a Table Lead-In Paragraph 229
Defining the Table Caption 230
Defining a Table Tag 230
Inserting Tables 233
Changing a Table's Tag Format 233
Multipage Tables 234
Referencing Table Captions 234
Correcting a Table Problem 236
Spot Color with Tables. 236
Using Corel Ventura. 236
Creating a Table Lead-In 236
Defining a Table Tag 237
Inserting Tables 237

Defining the Table Caption 239
Modifying the Table Format. 240
Inserting Graphics in Tables. 241
Using FrameMaker 241
Using Corel Ventura 241

6 Overriding the Other Layers 243

Redefining Paragraph Tags 244
Redefining a Paragraph's Text Attributes. 244
Redefining a Paragraph's Position on a Page 245
Using FrameMaker. 245
Overriding a Paragraph Tag. .245
Positioning a Paragraph on the Next Page 246
Positioning to the Top of a Column 247
Using Corel Ventura. 248
Overriding a Paragraph Tag. .248
Positioning a Paragraph on the Next Page 250
Modifying Text with Character Tags 251
Standard Character Attributes. 252
Using FrameMaker 253
Using Corel Ventura 253
Useful Character Tag Definitions 254
Defining Color, Symbols, and Bullets. 254
User-Interface Objects. 255
Software Engineering Character Tags 256
Defining Typographic Character Tags 257
Maintaining Character Tags 257
Using FrameMaker 258
Using Corel Ventura 260
Adjusting Spacing between Characters .260
Using FrameMaker. 261
Using Corel Ventura. 261
Dropping the First Character. 262
Using FrameMaker. 262
Using Corel Ventura. 264
Using Variables for Common Phrases 265
Why Use Variables?. 265
Variables That I Use. 266
Using FrameMaker. 267
Creating and Applying a Variable Definition 267
Updating the Entire Publication 269
Using Corel Ventura. 269
Creating a Variable 270
Inserting a Variable 271

7 Publishing the Book 273

Building Your Publication. 274
   Checking Your Publication. 274
   Inserting a Watermark 275
      Using FrameMaker 275
      Using Corel Ventura 277
Generating an Index. 278
   Using FrameMaker. 279
   Using Corel Ventura. 284
Generating a Table of Contents. 288
   Using FrameMaker. 288
   Using Corel Ventura. 292
Printing the Publication 297
   Determining Color Use 298
      Printing a Sample. 300
   Using FrameMaker. 300
      Selecting the Printer. 300
      Set Up Your Printing Option 301
      Printing the Final Publication. 305
   Using Corel Ventura. 307
      Selecting the Printer. 307
      Setup Printing Options. 307
      Printing the Final Publication. 309
   Providing Specifications to the Printshop 310
   Managing the Print Process 311
      The Blue Line 311
      Managing Quality 312
Backing Up a Publication 312
   Using FrameMaker. 312
   Using Corel Ventura. 313
   Backing Up with Tape Backup Units 314
The Future of Interactive Publications. 315
In Closing 316

Appendix 317

DTP Application Programs 318
Graphics Software Programs. 318
Plug-In Graphic Programs. 320
Major Font Suppliers. 321
Supporting Periodicals 322
Books 322
Miscellaneous Hardware 323

Index 325

PREFACE

With the explosion of desktop publishing (DTP) hardware and software products on the market, the dream for low-cost, professional publishing has finally become a reality for both the growing home office and corporate markets.

It should be no surprise, however, that although software technology continues to advance it can barely keep up with the speed at which hardware innovations take place. Nevertheless, the power of desktop publishing software coupled with high-performance hardware, has made DTP capabilities available to everyone. This is more than evolutionary—it is revolutionary.

Since the early Ventura and PageMaker days, DTP software was always highly capable. Unfortunately, the PC's speed, storage capacity, and graphics resolution was never really up to the task.

However, recently, technology trends like those listed here should make DTP software even more powerful, accessible, and easier to use:

- Color separation and prepress services integrated into the DTP package allow direct-to-press output from your PC. This will enable the emerging home office to produce high-quality manuals.

- Integration with complementary applications enable you to use best-of-breed applications for creating and accessing drawings, images, and other objects through OLE or the Windows clipboard.

- Competition has forced DTP products to provide more desktop publishing tools (including graphics, font management, image manipulation, and so on).

- Workgroup computing means graphics, images, and documents can easily be accessed, archived, and shared among multiple users on a network at the same time.

- High-quality graphics hardware is becoming more affordable, and DTP software tools are constantly being upgraded to keep pace with these hardware trends.

- Publications produced with DTP software are rapidly being made available to other users with suitable document viewing technologies such as Frame's FrameViewer, FrameReader, or Adobe's Acrobat.

The next great DTP wave is the emergence of the electronic book combining documentation, training, and multimedia technologies.

We will purchase an interactive book CD for our home PC much the way we now go to a local store to purchase a music CD.

Using DTP programs to create your books will undoubtedly make you ready for this electronic book revolution. Can you imagine an interactive book that walks you through activities and then tests you at the end of each topic (and records your results)? How about a book that lets you select from several endings? The whole education system is in for a shock not to mention making it more fun.

You may wish to consider the DTP software environment more as a document authoring toolkit that provides everything necessary to integrate graphics, text, and other information. All it needs is a customer base that has a suitably equipped PC.

So why did I write this book? If DTP technology is so plentiful, there should be little need for yet another author's interpretation of DTP software. But, even with all of these software tools, the DTP manual process is still not understood and output results are still not professional in many cases. Why?

Too many steps resulting in many errors   Writers continue to use a word processor to write their text thus requiring a conversion into a DTP application's format which has to be properly formatted and proofed before going to press. This is time-consuming and error-prone and requires figures, tables, indexing, text styles, and other elements to be redone. We simplify this effort (and others) by reducing redundant steps.

Professional drawings   There is little understanding for how to produce high-quality drawings to put in your manuals. How in the world do you produce professional drawings that can be used not only in manuals but in other promotional material? I'll show you which software tools you'll need to produce professional drawings even if you have little artistic talent.

Page design   Writers are typically not font or page design experts. DTP manuals do not really explain how to take advantage of "killer" (good) page design and fonts. I'll present guidelines that make sense along with sophisticated techniques (for elements such as sideheads and complex table numbering).

Screen capture fundamentals   Screen captures often look as if they were printed on a dot-matrix printer. There is no good reference available that shows writers how to make professional screen captures. You don't need special people to perform screen captures—you can do it.

Style guidelines   There are plenty of style manuals available, but is there a condensed version that applies to manual writers? Many of the so-called references are generally geared towards journalists. I'll present guidelines that are useful for manual writers.

Equality   Is there a way to make certain that documentation writers achieve "equal status" in the development organization? Writers are typically left in the dark during a project and then expected to achieve miracles at the end of the development cycle. I will dispel the myths and present techniques that work (note, your fellow product development engineers may not be happy with this information).

Graphics and separating color   Graphics formats and color separation fundamentals don't have to be that difficult to understand—all writers should understand the fundamentals. Most of the books that cover graphics get so complex most folks just plain don't understand it (and, frankly, pray that they never have to understand it). I'll present this information in a way that simplifies a very complex subject.

A Guide to Publishing User Manuals is designed as a practical how-to book for those folks whose job it is to write manuals, or for those development engineers forced to write a manual for a product they just invented.

Although this book focuses on writing manuals for the software industry, the contents also apply to producing usable documentation for most any product or service.

We review book building techniques in theory, then show you how to apply them using the best Windows-based DTP book building products (FrameMaker and Corel Ventura) while showing how great graphics tools (Visio, ImagePals, Photoshop, and others) can turn a small investment into a professional DTP operation.

On June 22, 1995, Adobe Systems announced the intention of acquiring Frame Technology. This makes this book even more important. This signals the war between Adobe's FrameMaker and Corel's Ventura.

Note that I do assume that you understand the fundamentals of using either Windows, FrameMaker, or Corel Ventura.

Chapter 1 explains the reasons for writing a manual and how the documentation effort fits into product development.

NOTE The OOP zealots will probably claim that C++ is not really object-oriented. Don't believe them.

Chapter 2 describes a view of the natural hierarchy of DTP documents and writing style guidelines. I present a way to look at the construction of a document that is reminiscent of an object-oriented C++ program.

Chapter 3 summarizes the base page layout fundamentals you should consider before you write a single word.

Chapter 4 focuses on the text flows and fully describes text style fundamentals and guidelines. There are plenty of bad examples to learn from.

Chapter 5 describes the incorporation of images, screen shots, drawings, tables, and other objects that frequently add pizazz to otherwise boring documents.

Chapter 6 discusses how to override page layout, text flows, and graphics (and other objects). How you do this is particularly important especially, if you have to make last minute changes.

Chapter 7 focuses on the printing task, when we finally see the output. I'll present techniques to minimize errors that result from the misuse of font technology, ill-conceived color separation, and other topics.

In the Appendix, I present my top list of great products and complementary books that will help you produce professional results.

This book was produced using FrameMaker version 5 for Windows using Type 1 fonts distributed by Adobe: Avantgarde, Helvetica Neue, Optima, Stone Informal, Stone Serif, Tekton, and Zapf Dingbat. Drawings were created using Visio version 3 and screen captures were taken and processed using ImagePals version 2. The operating system used for examples was Windows 95.

1 JUSTIFYING A USER MANUAL

Are you "getting grief" from your company's management about even writing a manual? Has someone said to you, "Nobody reads 'em, anyway!"

NOTE The terms manual and publication are used synonymously throughout this book.

Don't despair! No matter how intuitive a product claims it is supposed to be, your customers will always need a manual describing it, whether your manual is on paper or interactive.

We'll cover the following topics in this chapter:

- Why manuals are necessary.
- Why it's okay to use a PC.
- Documentation's role in the documentation process.
- Where the documentation group fits in with product developers and marketing.
- Choosing the right tools.
- Planning to be printshop-independent so that you can select the lowest-cost, highest-quality vendors.
- Establishing some basic DTP ground rules.

WHY EVEN WRITE A USER'S MANUAL?

As software becomes easier to use, is there still a need for documentation? Why is a user manual necessary these days?

To assist in the use of the product As the name implies, a user manual should be designed to assist the user. If the user feels like the documentation is not going to help him or her use the product, then the goal has not been met.

Aid in customer satisfaction I can only think of the so-called simplified documentation that comes with VCRs. No matter how easy the manual explains the operation of the VCR, it is next to impossible to learn how to program recordings for specific times. Just because you have documentation does not mean the user can make it operate correctly. Documentation should relieve stress, and the writer should put him or herself in the customer's shoes.

NOTE I prefer calling the technical support organization *customer support*.

Reduce calls to technical or customer support We'll get into this later—but your real customer is right down the hall! The sanity of your company's technical support depends primarily on the effectiveness of your documentation.

Use the best medium The term documentation does not necessarily mean that the delivery medium has to be paper. In fact, a combination of paper documentation plus on-line documentation is often spectacular and shows your customers that you are providing state-of-the-art information, where the manual can be thumbed through and the on-line assistance can interact with the user the instant a topic is being questioned.

By the way, don't think that if you are expected to put all documentation on-line, it will take less time to construct. It sometimes takes more time.

THE IMPACT OF GREAT DOCUMENTATION

The packaging of software products can influence the customer. Since shelf space is at a premium, streamlined and colorful product packaging has made it possible for major retailers to sell software as easy as they sell other products in their store.

The software industry has matured to a point where software merchandising now conforms to Retailing 101. Shelf space is minimal, retail pricing is now within the reach of the impulse buyer, and brand recognition attracts customers to purchase, yet requires your salespeople to know little about what the software does.

What does packaging have to do with documentation? The question actually should be the other way around. Documentation dramatically impacts product packaging.

Not including the media (which is rapidly becoming a single CD), packaging is designed around the documentation. The smaller the documentation, the lower the cost of goods (COGs), and the less shelf space is used, results in more choices and lower retail costs to the consumer.

A software product's documentation used to be less costly than the many diskettes in a product's packaging. Documentation has now become the prevailing cost of software packages and is becoming optional. For example, you can purchase a CD from Microsoft or Micrografx for software without paper documentation. For an additional charge, you can order the documentation.

On one hand, this is frustrating to a customer who says, "Documentation should come with the software! Why should I have to pay extra?" On the other hand, it gives the customer the option to buy the software for less if they find that they rarely refer to paper documentation. In most cases where printed documentation is optional or not even available, documentation is available on-line to assist the customer to still access how-to information.

Mark my words: the Mom-and-Pop software store will become a dinosaur replaced by retailers that sell software along with other commodity items such as books, music, and electronics.

Who will need trained salespeople knowledgeable about the software when advertising and magazine articles will take care of informing potential customers which software product is right for them?

Who will need telephone support when applications software is uniform due to user interface standards. If you do need help and can't understand the manuals, you can always call a 1-900 phone number or register with one of several customer support plans. It benefits *everyone* (especially your company and your customer) to produce great documentation.

Unfortunately, too often product development shops put little emphasis on documentation issues until after the product ships! Then, all of a sudden, quality of the documentation becomes a high priority problem.

More on this later...

SELECTING HARDWARE AND SOFTWARE

Before we answer this question let's look at the market.

Who's the DTP Market Leader?

NOTE By print-shop, I'm referring to the folks that perform the final production steps.

Many desktop publishing books focus on Macintosh-based DTP solutions. Until recently, there were few books on DTP fundamentals for Windows. For us Windows users, publishing books professionally can be a nightmare since most printshops still only support Mac files.

According to International Data Corporation (IDC), the worldwide Windows DTP market grew substantially to $172 million with close to 1 million units sold in 1993. The Windows trend is still dramatically growing. And this doesn't include the graphics, drawing, and imaging market.

As you might expect, PageMaker has the lion's share of the desktop publishing market. PageMaker is a spectacular DTP program, unfortunately with few book building features. Following in the distance is QuarkXPress, FrameMaker, and Corel Ventura. The remainder of the market is owned by those DTP products that are used primarily for single page, newsletter productions and not for full-scale manual publishing.

Figure 1.1
1994 NADTP
reader's survey.

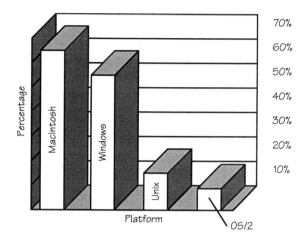

Source: National Association of Desktop Publishers (NADTP)

Figure 1.1 shows the response to a 1994 NADTP (National Association of Desktop Publishers) journal survey of its readership asking what platforms they use for DTP and graphics projects.

Surprisingly, Windows usage was very close to the Macintosh. In my estimation, Windows usage has probably surpassed the market share of Macintosh. With the introduction of Windows 95 and future object-oriented Windows, traditional Mac zealots will be scrambling for cover. Windows has definitely leapfrogged the capabilities of the Mac—even for graphics and DTP software.

The survey also showed that more than 30% of the readers who responded rely on multiple platforms in order to successfully lay out, illustrate, and complete DTP projects.

NOTE Darn, did I forget to mention Microsoft?

The only reason that Microsoft Word is not considered for inclusion in this book is due to its lack of high-precision object placement, convoluted multiple chapter handling, lack of registration marks, and no support for color separated printing. However, Word's features continue to rival that of most DTP products.

Even if your printshop only works with computer files produced on the Macintosh, you should have no problem producing high-quality manuals from your Windows-based DTP files.

Selecting Hardware

Not long ago, the following computer configuration was readily available to support desktop publishing software work:

- 80386 PC with 4 to 8 megabytes of memory.
- 300 dots per inch (dpi) laser printer.
- VGA monitor with 256 colors at 640 x 480 pixels.
- 200 megabyte fixed disk.
- Black-and-white or low-resolution color hand scanner.
- Just a few high-quality fonts (most of them expensive).
- Mouse and keyboard.

Now, what do we see?

- Fast PCs (Pentium processors and even faster) with at least 16 megabytes of memory.
- 1200 dpi laser printers.
- 21" monitor with video adapter supporting true color (in excess of 16 million colors) at 1600 by 1280 pixels.
- At least 1GB fixed disk.
- Medium-resolution color page scanner (at least 1200 dpi).
- Hundreds of high-quality fonts (worth the price of CorelDRAW to just get the fonts).
- Quad-speed CD ROM player.
- Network card (usually Ethernet compatible).
- Mouse and keyboard.

The only elements that appear to be similar in both of these lists are the mouse and keyboard! I recommend that you use as powerful a computer system as you can afford. "Killer" PCs should not just go to the programmers. DTP and graphics software applications really exercise a computer—any system with less than top-flight, accelerated hardware just won't do.

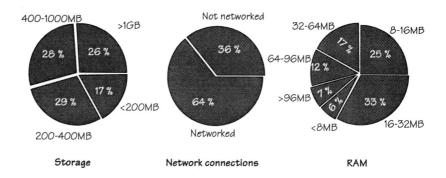

Figure 1.2
1994 Publish magazine reader's survey.

Source: Publish magazine

In late 1994, Publish magazine surveyed its readership to get a handle on hardware configurations used with DTP and graphics software. As the results in Figure 1.2 show, the trend is definitely towards using more RAM, sharing information on a network, and larger disk storage.

Now, I suspect that fixed disk storage used in DTP environments include 2GB, all systems networked, and RAM no less than 24MB. How times have changed.

Selecting DTP Software

We are going to use the following DTP applications throughout the book (presented in alphabetical order):

- Corel Ventura, version 5 (also applies to version 6) from Corel Corporation.
- FrameMaker, version 5 from Frame Technology Corporation.

If you haven't chosen DTP software for manual production yet, this book could actually assist you in selecting the best desktop publishing product for your needs.

In addition, these DTP products work extremely well under Windows 95 or Windows NT. In fact, the examples used in this book are taken using the advanced user interface of Windows 95.

How did I select the DTP products I just listed? In order for a DTP product to qualify for use in manual writing, it should possess the following features (not in priority order):

- Ability to handle long, multiple-file publications.
- Support for network access so that multiple writers can work on a publication at the same time.
- Ability to generate lists for tables of contents and indexes.
- High degree of control of typography.
- Styles for many DTP objects including paragraphs, characters, tables, and graphics frames.

How do the DTP programs measure up to our requirements? FrameMaker and Corel Ventura are easy choices—both are the best long-document DTP products available on the market. FrameMaker has just erupted onto the Windows scene, and although Corel Ventura had all but dropped out of sight under Xerox management, don't count out Corel Corporation's marketing prowess to turn around what I feared was essentially a dead product just a few years ago.

I'll highlight how specific user manual activities are performed with each DTP application.

Selecting Complementary Software Tools

I'll focus on several great products that can be used in conjunction with the already mentioned DTP products:

Drawing   Visio, version 3 from Shapeware Corporation.

Screen capture and image management   ImagePals, version 2 from Ulead Systems Incorporated.

Image and Painting   Photoshop, version 3 from Adobe Systems Incorporated and The Black Box, version 2 imaging filters from Alien Skin Software (yep, that's their name!).

Font management   FontMinder, version 2.5 from Ares Software Corporation and Type 1 fonts distributed by Adobe, Bitstream, and Monotype.

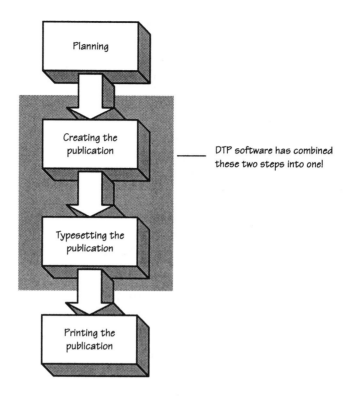

Figure 1.3
The documentation process.

DTP software has combined these two steps into one!

THE DOCUMENTATION PROCESS

Let's divide the process of user manual building into four simple steps, which are illustrated graphically in Figure 1.3.

1. Planning.
2. Creating the publication.
3. Typesetting the publication.
4. Printing the publication.

Planning   The first step is to plan the activities:

- Choosing personnel and the headcount needed.
- Choosing necessary software and hardware DTP tools.
- Coordinating with printshop.
- Generating documentation plans and getting buy-in.

Creating the publication   This step involves the creation of text and graphics (drawings, images, screen shots, and so on). Although this step usually requires the use of multiple software applications, publication files become the central storage container of all of the text and graphics objects to be included in the final publication output.

Typesetting the publication   Typesetting is the act of getting all of the publication's components in their final form so that you can go into final printing. This step is typically called production.

It is the role of DTP software to combine this step with the step of creating the publication. And why not? Sometimes the page design can actually influence the flow of text.

I guarantee that I considered how I place text around tables and figures which Wiley (my publisher) insists be at either a top or bottom page boundary.

As long as every writer in your organization follows typographic page design guidelines, you can skip the separate typesetting step. The publication will always be typeset during the initial design step.

There's another major benefit. This combined step could eliminate the need to hire someone to move text, graphics, and even chapters around later (and possibly lose the writer's original intentions).

Printing the publication   I know, I know. I've mentioned before that paper is not necessarily going to be the output medium. Whether you print on paper or create a CD, the fact is that you ultimately produce the manual on something.

What is documentation's role at print? Documentation should review the final masters (the blue line) returned from the printshop. The quality control of the actual printing should be performed by the distribution or production organization. The printshop should never be given the authority to modify the master documents.

Since documentation is vitally important to your company's product development activities, I'm going to assume that you need to understand and possibly control each of these steps.

FITTING INTO THE DEVELOPMENT PROCESS

Defining a Set of Milestones

Let's look at a typical product development life cycle in terms of well-defined milestones:

Concept   Marketing presents the idea to executive management in order to gain funding approval— development management is made aware of the concept in advance.

The documentation team is informed.

Proposal   Marketing and development managers jointly prepare a business plan or executive review. This could present a product's scope, competitive outlook, pro forma of revenue and profit, and rough schedule.

The documentation team is formed and is involved in some of the feature trade-off discussions—documentation plans are formulated and headcount identified.

Specification   Development produces prototypes from marketing's storyboards and completes specifications and user testing. Marketing signs off (in other words, approves)— the plans must match what marketing originally expected the project to accomplish.

The documentation team is involved in reviewing the engineering specifications and can assist with usability design issues.

Alpha   Product is functionally complete—but probably crashes a lot. At this point, internal users (within the company) can start working with the product.

NOTE Can't afford to bring in customers? Use your sales people instead!

Comprehensive documentation plans can now be written — writing starts in haste. This is a a great time to bring in key customers to have them look at your sample documentation changes and plans.

Once alpha is achieved, early draft documentation should be ready for review. Since the product's user interface is probably not stabilized, make reference to screen shots or diagrams that will appear in the beta milestone's documents.

NOTE Did you know that in the UK, beta is pronounced BEE-ta?

Beta Product you are documenting passes rudimentary tests, which uncover no crashes and is functionally complete. The product is available for external (customer) beta testing. For products that are or will be translated to other languages, now is the time to start performing some sample translations.

Draft documentation is ready to be distributed for review along with the beta product. Sample print jobs are delivered to the selected printshops for tests. It is assumed that page counts, use of color, page size, and choice of fonts are all finalized at beta.

NOTE It is appropriate to have a killer party with lotza beer!

Release Testing has been completed and the product is shipped. Congratulations!

Documentation should have been sent to the printshop in a timely fashion so that when the master diskette media (or CD ROM) is ready, the documentation is also ready.

Post mortem The team reassembles, and hashes out what went well and what went poorly during product delivery. At the same time, the product and all its components are archived.

NOTE Be careful that you are not violating any license agreements.

Copy all of the documentation files, drawing, graphics, and print files onto tape. Don't forget to backup DTP and graphics applications used to create these files.

Where does the documentation department fit into the development process? Is documentation part of the team or isn't it? If it is, do actions by the team to support documentation meet the company's expectations?

Role of Documentation Management

The role of documentation management is to be a valued contributor to the product delivery team. If the documentation team is not a key part of the development process, the quality of the documentation will most certainly be at risk.

But, where does the documentation group belong? Marketing? Get serious!

Figure 1.4
Documentation
department
reporting into
development.

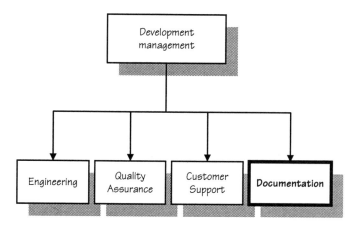

Do the right thing by integrating documentation as a key member of the development staff as shown in Figure 1.4.

In this organizational structure, documentation contributes on an equal footing with the other key development organizations: engineering, quality assurance (SQA, for short), and customer support.

Each organization may have different pay scales and different responsibilities, but no creative product organization can survive without tight teamwork between these departments.

Want to go one step further? For customer support to really be effective with customers, the documentation had better serve their needs. Customer support personnel must take an active role in making sure that the documentation serves their needs, and documentation folks need to be open to customer support's suggestions.

The organization shown in Figure 1.5 demonstrates this commitment if the documentation group needs a single manager (or director) to direct that documentation and customer support members become "blood brothers and sisters."

To make matters even more interesting, why not include the instructional design group with them? Instructional designers create the material for training. Sharing information between documentation and training encourages communication between all departments so that information is shared in a timely fashion.

Figure 1.5
Revised
documentation
management
chain.

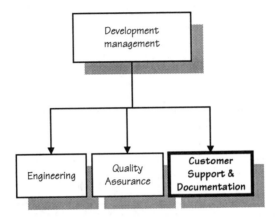

Where is marketing in relation to these organizations? I've seen product managers be a part of development, too. You know, product marketing managers are the ones who dictate which features need to be in the product in order to be competitive and to grow the business.

This may be a good idea when organizations are initially being formed as in a start-up company. In the long run, the organization that works best is one in which sales, marketing, and development are separate organizations, each leading its own turf while aiming toward one common company goal.

What should be the goal? To produce quality products on schedule. Pretty simple, huh?

What's in a name? In some companies, the documentation department is known as technical publications or TPUBS. It doesn't matter what the group is called as long as the name accurately reflects the work being performed.

Should You Be Required to Be the Expert?

Writers are sometimes considered to be English-literate people who aren't technical. In fact, documentation is rarely held accountable for knowing how a product works. Oops.

Well, if that is true, how in the heck can a writer produce manuals if he or she can't understand or gain access to the product that's being documented? Writers need to understand how to use the product.

Figure 1.6
Duties of each
development
group.

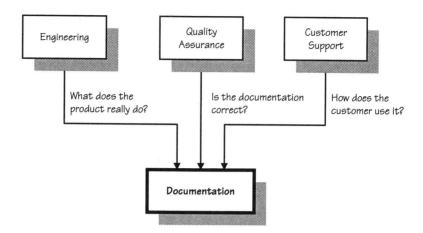

How can the other development groups help the writer? Simple. Figure 1.6 shows the information trail.

Before you go very far into creating a publication, you had better learn the product. Go to training, study the existing manuals, whatever—just learn the product as early in the product development process as you can. There is no excuse for you to wing it. If you do, chances are your customers will notice that they know more about the product than the documentation delivers.

And what should each department's interaction be with documentation?

Customer support   These stressed-out people need to determine what kind of information should be presented. Most important, they recognize how a customer will use the information.

Quality Assurance   This group may become involved with documentation much later in the product delivery process (at the beta milestone, most likely). They should be able to validate that the instructions in the documentation make sense.

NOTE I expect a lot of assistance from engineering!

Engineers   The software engineers should be required to give you information and to present you with early versions of the product under development so that writers have the necessary information to produce successful results.

Is the Writer Really Accountable?

It is easy for writers to proclaim that they can't write successful manuals. Here are some obvious reasons:

- The product keeps on changing.
- There's no time to investigate any facts on this aggressive schedule.
- "We're the last to know when things happen with the product and when I ask for information, we're considered pests."

How do you get feedback from those who don't have time to give it to you or with a development process that doesn't treat the documentation department as a valuable team member? This is, by far, the most serious frustration of any documentation writer—how to deal with uncooperative product engineers. Let's take a look at this in more detail.

Both the product and the company will suffer if the writing team takes the stand that without accountability and the information to complete the writing task, the documentation will simply not be complete or meet the required schedules.

What if the Product Continually Changes?

Most software products you document change during the development process. Depending on your mood or history with the company, you may consider any change to be totally unacceptable regardless of the importance to the customer and to your company's business.

But, you better expect change and plan for it. Let's summarize some reasons for change and why it may be taking place:

The product doesn't work.   The engineers responsible are not testing the product before passing it on to other team members.

Specifications keep on changing.   Chances are, constantly changing specs are affecting everyone on the team—not just the documentation department.

If you can nail down those features that will *not* change and those that have a high degree of probability of change before you start to write, you should be able to plan accordingly.

If, on the other hand, the product being developed is changing from day to day, the documentation group is probably not the only department suffering. This usually reflects an unfocused product management department or an engineering group out of control. Elevate the problem to your management and resolve the problem.

Leaving Time for Research

NOTE Most developers like to present issues as "concerns." What I prefer are "risks" with potential resolutions.

Folks who work with me know not to use the words "research" and "concern." Research means to me spending a lot of time figuring out what details a writer is expected to know or learn. When research becomes a special milestone that potentially puts the overall product schedule at risk, there are usually other deep-seated problems.

Prior to the alpha milestone, the documentation team ought to be chomping at the bit to start writing!

Documentation Isn't Informed

A horrible situation is when the documentation team is not informed of important project decisions or status. It signals the department that their involvement with a product team is considered not very important.

Resolving Conflicts in Opinion

Avoid long-term stalemates.

If you can't seem to get anyone on the team to agree to your documentation plan, outlines, or review copies, it is your responsibility to force two action steps.

1. Elevate to the development boss (more commonly known as the King or Queen of Software) for immediate assistance.

2. At the next product team meeting, development management could reinforce the need for all groups to cooperate.

Figure 1.7
Proper way to
resolve conflicts
of opinion.

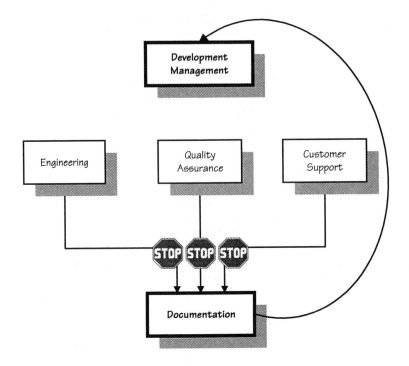

These steps can keep team conflicts and poor communication from becoming personal.

NOTE The impact of poor documentation may have a huge effect on customer satisfaction.

Early in the development cycle, documentation should set expectations that if there is little or no feedback by a certain milestone, you will document in the team minutes that information has not been made available. Should this occur, management should "be shot," since teamwork has obviously broken down with the risk that documentation will not be as accurate as it should be.

Prioritizing Documentation Tasks

NOTE This order works for both established companies as well as start-up companies.

Development decisions must be made based on the following pecking order:

1. Customer.

2. Company.

3. Employee.

This simply means that most product decisions must be

made first and foremost for the good of the customer (in other words, the market). If the customer is satisfied, then there is a strong chance that the company will prosper.

And if the company is succeeding, the employee should feel that his or her contribution is truly making a difference.

You may have a philosophical problem with this decision hierarchy if your company suffers from weak management, politics, lack of strategy, burnout, and so on. Following these priorities clears the air for making the best decisions and definitely impacts documentation. Let's go through a real example.

I participated in a team meeting during which we were trying to figure out how to organize a specific set of documentation manuals. The choices were:

1. Combine product module manuals into one single manual.

2. Separate manuals for each product module.

The documentation manager actually made the statement that, "I know the customer would like to use only one manual, but it would be difficult for us to combine each of the manuals. The right decision is to keep them separate since that is how we've arranged our DTP files."

There was a moment of silence. The meeting had dragged on for at least 45 minutes and representatives from sales, marketing, customer support, engineering, and documentation were exhausted. We had all of the right people in the room to make a decision.

The engineering manager spoke up, "You may have organized the documentation files a certain way, but I thought we stood by the rule that customers are first. This decision makes it easy on the writers but harder on the customer. Customers want just one manual."

It was as if a bucket of water was thrown on the team. The engineering manager, of all people, was absolutely correct and a single manual was chosen as the right decision. In this case, the documentation manager had mistakenly prioritized the employee need ahead of the customer and company.

Translating a Publication to Another Language

Once a publication has achieved a certain stability level, it can be translated to another language. Translating too early will result in lots of rewrites. Translating too late will result in a missed schedule with potential loss of revenue (in foreign country versions).

1. Decide early into which languages the manual needs to be translated and arrange for the work to be performed with language translation shops once a product's concept milestone is approved.

NOTE The best results are achieved by individuals residing in that country.

2. As drafts and early outlines are created, distribute them to language translation shops so that they know what is going on. If DTP template formats are finalized early in the product development process, they also should be given to the language translation shops.

3. Once certain manuals (or even just chapters) stabilize, release the DTP files to the language translation shop. Don't forget to include the software product (even if it is early) that you are documenting.

4. Once the production is released, send final DTP files with all graphics to the language translation shop. Don't forget instructions indicating what has changed from early releases. Even if minor changes have taken place in the DTP files, include revision bars.

Using Documentation Contractors

If possible, stick to using your employees to perform all documentation activities, except possibly the printing (there are plenty of printshops out there that are better equipped to handle that task).

Should you depend on outside contractors to write manuals? When your company is small and just doesn't have the financial backing to support an in-house documentation effort, then the use of a professional consultant can get you by. However, documentation that is authored by those that are not truly integrated into your company's product development team may not have a vested interest in learning your industry's terminology and customer profile. This can result in a shallow product.

I can think of two examples.

One major up-and-coming graphics imaging company initially used contract writers. The software product they documented is incredible; however, the documentation is not only inaccurate but it looks like someone used the right terminology but hadn't a clue how the product would be used. Management has gotten so much negative feedback from (guess who?) customer support that an internal documentation group is now being set up. Also, they've had to ship out replacement manuals to frustrated customers.

In another company, a documentation group needed training material constructed, and a contract writer was brought in. The writer didn't know the software product's specific industry but she had great credentials and was confident that she could do a smashing job. After three months of work, the writing covered the main topics. But the lack of knowledge in the subject (that could have been gained by working alongside the other team members) resulted in a document that just plain didn't work. The project, unfortunately, was scrapped.

How Engineering Can Help Documentation

It's amazing to me how often a publication is criticized after it hits the customer's hands. Yet, when it comes to helping documentation before the product is finished, everyone including management runs for the hills. At times, a documentation group feels either they are set up to fail or they must fight for information, any information.

Engineering has a responsibility to present the appropriate information to the documentation group in a timely manner. It is the documentation group's responsibility to ask for the appropriate information at the appropriate time. What is appropriate?

Well, if you just ask the question, "How does this thing work?" the engineer will probably get frustrated with you since you have not properly prepared to ask probing questions. One week before the beta milestone is the wrong time to try to get the attention of the product engineer. Be considerate of your team member's valuable time.

Both quality assurance and engineering share in the responsibility to read and verify the documentation once it is written. If these individuals don't have the time to spare because of their own responsibilities, their managers should be prepared to assist documentation. That's right—their managers! They can always figure out creative ways to get the information to you if they don't know the information themselves.

How Marketing Can Help Documentation

NOTE Marketing includes both product management as well as marketing communications activities.

How can marketing help documentation? Easy: By clearly identifying the customer.

First, get everyone in the team to approve your documentation outline with the expressed intent to make certain that you have clearly identified the customer. You need to put yourself in a typical customer's shoes.

Marketing determines what a product's features are, as well as the image the product needs to portray to the market. Although you may think differently, marketing has a thankless job. They have to balance the needs of the customer, the frustration of sales, and the reality of development.

Product marketeers need to agree with your document plan and, to some extent, set the tone for the documentation. Let's take two sample directives from marketing to the documentation team. Which do you like?

1. The manual must be 7"x9", black ink, and no longer than 250 pages. If more material is needed, then put it on-line.

2. Our customer base expects a standard size manual (preferably, 7"x9"), preferably one color (but if you can justify a spot color without much more expense—great), the manual should not exceed 1" in depth to meet our packaging goals. I'd like a specification within two weeks so that we can get a shipping box designed.

If you are like me, you'd appreciate the latter instead of the former. It sets the tone but does not dictate how you should do it. This gives the documentation group the ability to design the appropriate page size and, if more pages are required, a different type of paper can be used.

What about page count? If you reduce customer calls with more thorough documentation (in other words, more pages), you have saved the customer and your company's support and sales staff frustration!

Although we'll touch on this later, PageMaker's manual is about the same depth as Word's manual but the page count is 460 versus 825. How is that possible? In this case, the choice of paper stock made the difference.

Page count restrictions are viewed by someone in documentation the same as an engineer who is instructed to cut down the features because the product must now be released on one diskette instead of two. Should that happen, the product ships on two diskettes—no questions asked.

There are more critical battles to fight than page count.

Before we leave marketing's role, note that marketing should take an active part in reviewing the quality and accuracy of the documentation while it is being developed.

USING THE RIGHT TOOLS FOR THE JOB

There are still companies that practice the "beg until you really scream" type of attitude when it comes to purchasing software or hardware tools to do the job.

Some DTP books present pages and pages of details on specific versions of software and hardware products that you can use to create publications. Unfortunately, these product specifications become outdated soon after the book is published. I've been using certain tools for several years, and although they are updated about once a year, I'm still committed to using these outstanding tools.

Normally, programmers are able to justify software and hardware purchases. Writers' requests, on the other hand, tend to get a lot more scrutiny by management. And with this scrutiny comes dissatisfaction and a feeling that documentation is a third-class citizen since it seems like software engineers get anything they ask for.

At a minimum, here are some software tools that I suggest you have in your DTP arsenal:

- **Desktop publisher**   In my case, the desktop publishing product of choice is FrameMaker. Forget a word processor—you don't need it!

- **Drawing**   Use Visio to create simple diagrams for your manual. Visio is what I use throughout this book. For more sophisticated drawings, there's always CorelDRAW.

- **Screen capture**   The Windows screen capture facility (you know, the **PRINT SCREEN** key) is hardly suitable for taking any screen shot. You need something that can take not only screen shots of parts of your Windows screen objects (title bars, icons, windows, and so on) but you need something that can automatically convert, for example, color to grayscale.

  For this reason, I have chosen what I believe to be the best screen capture software tool on the Windows market: ImagePals Screen Capture by Ulead Systems.

- **Imaging**   You simply can't beat Adobe's Photoshop. You can create an image, create floating objects; and with plug-in filters, the possibilities are virtually unlimited.

  Ulead Systems' ImagePals imaging software product includes another useful application: the Image Editor that is a poor person's Photoshop. Since version 2, this wonderful application supports most of Photoshop's plug-in filters available from many third party sources.

- **Image management**   Image and drawing files do not normally have descriptions in order to organize them in some order that makes sense for the documentation. I use the fabulous Album program in (once again) ImagePals.

- **Font management**   To catalog fonts, there is none better than Ares Software Corporation's FontMinder. The performance of Windows slows to a snail's pace when you have loaded more than 200 fonts. This tool allows you to group fonts into font packs. One pack is installed at a time. FontMinder makes sure that those fonts referenced in the pack are properly recognized by Windows.

MAKE YOURSELF PRINTSHOP-INDEPENDENT

Right from the start, consider the role of the printshop.

Does Your Printshop Speak Windows?

The Macintosh market has all but owned the printshop business even though the DTP business is becoming more and more Windows-based. Years ago, Mac software and font suppliers practically gave away technology to win the hearts of printshops needing to migrate to computer-based typesetting. It worked. For years, many printshops would only accept Mac files.

Postscript and Type 1 font standards allowed publications to be created and printed on low-resolution lasers before committing to high-resolution typesetting equipment.

When you need to submit your documentation to print, the printshop will usually talk about Mac software formats. If you are dealing with a printshop that doesn't know anything about the PC, don't walk away—RUN! You will be in for a terror ride if you are under any stringent deadlines.

I would strongly suggest that you deal with those printshops that actually use the PC and have in-house personnel familiar with CorelDRAW files or Corel Ventura files. That is a good signal that they are PC-literate and can probably handle any mainstream DTP and graphics program publication files.

The spectacular Corel magazine usually prints a comprehensive advertisement that lists Corel approved training and service bureau centers. Chances are these same centers have the knowledge to successfully print publications created with the key Windows DTP program.

Last-Minute Printer Modifications

Make certain that you are designing and creating your manual in a way that reduces the risk of last-minute panic to handle problems like:

NOTE These are all no-no's.

- Photo reduction of full-page documents to fit on smaller page dimensions.
- Any editing or corrections that the printshop must make with its printing software.
- The printshop doesn't have the fonts you've selected available (this may not be a problem if you've delivered your DTP file as a Postscript print file).

The way to avoid major problems like this sample list is to construct a simple shell for each of your chapters and perform a sample print run at the beginning of your project. It may cost you a little time, but this initial test will dramatically reduce significant risk at the end of the project (when you don't need the stress or delays).

Treat your printshop as a source to perform only the final printing. They should not be allowed to perform edits, scaling, or modifications of any kind that could ultimately result in print errors.

KEN'S TOP 10 GUIDELINES

Here is my top ten list of DTP guidelines that I think are the most important things you can learn from this book:

1. Provide manual outlines, prototypes, and plans in order to gain early buy-in with your editors and fellow product team members.

2. Identify your customer and make certain that you are truly developing documentation for that customer. Your best customer is the support staff in your own back yard.

3. Select appropriate page layouts, styles, and icons to be used throughout your documentation. The style you

choose will leave a lasting impression on your reader (in other words, the customer).

4. Perform prototype printing early—don't wait till the end to find out that your print job doesn't work properly. If you don't have a Postscript printer, purchase a Postscript-compatible cartridge. If you don't do early tests, I guarantee that every time you go to final print, you'll encounter problems.

5. Back up your work all the time. Why risk not having backup copies of all of your hard work?

6. Even though you may be dependent on other team members for product expertise (like software engineers), you are responsible for the accuracy and usability of the documentation. Own the problem; no one else will. If you are not getting the information to do your job, elevate the problem to management!

7. Do not use a word processor to create the documentation—use your favorite DTP program instead. And don't forget that your document needs to be designed in a way that enables it to be turned into an on-line, interactive manual.

8. Use supporting tools (image editors, drawing programs, image/drawing catalogs, and screen captures) that are independent of the DTP program. Common artwork can be used for marketing material, too.

9. Use a printshop that has a PC on the premises and has experience using PC-based DTP and graphics software. If they don't have the experience but think they can, go elsewhere. Chances are you will be frustrated (I've been there many times).

10. Your writing style and page design style must present topics in a way that is very simple. Even if you think you have presented topics simply, simplify further.

OK—I lied, there are eleven.

11. Most manuals don't indicate the date of printing or, most important, the version of the product being documented. Also, get an ISBN number from the Library of Congress to "legitimize" your manual as a book.

2 *STYLE DESIGN GUIDELINES*

s a user manual writer, you need to adopt a style that is both consistent and easy to follow for your readers (in other words, the customer).

NOTE If you are already a DTP and writing genius, you may want to skip this chapter and go right to Chapter 3.

If you are more technical than literate and dread the prospect of writing a manual, this chapter will take the time necessary to get you up to speed with standard style basics (both page design and writing styles). If you follow these rules, you'll look like a genius!

We'll cover specific features of Corel Ventura and FrameMaker starting in Chapter 3.

ABOUT THIS CHAPTER

We'll cover the following topics:

- Thinking through page design fundamentals.
- Defining a hierarchy of document objects.
- Writing style guidelines.

COMPONENTS OF A PUBLICATION

We've all seen some pretty dull manuals before—you know, the boring ones that you hate reading. I like making publications interesting.

There are some basic components of every publication.

Title   The title page should mimic the cover (which is typically four-color artwork). If you can't justify the luxury of color, at least use similar title text so that it looks like the title page and the cover represent the same product.

Table of Contents   The table of contents is generated by the DTP program from the headings that you designate to be included. The DTP program creates a file with the heading text and page number along with an implied paragraph format (which you can modify to suit your needs).

Preface   A preface provides a great opportunity for you to introduce your company and your product to the customer. Page numbers usually are roman numerals without a chapter number (or title). The preface can also include basic information such as upgrade information, registration, license agreement, and support information.

Chapters   Each chapter automatically increments the chapter number and continues the page number counting throughout the entire publication (unless your page numbering scheme includes both the chapter number and the page number within that chapter).

Appendixes   Although nothing more than a chapter with an alphabetic counter, an appendix is typically used for glossaries or other reference information not typically needed in the main chapter context.

Index   The index is typically a two-column alphabetized list of index entries and page numbers (or page ranges). The list is generated much like a table of contents. Index entries, however, are not created based on a heading style—they are generated from writer-input special indexing codes.

WHY WORRY ABOUT STYLES?

So, you are a writer with "lotza" style and you perceive there is little room for improvement in your writing style, right?

Wrong.

You'd be surprised how different your style is depending on your stress level, interest in the subject being documented, and even between the first chapter and the most recent chapter you've been working on.

What about style differences between several writers working on one manual together? Whew! If one writer's style is consistent but someone else is not, what is the reader going to think?

What do I mean by style? There are two types of styles that I would like to discuss:

- **Design style**   This refers to the page design style that includes things like page layout, use of fonts, tasteful use of color and borders.
- **Writing style**   This has to do with setting a tone, and certainly punctuation.

Every paragraph throughout your publication should use a consistent style. As you write, think about your audience and make certain that the style is appropriate and consistent.

How important is mastering both styles to the creation of a spectacular manual? Here are some things to consider:

- A great style communicates authority and content confidence.

- A user who can understand the manual's subject will be a happy customer. (This assumes that the product being documented works as documented.)

- Styles should always communicate simplicity and should always try to present information in a way that is clear to the typical customer of that product.

You need to develop a style that is consistent and that is easy-to-follow for your readers. What are the effects when a manual incorporates inconsistent style?

- the documentation is difficult to follow.

- users become frustrated and automatically call customer support.

- treating the novice user as if he or she is experienced can be intimidating or even demeaning.

Notice that we immediately broke a style rule already?

The above bullet lists should have started with capital letters.

To make matters worse, a reader trying to decipher a manual's inconsistent style can lose confidence in the material (and maybe even the product you have documented).

The bullet list should have been written as:

- The documentation is difficult to follow.

- Users become frustrated and automatically call customer support.

- Treating the novice user as if he or she is experienced can be intimidating or even demeaning.

For some users this is no big deal. However, readers that dissect user manuals could have a real problem since the use of capitals letters, bold print, and italics could have significance.

DEFINING A PAGE DESIGN STYLE

A Guide to Publishing User Manuals takes page design issues at all levels and presents a practical guide on how to take advantage of each of these levels with DTP software applications.

Let's talk first about what goes into creating a successful publication design style:

- Logical organization of files belonging to a publication.

- Templates that dictate a common format for any and all publications documents.

- Factors influencing the organization of a publication such as binding, page size, and page design.

- Storyboarding and presenting a sample outline of a publication before you write.

You can think of DTP document files as a hierarchy of levels that can actually make creating complex manual projects more comprehensible and maintainable.

Organizing Files In a Publication

A publication includes references to multiple document files. Each chapter that you create can be saved in individual chapter files as shown in Figure 2.1.

These files provide information that the DTP program uses to generate list files such as an index and table of contents.

Figure 2.1
Files in a
publication.

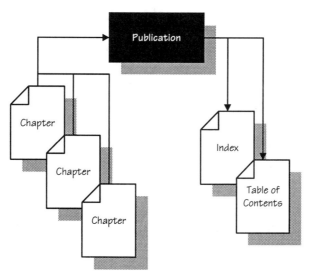

Chapter document files   Generated document files

Each of the chapters may have a slightly different format since a preface or appendix, for example, may present information radically different than what is contained in a mainstream chapter. A publication file acts as the glue that keeps track of each chapter and generates document files.

Each chapter in a document should be stored in its own file, as should each of the generated list files (the index and table of contents).

I've seen publications that have multiple files per chapter. I don't recommend this practice. Too few files make the documentation project difficult to handle, too many files can get confusing; especially once you try to submit these files directly to your printshop for final proofs.

Since the publication file is nothing more than a holder of references to the other files in the publication, it points to other files that are included in the publication. And, naturally, each chapter points to other files (graphics, screen shots, drawings, and so on).

Using Publication Templates

How do you keep track of your publications so that you don't have to recreate the style (you know, layout, fonts, and so on) every time you write a new book? The answer is a template as shown in Figure 2.2.

A template is often used as a model for creating publications with similar layouts. When you create a new publication, you'll typically use a template as the basis for the new document. In fact, a template is nothing more than a sample document file without body text.

Templates are used only during creation stage of a new publication. Otherwise, templates could be accidentally modified by inadvertently saving a publication as a template. *So, keep backups of your templates.*

You should have separate template document files for each key document type. For example, a single chapter template should be used as the basis for all chapters in a publication.

Figure 2.2
Using templates to create a new publication.

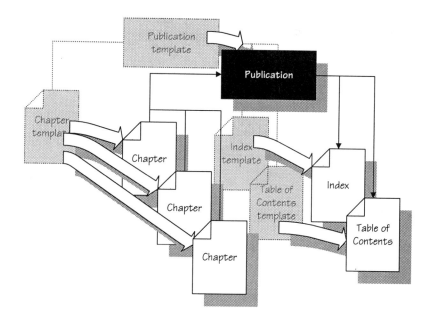

NOTE Style sheets used by a template may, however, persist in a new publication. More on this in the next chapter.

Templates are never persistent. This means that as soon as you use a template to create a new publication, the template should have no bearing on further changes made to the publication. In other words, the connection between the template and the newly created publication is broken.

The template becomes important only when a new publication (or chapter) is created based on that template.

Planning the Publication

Binding Your Manual

Who cares about binding? Well, your customer, for one. The manual may look great on someone's shelf but if it snaps closed when your customer is trying to use it, he or she will become very frustrated. The typical types of binding are:

- Perfect binding.
- Plastic comb binding.
- Wire spiral binding.
- Three-ring binding.

Figure 2.3
Perfect binding.

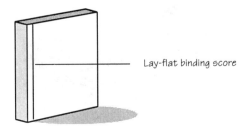

Lay-flat binding score

There are strengths and weaknesses of each type of binding.

Using Perfect binding

Figure 2.3 shows the preferred binding for manuals known as perfect binding. It more closely resembles the popular paperback book binding. Unfortunately, when dealing with a printshop you must indicate that the binding has to have a lay-flat binding that allows the book to stay open.

Lay-flat binding usually can be detected if the binder has a noticeable score (one or two cuts) on the outside of the cover. Many established binderies or printshops will know how to provide this to you—*but you'll need to ask for it!*

Perfect binding has become the standard for software documentation and, in large quantities, can actually be the cheapest to produce.

Using Plastic comb binding

This is a great solution for oversize (8.5" x 11") manuals because it allows the manual to lay flat better than any other binding. However, it is generally used for presentation material such as a request for proposal or for material you would give to product marketing for approval (well, it looks better than staples). It also works well for training material that often requires oversize documents so that the user can write in the margins during class.

The plastic comb binding's disadvantage is that it may not last and pages sometimes slip out of the holes. It is really only a temporary, low-usage binding technique. There are binding devices that you can purchase that are very inexpensive. For this reason, it is a good choice for internal company material.

In any case, I would recommend this binding only as a last resort and with short documents less than 50 pages.

Figure 2.4
Wire spiral binding.

Wire spiral binding   Spiral binding is the thin, wire binding (sometimes called wiro) that was popular for manuals several years ago due to its ability to provide long-term binding for any manual, shown in Figure 2.4.

The wire is actually threaded by a machine into every hole and is doubled up at every punctured hole.

Wire spiral binding looks professional and it is robust. This is the perfect binding for training material where the page count is less than 200 pages. If the page count is much higher than that, you should really consider either perfect binding or three-ring binding.

Three-ring binding   Remember elementary school and the three-ring binders that would sometimes snap onto your thumb? Ouch! Well, you can still use them for manuals.

In the early days of PC software, three-ring binders were plentiful, with cover stock ranging from plastic to expensive cloth. With every new release of software you were never quite sure what the binding and page size would look like.

Today, the majority of all software manuals resemble paperback books.

If you are shipping product to thousands of customers and the product updates are relatively infrequent, then choose a binding that is more permanent such as wire spiral binding or perfect binding.

If, on the other hand, your customer base expects updates regularly, a three-ring binder may be more appropriate. They can be of any size (8.5"x11" or 7"x9") and can look very professional. All you have to deliver is page inserts to your customer since they already have durable binding.

Figure 2.5
Unusual page
design—but does
it actually work?

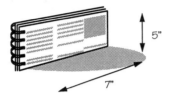

5"

7"

Binding as Copy Protection

NOTE Also, the
cost of CD publish-
ing is getting very
inexpensive.

One last important point may be worth mentioning. As with many software products these days, diskettes can be freely copied. If your documentation is bound so that it can be easily copied (any technique other than perfect binding), you run the risk of customers copying your entire product (documentation and all).

Determining the Document Size

Determine the page size that best fits your customer base. The 7.5"x9.25" is becoming the standard for most manuals. This book uses that very page size.

On the other hand, I've seen some pretty unusual manual sizes. One software product of note has used spiral binding on a document size that is 7"x5". To top it off, each page is divided into three columns as shown in Figure 2.5.

This is a great size to fit into creative packaging (like in a paint can, for example) but it is more difficult to read. In manuals, multiple columns can actually be intimidating and the size is just so odd, that each page cannot have much information on it. The customer could be reading several pages to understand concepts that shouldn't exceed a single page.

Designing the Page

There are many things to take into consideration when designing your page: number of columns, size of fonts, use of color, room for sideheads, and so on.

Whatever you do, design your pages so that the user can easily find information and, once found, can understand that information. As ridiculous as this sounds, a poorly designed page can make finding anything like an Easter egg hunt.

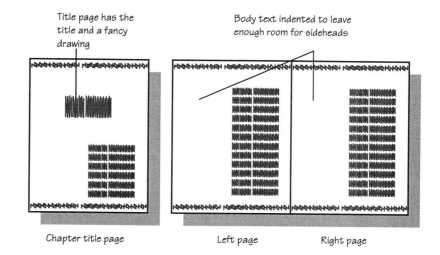

Figure 2.6
Showing a
manual's style
with a storyboard.

Title page has the
title and a fancy
drawing

Body text indented to leave
enough room for sideheads

Chapter title page

Left page

Right page

Storyboarding the Publication Style

At the very beginning of publication planning, you will need to gain approval of the publication style with key team members such as customer support, sales, and marketing.

Although Figure 2.6 looks crude, it is the first step to showing your product team how you plan on setting up the manual's style. You'll need to pull together as much planning information as possible (obviously, the figure here doesn't go into enough detail).

Outlining the Manual

Once you've storyboarded the documentation with some samples, the next thing to do is to outline the manual in a way that a reviewer can get a sense of the flow.

It is an outstanding idea to also estimate the amount of pages and artwork so that your production people can start estimating the costs and the marketing people can start commissioning artwork for the packaging design.

The most productive way to outline a manual is to generate a table of contents composed of all chapter and heading names from the real document files. Creating a draft outline (to be filled in later with actual text) is similar to the technique used by software engineers when they initially create software modules.

Here's a sample outline of a fictitious manual entitled *CommTerm User Guide*:

- Table of Contents (4 pages)

- Getting Started (12 pages, 2 drawings, no screen shots)
  What Is CommTerm?
  Installing CommTerm
  Getting Help

- Chapter 1, Using CommTerm (36 pages, 10 drawings, 20 screen shots)
  Introduction To Data Communications
  What Does a Terminal Emulator Do
  Starting CommTerm
  Configuring CommTerm
  Connecting with a Host
  Uploading and Downloading Files
  Miscellaneous Features
  Exiting CommTerm

- Chapter 2, Command Reference (50 pages, 4 drawings, 30 screen shots)
  File Menu
  View Menu
  Communications Menu
  Options Menu
  Help Menu

- Index (4 pages)

Once the outline is approved, you just start filling in the blanks (with text). *Easy for me to say!*

DEFINING A PUBLICATION HIERARCHY

A publication's structure has an implied relationship between all of its components. You could ask the question, "Is there any way that each component can share the same properties so that they don't have to be redefined all of the time?"

Figure 2.7
The layers of each
manual.

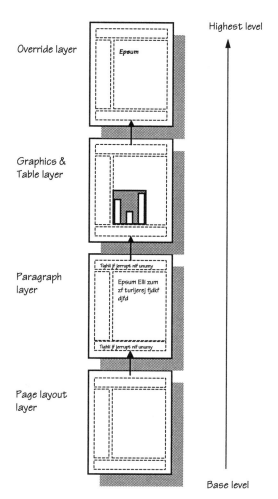

Of course there is!

In Figure 2.7 I have defined four layers of relationships that all of a manual's components need to share.

Just like object-oriented programming fundamentals, manuals rely on layers that build upon each other. In some respects, a master page is used to define these layers, and a manual actually uses (or, in object-oriented terms, inherits) these definitions.

Thinking of DTP-based publications as a hierarchy of layers gives each layer some level of independence. Each layer depends on the level below it while not being really aware of the lower layer's characteristics.

As we'll see in the descriptions in the next few pages, although the text layer must rely on the lower layer page design it really doesn't "know" much about the characteristics of the page layout layer such as paper size, margins, number of columns. Without the page layout layer, however, the text layer cannot exist—an upper layer depends on the existence of all lower layers.

In contrast, the page layout layer is set up to handle the text layer but it is not affected if there isn't any text written in the text layer.

I devote Chapter 3 to explaining how different DTP programs treat each of these layers, but let's do a quick review of each layer starting with the base level.

The Page Layout Layer

The page layout layer defines the page format and the text flow. It is the blueprint on which all of the document objects are built, namely:

- Body text flow.
- Sideheads and margins.
- Headers and footers.

As just noted, the top three layers of a manual generally have little idea what is going on in the underlying page layout. If you have designed a manual for a specific page size (7" x 9") and at the last minute need to change it to a different size (say, 7.5"x9.25"), you should be able to modify the manual's template page layout characteristics without much impact to any of the upper layers (such as retyping the text, repositioning graphics, and so on).

The page layout layer must define rules on how body text will flow from page to page. Figure 2.8 shows the automatic transition of text from one page to the next. The page layout level normally defines the rules so that text can "find a home" even if the page design elements change later.

Figure 2.8
Flow defined in
the page layout
level.

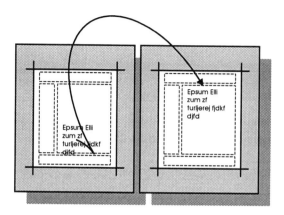

When you eventually add body text (in the paragraph layer), text that can't fit on one page should automatically continue to the next page. This defines the text flow used in your manual.

Don't assume, however, that the concept of text flow is simple because the flow rules may vary depending on the page. A case in point is a newspaper where text flows from page to page (sometimes not in any reasonable page order).

NOTE Headers refer to fixed text found on the top of most pages versus headings, which denote a hierarchy of topics in the body text.

Headers and footers normally include repeated text with certain fields of information that are updated based on changing elements such as page numbers and headings.

All of these "rules" are based on the concept of frames—rectangular units that specify attributes such as horizontal width, vertical width, text flow, and so on.

One final note—you may have noticed that some documents use graphics or text that is somehow permanently set in the page layout. Most manuals allow graphical or text objects to be defined on the page layout layer. These repeated objects are automatically displayed and printed on every page. This is how logos or the word CONFIDENTIAL, for example, are placed on every page.

The Paragraph Layer

The text flow defined in the page layout layer acts as a roadmap for body text. Body text is placed in the paragraph layer. Your wise choice of font technology and text placement is absolutely essential for the consistent presentation of material from chapter to chapter.

Sometimes called tags, paragraph styles are used to define attributes of certain objects so that they can be invoked for similar objects throughout the document. They are great time-savers and ensure a consistent style.

In particular, paragraph styles are used to define attributes of paragraph text objects such as:

- Font family, weight, angle, size, and color.
- Alignment and spacing (both horizontally and vertically) between lines of text and the underlying page design.
- Borders associated with text (lines above, lines below, lines around, and so on).
- Kerning and hyphenation properties.
- Tab stops.

NOTE
Get used to using styles. All text should use a named paragraph tag.

Without styles, you would have to define these attributes over and over again. When you define a style, assign a name to it. Every unique style should have an easy-to-remember descriptive name. I use names like Body, Body Next, and Heading 1. Then, whenever you wish to select a style for a given paragraph, you click on the paragraph and then select the style name.

Your choice of fonts is important at the beginning. Windows provides TrueType fonts automatically. And they are high-quality fonts. If your selected printshop does not handle TrueType fonts, you better get that straightened out at the beginning. Your company should actually define font standards, too. Most do.

If you must use a printshop that supports only Postscript files, chances are their imagesetting equipment will only accept Type 1 fonts. This requires you to use the Adobe Type Manager (ATM) with Windows with Type 1 fonts.

Whatever you do, choose fonts other than the classic Helvetica and Times Roman. There are too many font options available to limit yourself. But choose a small selection of fonts and try to use them consistently in all of your publications.

The Graphics and Table Layer

Although you could argue that graphics and tables should be treated as part of the text layer, I have chosen to distinguish them.

What characteristics do graphics and tables have in common?

- The frames around the graphics (or table) object should be able to automatically adjust depending on their size.

- The graphics or table object should be placed within the body text flow. Then, if the text preceding a graphics/ table object moves, so does the graphics/table.

- Backgrounds can be shaded and border widths (tables and graphics) defined.

- Captions can be "attached" to the graphics/table object.

Writers are not usually artists, so the prospect of creating drawings is a little scary to them and the way they deal with it is to avoid doing any art. But, graphics do communicate better and that is why we focus so much attention (see Chapter 5, "Graphics and Tables") on using tools that will make drawing less stressful.

What is included under the term graphics?

- Drawings (vector, object-based creations using products like Visio or TextPlus).

- Bitmap images (created using products like Photocells).

- Screen captures (grabbed by products like ImagePals).

Each of these graphics files has particular characteristics that you will need to understand. If you expect your printshop to be able to automatically solve format incompatibilities with their imagesetting equipment, you are in for an unpleasant surprise.

For example, imported graphics or graphics embedded using OLE cannot be easily color separated. In addition, bitmap images that include text will look horrible when printed.

Finally, screen captures (which are also bitmap images) normally require brightness and contrast changes especially if your screens have any amount of gray background in them.

There's a lot of detail that you need to be aware of early in the documentation process so that you can create the graphics right the first time. We'll focus on the details in Chapter 5.

With both tables and graphics, you may wish to assign a numbering scheme in order to affix a caption or title that goes along with each. You would also expect that this numbering will increment automatically whenever you are ready to print the publication.

The Overrides Layer

Last but not least, the overrides layer can be used for exceptions to a defined style. Just because you define a paragraph tag (or style) as Palatino, 10 point, normal font does not mean that you cannot also define special text in that paragraph as Zapf Dingbat font at 12 points.

Overrides are important because they modify only certain properties defined in underlying levels. Overrides do not just apply to text. Overrides can modify:

- Margins and columns.
- Graphics and table formats.
- Graphics and text placement outside of the normal page layout flow.

WRITING STYLE GUIDELINES

You and your fellow writers need to follow consistent rules so that your readers aren't confused. Most companies have writing style guidelines, but in case yours doesn't, let's present some fundamentals that are aimed at manual writing.

Here are some standards that I recommend, but whatever editing guidelines you and your company use, be consistent.

Two Different Approaches

There are basically two approaches to writing manuals:

- Reference.
- Task.

Using a Reference Approach

A reference manual normally presents a very methodical summary of all the features of the product being documented.

Generally, a reference manual presents information in some order (based on the menu names, for example) or in alphabetical order (used for documenting call libraries for compilers).

For some readers, a reference approach makes the most sense. They have no interest in anything other than the information.

Using a Task Approach

On the other hand, if a manual needs to present procedures to accomplish tasks (most do), you may want to illustrate the topics in well-defined steps. For those readers who want to be "walked through" topics, the task approach is great.

Which approach makes sense for you?

Each approach has its purpose and its audience. If your typical customer just needs the facts and has no need for specific how-to information, the reference approach works just fine.

For most of us, however, the task approach works the best. In fact, a manual that is task-oriented yet also has a reference component (or, better yet, a separate reference manual) is the most effective.

Pick up one of the early Xerox (pre-Corel Corporation) Ventura manuals. Reference to the max. The information was presented in menu command order but the reader was given absolutely no idea how to perform basic tasks. (I suspect that is why Ventura training classes were so popular!)

On the other hand, pick up one of the FrameMaker manuals and you will see a document that somehow manages to anticipate the task you want to perform next. Even a complicated product like a DTP package can be simplified.

The reference approach is great for:

- Programming guides.
- For accessing quick information (not unlike a dictionary).
- The manual used only as a last resort.
- Topics presented in some sort of hierarchical or collated sequence.

The task approach is great for:

- Processes that require well-defined steps.
- An audience that could easily be somewhat intimidated and needs to feel comfortable going through the manual.
- The audience that actually wants to understand how to use the product.

Writers would rather concentrate on a writing style that is task-oriented. However, if the customer only requires a reference approach, then the document had better be written that way.

However, there is a compromise that you should consider. If your customer base can benefit from both styles, you can always produce a task-oriented user's guide that is also a reference manual.

One of the best examples of this approach is Borland's C++ manuals. Their user guides provide programming information to help a programmer through the use of the C++ compiler, and their reference guide is organized based on alphabetical order of all C++ library functions.

Showing Keywords

NOTE My editors prefer italics for keywords.

Keywords should be set in a different text attribute only the first time it is used. This example shows keywords set off in italics:

The term *asynchronous* refers to the random method in which data communications information occurs. This terminal emulation software application only supports asynchronous communications.

Keywords should be highlighted from normal body text using either *italics* or ***bold-italics***. I prefer bold-italics with a spot color (or 50 percent gray) much like you would see in those expensive college text books.

Showing Out-of-Context Terms

NOTE Use curly quotations to surround a word or phrase and not the straight quotes.

When text is used in a context that is out of the ordinary, it is best to highlight it in quotation marks. For example:

The software will go "belly-up" if you type too many characters.

Out-of-context phrases should be surrounded with quotation marks every time they are used.

Handling Dashes and Spaces

Dashes and spaces are particularly challenging since there are several types. You should be able to type an en dash (short dash), em dash (long dash), en space (short space), em space (long space), and thin space (one or two pixel width space).

Dashes should also be nonbreaking so that if the dash appears at a right margin, the entire word including the dash is automatically moved to the next line by the DTP program.

One last key feature I don't want to forget: A DTP program should guard against you entering more than one space in a row—that is what an em dash is for!

FrameMaker does a spectacular job of providing support for all of these dashes and space types.

Using Hyphenation

All DTP products support hyphenation options based on the DTP program's internal dictionary capability.

The DTP programs allow the writer to enable or disable hyphenation in a publication or for specific paragraph tags.

NOTE The term for documents that don't hyphenate or line up to the right margin is ragged right.

For manuals, though, I just don't suggest you use hyphenation unless the page layout design requires that all text must align on the right. I have heard of studies indicating that the use of excessive hyphenation can even be stressful to a reader.

Showing Keyboard and Display Text

NOTE A good example of mono-spaced fonts are DOS applications.

Screen display text should be presented in a monospaced font if the product you are documenting is monospaced:

```
Please choose COM1 or COM2:
```

My favorite font for monospaced paragraph tags is Letter Gothic. Most all of you should have the Courier or Courier New font but it just doesn't print well on the page.

Graphical user interfaces like Windows show text that takes as much as much space as the letter needs to. In this case, the text is not monospaced and you should use a good sans serif font:

Please choose COM1 or COM2:

My favorite font for display and keyboard text is Helvetica Neue. If you can't tell the difference with the previous monospaced example, compare the spacing between the P, l, and e.

To distinguish displayed and keyboard text within a paragraph, it should be in a type size that matches normal body text but in the appropriate sans serif font (such as: Please choose COM1 or COM2) or monospaced font (such as: Please choose COM1 or COM2:).

Menu commands are presented with the menu name followed by a colon (or upright bar or "pipe") and the pull-down menu item. For example, if the user is to choose the Copy command from the Edit menu, this command could be presented as Edit|Copy or as Edit>Copy.

Keyboard entry is shown in bold with specific keys noted as separate keycaps in uppercase (as the **ENTER** key below):

C:>BRKOUT**ENTER**

Combination keys that require you to hold one key while you press another should have a + (plus sign) between the keys. For example, to display context-sensitive help you would hold the **SHIFT** key while temporarily pressing the **F1** key. This would be presented as **SHIFT+F1** in a publication.

Creating Tasks

This paragraph uses an arrow symbol in the margin followed by a sentence representing the task, for example:

➲ **Do this task first.**

Distinguishing tasks from numbered lists shows the reader that tasks are not just a numbered list or a heading—they are something of both. Using both a symbol (like the arrow) with text set off in a spot color (or gray) helps focus the customer's eyes on tasks that they should concentrate on using or doing.

Using Sideheads for Notes

NOTE This is a sidehead.

I like to use sideheads to help communicate important information separate from the main text. When presenting technical information, casual sideheads can really help relieve the pressure of learning new material.

Make the sidehead font a little smaller than normal body text with a slight flair (like the Tekton font used in this book).

Documenting Menu Commands

You can present pull-down menus with the aid of your DTP program's table editing facility or perform a screen capture of the software program's menu.

Figure 2.9
Two methods of
showing a
pull-down menu.

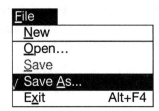

Menu pull-down created using the table feature

Screen captured menu pull-down

Figure 2.9 shows two methods of showing menu pull-downs. The drawing on the left is actually a table without a caption. Each menu command (including the top menu File) is actually text within a table cell. It is fairly easy to show menu shortcuts with an underline, checkmarks, and highlighted menu commands. By turning on and off specific cell line borders, the menu commands can closely look like the "real McCoy."

Using a table is far easier than most drawing software tools and a great way to prototype menu structures if the software application you are documenting hasn't been written yet.

On the right, I used ImagePals to take a screen capture of the actual menu pull-down. The cursor is disabled and the capture source is set to the Menu Under Pointer option. This looks more realistic.

By the way, don't forget to use text that is sans serif to more closely resemble menu commands displayed on the video. I like the Helvetica Neue font. The highlighted menu command would be denoted as File>Save As. The ellipsis following the menu command (...) only means that choosing this menu command will bring up a dialog box.

Creating Programming Styles

NOTE I'm assuming you are documenting C or C++ programs.

For those of you writing manual information for programmers, try these formatting standards on for size. The Helvetica font family works great for programming styles.

- C++ class names and function members should be in a sans serif bold format: Class **aflni**, function **main()**. By the way, anytime you refer to a function, always append a pair of parentheses.

- Definitions (#defines ifupper) could use a basic sans serif font while declarations (int _ix) uses a bolded sans serif— usually not as bold as a function name.

- Parameters (or function arguments) could be bold-italics in either a spot color or a gray (like 50% black). For example, **main**(*argc*).

- Programming code should simply be set as monospaced sans serif font (like Letter Gothic):

```
//    This is a comment
int y = x * 80;
```

Referencing Files

Filenames should always be shown in capitals (for example, SETUP.INF) unless you are taking advantage of the long filename capabilities becoming available with Windows 95 and Windows NT where case-sensitivity is important and files may have names with uppercase and lowercase letter combinations. File extensions (such as .EXE and .BAT) have a special relationship as a file type and are not normally explicitly mentioned.

Otherwise, the standard eight and three filenames (also known as 8.3) should always be referenced with *both* the filename and the associated extension.

3 PAGE LAYOUT

Now that you are familiar with all of the terminology and styles you need for producing good (I mean "great") user manuals, let's create a sample page layout for a publication.

ABOUT THIS CHAPTER

In this chapter we will cover:

- Planning the publication.
- Designing the page layout.
- Defining a header and footer.
- Working with publication files.
- Putting finishing touches on the publication.

Where do you keep notes for your documents? You need to develop a good way to keep track of comments, production notes, and other information.

It would be best to be able to keep this information with the publication somehow. I strongly suggest keeping a log that defines the following information:

- Location of all files (DTP, graphics, images, and so on) used in the document.

- Printing instructions and actual thumbnails of special pages pointing out spot colors, page dimensions, and so on.

- All documentation specifications used throughout a project's development.

PLANNING THE PUBLICATION

The following is a typical conversation when people begin to plan a publication.

"A document is important. Let's keep the cost to a minimum, okay? Yeah, I still like the old three-ring binder. It's easy to add pages to it."

"I'm concerned about price and page count. Color? You want color? Color will add cost! Nope, black and white will do just fine. Hey, isn't that two color? Black and white?"

"Well, I talked it over with the VP of marketing and the page count must be no more than 250 pages! Black and white will do fine and you only have three months to put it together! That should be no problem, right? After all—that's what you are paid for."

Sound ridiculous?

I've heard some version of this discussion several times!

Keeping Production Costs Under Control

Although we don't get into detail on production issues until the end of the book, there are some considerations that every documentation group (and writer) needs to consider early in the process of planning.

NOTE The term production refers to the activity of mass producing documentation material after the master and pre-press work is completed.

- Production quantity required for print job and on-hand inventory.
- Page size.
- Use of color in the manual and on the cover.
- Paper quality.

What Size Should the Manual Be?

The size of the documentation should be determined by your intended audience and the prevalent standard for your industry. For example, in the mid-1980s the standard was small size three-ring binders with pages 5.5"x8.5".

You could tell that the writers often were software engineers being forced to put something on paper. It probably didn't help that there were no user-interface standards in DOS-based applications. It seemed like every company had its own software program and documentation style.

In the case of documentation, white space (you know, margins, spacing between headings, and other areas not used for text or graphics) was not much of a design issue. In other words, looking back at many of the manuals developed in the 1980s, you were lucky if there was any white space!

Context-sensitive help was almost nonexistent and if it was present, couldn't easily use the original publication's text—it had to be created and entered in some other format.

Now, the bigger-than-paperback size is the most common: 7.4"x9" or 7.5"x9.25" with a very fancy, four-color art cover. Almost all manuals now use the familiar paperback or perfect binding, diskettes have been replaced by CDs, and the manuals are getting more compact with lots of information available on-line.

Does this remind you of the transition made in the music industry from LPs to CDs or the transition of the book industry from hardcopy to softcopy? There are a lot of parallels.

Competitive pricing, huge advertising budgets, compact product packaging, standard user interfaces are all contributing to the fact that the software business is becoming more of a commodity industry. All this because of a manual's page size?

Not really—but the types of manuals we see everywhere now are a visible reflection of the state of the industry.

What about Page Count?

Page count should be estimated early in the development process to help determine the cost of goods. It is totally unacceptable for a documentation group to not be able to estimate the page count. I can hear it now: "How can I predict the page count until I write it?"

In the DOS days, how did a programmer know that a program to be created would fit into 640K of RAM? Professionals are always given opportunities to estimate tasks and hacker programmers (and that goes for hacker writers, too) can always make the excuse that they've got "no idea."

The statement mandated by management that a manual is "not to exceed *X* pages" does, however, bother me. This proclamation typically comes from a marketing manager who wants to portray a certain product image. But what image?

Complexity   There is a perception that larger manuals result in a customer expectation that the product being documented is difficult to use and needs lots of explaining.

Cost   If the documentation is on-line (in some user's minds it *must* be) then the software supplier's costs should be lower and the cost benefits passed to the customer. Micrografx has already started this trend and you may see more of this in the future. On the other hand, for the documentation to be on-line you will need lots of disk space dedicated to it, or you will need to have the correct CD always inserted in your CD drive.

LAYING OUT THE PAGE

Setting up the page is one of those tasks that has you saying to yourself: "I know I've gotta do it but I'll start typing and then worry about the page design later."

This approach is often why desktop publishing projects gets into trouble once the writing is half done. This "design avoidance" phenomenon keeps writers working in a word processor until the final desktop publishing production nightmare begins. Besides, "aren't we writers and not desktop publishers?" Nope. Not anymore.

NOTE We will assume pages of the same size are used in a publication.

All desktop publishing products allow you to configure the page to almost any size you desire. A page design can take one day to design or can (through long-winded consensus) take weeks. However, sometimes it is not easy to master page design since there can be some confusion about:

- The master page versus the body page.
- The difference between the target page and the underlying page.
- How to change page sizes after you have already started your document.

Let's begin by getting a firm understanding of page layout concepts.

Master Page vs. Body Page

NOTE Even desktop publishing folks can talk in terms of objects!

Every desktop publishing product supports the concept of a master page. The master page provides a template for body pages that inherit the attributes of a master page (Figure 3.1).

The DTP program should provide the mechanism to define multiple master pages since some pages will not use the same page layout attributes.

FrameMaker does provide a named master page capability that can be assigned to specific body pages where your text and graphics are stored. Corel Ventura, on the other hand, supports an implied master page capability by letting you redefine page design on any body page.

Figure 3.1
Base (master)
and derived
(body) page
layouts.

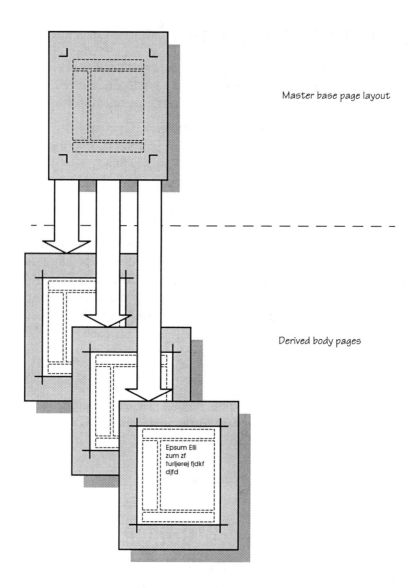

Master base page layout

Derived body pages

Epsum Elli
zum zf
furljerej fjdkf
djfd

What attributes? How about these?

- Margins and page size.

- Location of headers and footers.

- Number of columns and inter-column distance.

Note that the page size may not be the same as the page size of the film or paper that you use to print the target page. See Figure 3.2.

Figure 3.2
Target page versus underlying printed page.

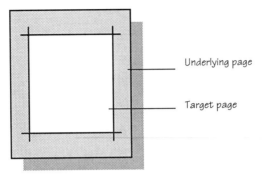

Underlying page

Target page

In this book, the page size always refers to the target page size as the final publication page size.

NOTE We'll cover this topic in Chapter 7.

In order for a publication to print properly, it must be printed on material (paper or film) that leaves enough room around the target page for registration marks. For example, the target page may be 7.4"x9" but the underlying page that includes the registration marks may be 8.5"x11".

CREATING A PUBLICATION

A publication's components include chapters, titles, and generated index and table of contents. Pages are double-sided (left and right). Each chapter should have an even number of pages so that the chapter is on the right side.

Figure 3.3
A new chapter.

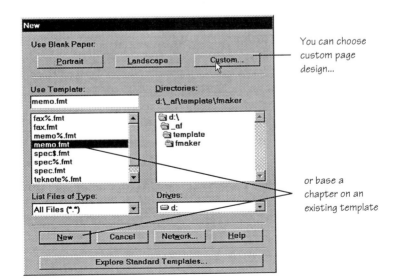

You can choose custom page design...

or base a chapter on an existing template

Figure 3.4
The page
attributes.

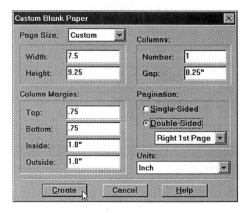

Using FrameMaker

Creating a Chapter

In FrameMaker, you create a chapter before creating a publication. Start FrameMaker. Create a chapter by selecting the File>New menu command. See Figure 3.3.

Click on Custom and FrameMaker will ask you to specify the attributes of the page (Figure 3.4). We'll fill in our own values to match the page dimensions of this book.

As you change the Width field, the Page Size field automatically changes from US Letter to Custom. Change the Width, Height, Top, and Bottom margins as well as selecting Double-Sided fields.

Click on Create when you have set the fields to your liking and you will be rewarded with a blank page.

NOTE To display the tools palette, click the triangle button above the vertical slider.

Select the Format>Page Layout>Column Layout menu command. Although you are presented with some of the same information (such as margins), check Room for Side Heads and set the Width field to **1.15"**, Gap to **0.1"**, and the Side field to Left.

Figure 3.5 shows the new window with the page setup for your page values.Click on the Smart Selection tool in the Tools palette at the upper left corner of the text flow area (inside the margins) until an insertion point is established.

Figure 3.5
Created
document page.

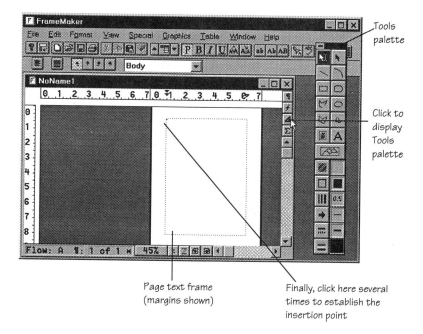

Tools
palette

Click to
display
Tools
palette

Page text frame
(margins shown)

Finally, click here several
times to establish the
insertion point

Type a couple lines of text. Don't be alarmed if you don't see a header and footer appear. I'll show you how to create headers and footers starting on page 71.

FrameMaker defines flows that automatically connects text frames between pages.

It is possible to define multiple flows, each representing a different article or column of information. Setting multiple, complex text flows is a nice feature if you were creating a newsletter or newspaper. For manuals, one text flow is normally sufficient.

The flow of a particular frame can be viewed by first clicking on the Object Selection tool in the Tools palette. Click on the margin frame denoted by the dotted rectangle.

In order to change or view the flow name, select Format>Customize Layout>Customize Text Frame. The Customize Text Frame dialog is displayed (Figure 3.6).

NOTE The page is referred to as a rectangular frame.

For normal publication uses, make certain that the Flow Tag is set to **A** with Autoconnect checked. You'll notice that there are other text frame properties that can be viewed and even changed. For now, click Set to return to the document.

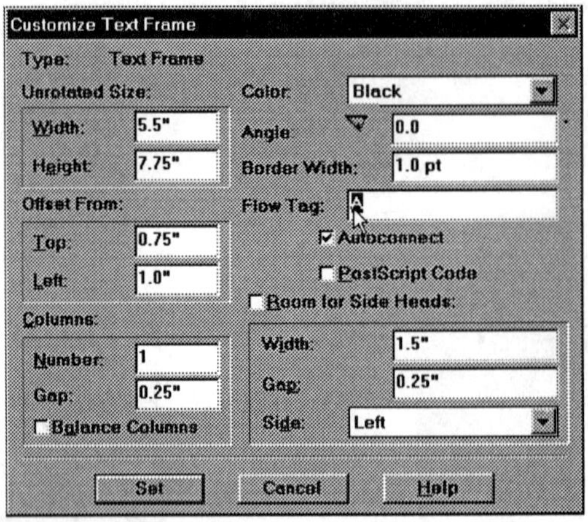

Figure 3.6
Examine the text
flow.

Figure 3.6
Examine the text
flow.

Set up the page numbering system by selecting the
Format>Document>Numbering menu to display the
Document Properties dialog (Figure 3.7).

The 1st Page # field is automatically set by FrameMaker, but
you can change it to a specific page number if you wish (I
wouldn't recommend it). The Page # Style can be set to an
assortment of formats with Numeric (4) being the most
common. Also, select Format>Document>Text Options in
order to allow Smart Quotes and Smart Spaces.

Note that you should let FrameMaker make certain that all
chapters end on an even-numbered page. Click on the Make
Page Count Even option by clicking on the list pull-down
(shown behind the arrow pointer in Figure 3.7).

Click Set to return to the document.

Saving a Chapter

NOTE In Win-
dows 95, file
extensions
become file types.

To save the chapter, just select File>Save (or Save As). Select
the proper subdirectory and select a filename. Even though
FrameMaker uses the file extension of .DOC, I prefer to use
.FMD (for FrameMaker Document).

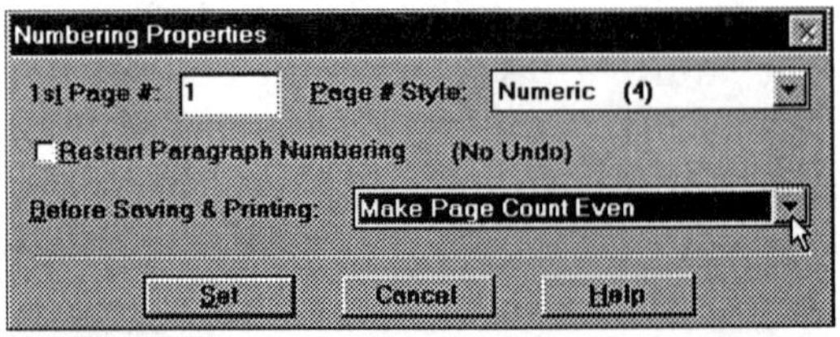

Figure 3.7
Portion of the
Document
Properties dialog.

Figure 3.8
Create a book.

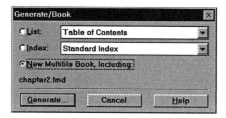

If I wish to save this file as a template, I use .FMT.

Let's save the chapter as CHAPTER1.FMD and then copy it by saving another version as CHAPTER2.FMD using File>Save As menu command.

Creating a Publication

FrameMaker allows more than one document to be viewed, which means you can display your entire publication with each chapter in its own window.

Now that you have a couple of chapters defined, let's create a publication. First, click in the CHAPTER2.FMD window. Click on File>Generate/Book. You have three options: to generate a list, index, or a book (Figure 3.8).

Click on New Multifile Book, Including: and then click Generate.

A book is normally created with the .BK file extension. The chapters in the book are listed (there's only one chapter currently). A book file is synonymous with the concept of publication file. Although it only points to document files and has no real content, it still needs to be saved.

Select File>Save (or Save As) and the Save Book dialog will be presented, as shown in Figure 3.9. Rename the Save in File field to a filename that is more meaningful (such as PUB.FMB). You'll notice that the Format field is automatically set to Normal FrameMaker Book.

You've just created a publication with one chapter!

Please note that the directory structure that I use is on a network drive H. You will probably use drive C with some other directory.

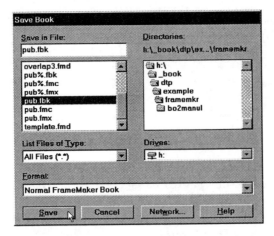

Notice the file PUB%.FBK? FrameMaker appends a special character to files (such as % for backups and @ or $ for saved files in the case of a system crash). Frame Technology Corporation really put in a lot of thought to providing a fail-safe system for you.

Using Corel Ventura

Creating a Publication

Corel Ventura has a new facility with all sorts of quick format tools that can help you through processes that used to be time-consuming. I'll stick to the more traditional methods of this feature-rich product.

Many things have improved with the latest version of Corel Ventura and the old method of creating a publication a chapter at a time has all but disappeared. Now, you first create a publication and then the chapters.

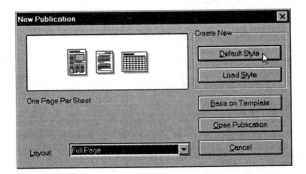

Figure 3.11
Setting the page
layout.

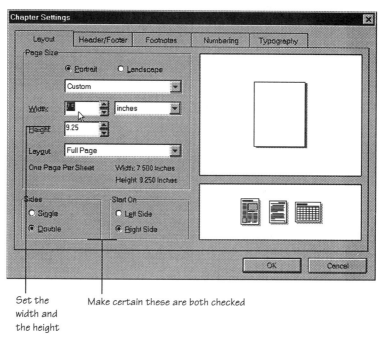

Set the
width and
the height

Make certain these are both checked

Start Corel Ventura. Click File>New menu to bring up the
New Publication dialog (Figure 3.10). You should experiment
with the different layout options—there are many neat ones
(including one for folded brochures). For now, though, select
Full Page and click Default Style.

If you wish to open a new publication and you have defined
another publication with a style sheet you'd like to use, click
on Load Style instead. You now have created a blank
8.5"x11" chapter.

Let's change the target page size to 7.5"x9.25" (Figure 3.11).
Click Layout>Chapter Settings (or **F5**).

As you change the default Width field from **8.5"** to **7.5"**, the
Page Size field automatically changes to Custom. Change the
Height field to **9.25"**.

Click OK.

Your target page size is now set. To set the margins, click the
Pick tool ⊾ to select the page frame. Right-click and select
Frame> Margins (Figure 3.12).

Change the Top and Bottom margins to **.75"** and leave the
Left and Right at **1"** for all pages. Click OK.

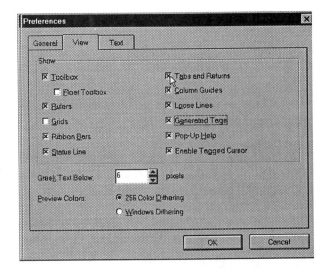

Normally, Corel Ventura doesn't show borders and symbols. You'll have to enable that yourself.

Select the View tab (Figure 3.13) in the Preferences dialog after choosing the Tools>Preferences menu command. Check the view preferences as I've done. You'll now view the page with all of its typographic symbols and page layout borders (Figure 3.14).

There are two items on the page that stand out: the insertion point and the text flow frame which acts as the boundaries to the chapter page.

Figure 3.13
Setting viewing
preferences.

Figure 3.14
The newly created
text frame.

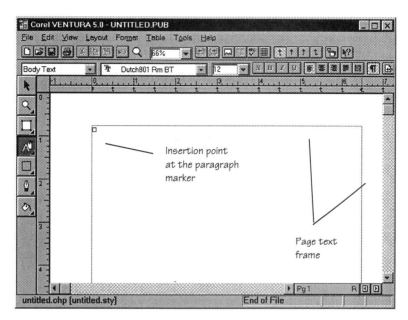

Before saving the chapter, let's set up the page numbering system.

Using the Pick tool , click and select the entire page frame so that square handles are displayed on all four sides of the document.

Either right-click to select the Chapter>Numbering menu command, or use the keyboard shortcut key (**F5**) to display the Chapter Settings dialog. Click on the Numbering tab if not currently viewed (Figure 3.15).

If the chapter is the first (or a preface), you'll want to uncheck Continue From Previous Chapter and set the Starting Number to **1**.

If it is a chapter that continues from a previous one, check Continue From Previous Chapter and select the Number Style from the list box (you'll normally use style 1,2,3).

Select OK when you are ready to return to the document. Corel Ventura has really improved the usability of setting the page numbering scheme.

Figure 3.15
Setting a chapter's numbering format and starting point.

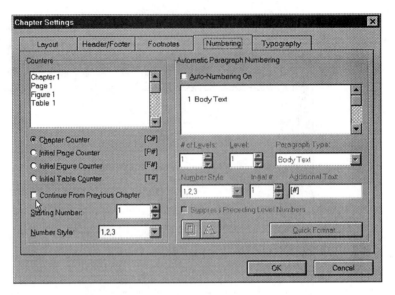

Saving the Chapter

You should now save the style template, which includes page formatting information, into file CHAPTER.STY. Select Layout>Save Style Sheet As. (You can always load another style sheet with the Load Style Sheet menu command.) Save CHAPTER.STY into your publication's TEMPLATE subdirectory.

Save the current chapter as CHAPTER1.CHP in the CHAPTER subdirectory using the Layout>Save Chapter As menu.

To save the entire publication, select File>Save As. Corel Ventura uses a file extension of .PUB for all publications.

Adding Chapters to a Publication

To add another chapter to a publication, select Layout>Add New Chapter. Corel Ventura may ask you to save the currently opened chapter if changes were made to it since the last save. You'll know that you created a new chapter because the Status line shows: untitled.chp [chapter.sty] . Like other Windows applications, a filename called UNTITLED means that the file is new and hasn't been saved.

Opening an Existing Publication

To open a publication, select File>New. You used to be able

to open just a single chapter from the File menu—no more! Click on the Open Publication button. Browse through the directory structure and select the desired publication file.

You can also select a file from the latest file cache list at the bottom of the File menu if the publication has been one of the latest publications selected.

DEFINING HEADERS AND FOOTERS

Headers and footers have interesting characteristics:

- They are located in frames that are typically outside of the normal body text flow.
- They include references to changing information such as page numbers and repeating heading text. References that are repeated but whose contents change are typically called running header/footer variables.

NOTE I'll discuss sans serif and serif fonts later.

- They are usually set in a sans serif font that is smaller than normal body text and sometimes set in a different spot color.

Our headers and footers will be somewhat complex in order to show you how to do great things (you may choose to do far less than this example).

Our example will include the following:

- A header in a spot color that alternates the topmost heading level (using style Header 1).
- A footer in a spot color for the text with a larger, black page number.
- A chapter thumb tab that displays the current chapter name and the chapter number (also larger than the chapter name). In fact, this text is printed in a format much like a header so that it can stand out on the spot colored rectangular background. Chapter tabs, in our case, are placed on odd pages only.

Figure 3.16
The header and
footer page view.

Header (all in spot color) of
the most current topmost
header level

Chapter tab with the
current chapter number
and title

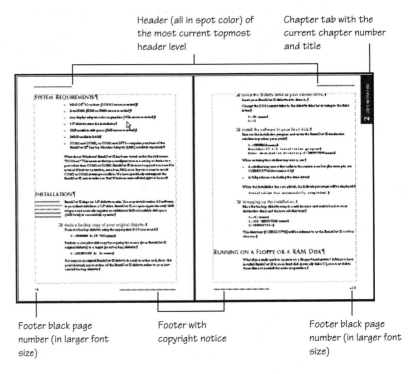

Footer black page
number (in larger font
size)

Footer with
copyright notice

Footer black page
number (in larger font
size)

I've chosen a spot color instead of black for the header and footer.

Our page design uses the concept of mirrored headers and footers where the location of header/footer elements are absolutely presented in reverse order on left and right pages.

Figure 3.16 is a miniature illustration of our three elements in facing page view. The chapter title page has a footer even though you would normally consider it the first right page.

The chapter tab can be regarded as a repeated frame that has a background color with a single line of text flow inside, composed of bolded, white (called reverse) text including the chapter number and the chapter title. It is assumed that the chapter title does not change for a given chapter.

NOTE Don't forget that our target page is 7.5"x9.25".

For example, our chapter tab occupies .5"x2" at a horizontal location 7" from the leftmost target page edge. For the first chapter, the chapter tab's leftmost corner would start at vertical 0", the second chapter would start at vertical 2" from the target page's top, and so on.

Figure 3.17
The placement of
chapter tabs.

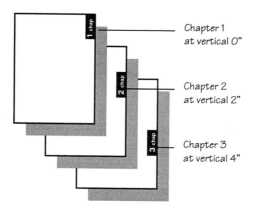

Chapter 1
at vertical 0"

Chapter 2
at vertical 2"

Chapter 3
at vertical 4"

Figure 3.17 shows what consecutive chapter tabs in a three
chapter publication would look like.

When you have many chapters and the tab for a chapter runs
out of vertical space at the bottom of the page, just start over
at vertical 0" from the top.

Using FrameMaker

Viewing Facing Pages

Select the Facing Pages view in the Page Scrolling field under
the View>Options menu to look at both pages.

Creating the Header

You can only create or modify a header from a master page.
Select the View>Master Pages. **PAGE DOWN** (or **PAGE UP**) in
order to select the Right master page.

Click the Smart Selection tool ▉ . Double-click at the right of
the header until an insertion point is established at the right
margin (Figure 3.18).

I use FrameMaker's system variable mechanism to refer to a
running header. Click on Special>Variable and then scroll to
Running H/F 2. See Figure 3.19.

Click on Edit definition and enter the following text by
clicking on Building Blocks:

<$paratext[Heading 1]><Default ¶ Font>

Figure 3.18
Create a header.

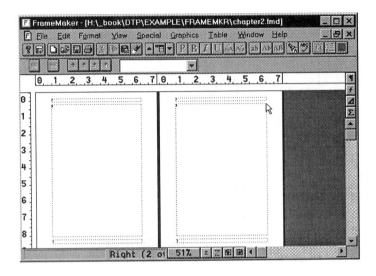

This is a variable building block that displays the running (or, better put, changing) contents of the first level heading represented by the tag name of Heading 1.

NOTE Tags are described in the next chapter.

It is good practice (but not necessary in this case) to return to the default text style. Click on Edit, then Insert. Do the same to the left page's header at the far lefthand margin. Your heading is done.

Creating the Footer

The footer is created in a similar way except that you click the insertion point on the leftmost position in the footer frame and type the book's title, copyright (that's what I use), or whatever you want.

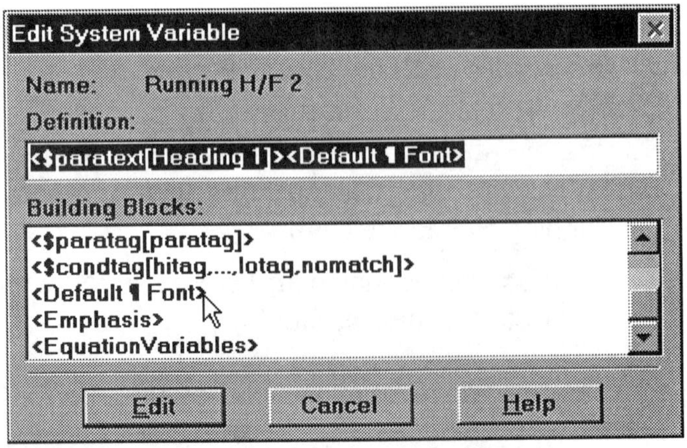

Figure 3.19
Create a running header variable.

Edit System Variable

Name: Running H/F 2

Definition:

`<$paratext[Heading 1]><Default ¶ Font>`

Building Blocks:

`<$paratag[paratag]>`
`<$condtag[hitag,....,lotag,nomatch]>`
`<Default ¶ Font>`
`<Emphasis>`
`<EquationVariables>`

Edit   Cancel   Help

As long as you are not referencing changing paragraph's contents (like chapter or a heading), you don't need to use a FrameMaker Running H/F system variable.

Press **TAB** a couple of time to position the cursor to the right margin of the footer text frame. You'll need to insert a page number reference here. This page counter is similar to a running system variable since it automatically changes on every page.

Click System>Variables and then insert the Current Page # definition. Highlight the # (inserted by FrameMaker) and change the font size to **10.0 pt** with the Format>Size menu.

NOTE Setting paragraph tab stops will be shown in detail in the next chapter.

If the text is not lining up properly it is because your tab settings are not correct. In the Footer paragraph tag designer, set Tab Stops (in Basic properties) to a centered 2.75" and a right-justified 5.5". This can be changed later.

Creating the Chapter Tab

NOTE As you drag the rectangular frame, the size of the frame is constantly being updated in the Status bar.

Click the Graphics Frame tool [icon] in the Tools palette and create a frame (dimensions .5"x2") positioned at the upper right corner of the page (located at the top at 7" left at 0") by dragging the frame from the upper, left corner to the lower, right corner.

Within that frame, insert a Text Frame tool [icon] with these parameters: Top: .125", Left: .25", Width: 1.75", and Height: .25". Then under the Graphics>Rotate menu, rotate the text frame 90 degrees counterclockwise. The technique of using a text frame inside of a chapter tab frame will be used throughout all of the chapters of your publication.

Change the cursor to a text cursor with the Smart Selection tool [icon] and double-click in the text paragraph frame until an insertion point appears. Click Special>Variables, then Running H/F 3. This system variable will be used for text in the chapter tab.

Finally, click on the Edit definition button. In the Definition field, create:

```
<BOLD BIG><$paranum[Chapter No]><Default ¶
Font>\sm<$paratext[Chapter]><Default ¶ Font>.
```

Figure 3.20
Setting a color
reference.

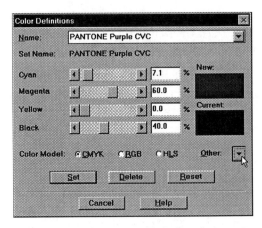

This definition results in a large chapter number followed by the paragraph text of the current chapter. Click Edit to accept followed by Insert. We'll change the color of the chapter tab text to white and define the character/paragraph tags referenced in this definition in the next chapter.

Finally, let's fill the chapter tab frame with Pantone Purple CV. But, how do you refer to a spot color that isn't your normal color choice?

Click View>Color>Definitions. Now, you are presented a wide choice of color models. Click the Other button and select Pantone.

When presented the PANTONE Colors dialog, type **Purple** in the Find PANTONE field, click on the Purple color swatch, and then return to the Color Definitions dialog by clicking Set followed by Done. The Pantone color matching system automatically presents the color as PANTONE Purple CVC (Figure 3.20).

You may have noticed that FrameMaker shows that for some reason, the color purple is a CMYK color even though we chose a Pantone spot color. The Pantone color matching system actually tells FrameMaker what Purple's spot color equates to as a mixture of cyan, magenta, yellow, and black.

Select the chapter tab graphics frame and click the Color pop-up menu ▤ from the Tools palette. Choose PANTONE Purple CVC. If the chapter tab didn't fill with color, select the 100% fill by clicking the Fill pattern pop-up menu ▨.

Figure 3.21
The completed chapter tab.

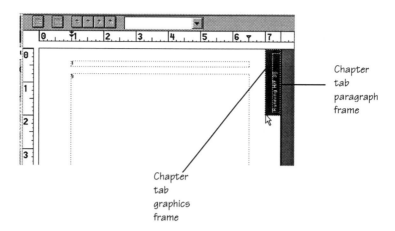

Chapter tab paragraph frame

Chapter tab graphics frame

NOTE Don't forget to save the chapter!

Figure 3.21 shows the finished chapter tab. Now, click on View>Body Pages to switch back to the body page. FrameMaker will automatically alternate the Left and Right master pages as you create your chapter.

In addition, running header fields will be automatically generated.

Using Corel Ventura

Viewing Facing Pages

To view facing pages, click on View>Facing Pages Preview. This displays both pages side by side (Figure 3.22).

Figure 3.22
Facing views.

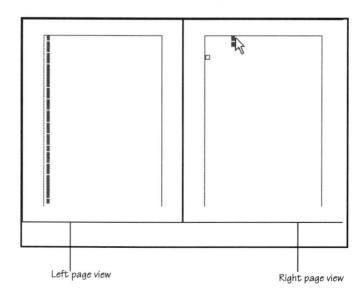

Left page view

Right page view

Unfortunately, you cannot edit when facing views are enabled—it is just a preview capability. You can always **PAGE DOWN** or **PAGE UP** through your chapter. By the way, when you haven't inserted body text that extends over one page, you only view the first right page.

Uncheck the Facing Pages Preview menu command to return to normal view.

Let's create the header, footer, and chapter tab. Keep in mind that we won't be able to finish these items properly until we complete some of the text work in the next chapter.

Creating the Header

Select the entire page frame, right-click, and then choose Chapter>Headers and Footers. You'll be presented with a dialog that looks pretty intimidating (Figure 3.23).

NOTE You can disable headers or footers on selected pages with Layout>Hide Page Header (or Footer).

Before we forget, check all four of the Enable boxes informing Corel Ventura to allow headers and footers to be generated for all pages in the chapter. As you can see, there are lots of buttons that assist in the building of headers and footers that were simply not available in earlier versions of Corel Ventura. These buttons should initially be grayed out.

Select the Right Page Header from the Define list. Click the cursor into the Right field to place an insertion point.

NOTE If the Tags dialog box is not displayed, you are probably low in available memory. Terminate other applications and try again.

Once you place the insertion point in one of the text fields, the buttons can be used. Click on the first matching tag button (the second button from the right).

You will be shown the Tags dialog, which, currently has a very small list of predefined paragraph tags. See Figure 3.24.

Double-click on the MainHeading tag. This tag is inserted into the Right field as [<MainHeading]. Highlight the word MainHeading and replace it with the tag **Heading 1**, which will be defined later in the next chapter.

Click Mirror to Facing Pages so that the left page header. If you wish to look at the results, click on Left Page Header pull-down option and you'll see [<**Heading 1**] in the Left field (as it should be).

Figure 3.23
The initial Chapter
Settings dialog
box.

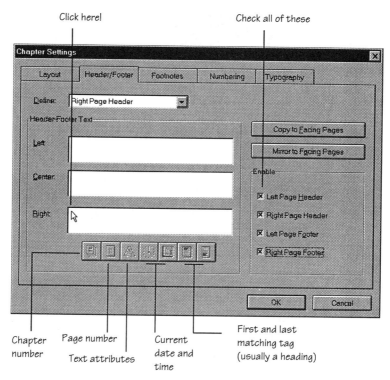

The paragraph tag is actually a running header. Corel
Ventura automatically updates the header as the paragraph
tag (in this case, Heading 1) changes.

Click OK to accept the header.

Creating the Footer

With the page frame selected, right-click and select
Chapter>Headers and Footers from the pop-up menu.

Figure 3.24
Select the first
matching
paragraph
heading.

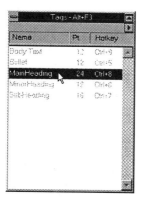

Figure 3.25
Setting the page
number text size.

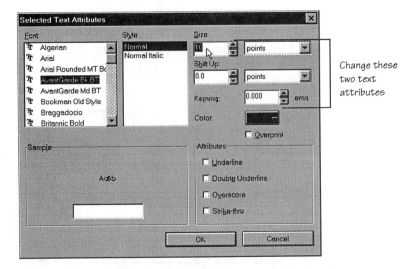

Make certain that the Define field is set to Right Page Footer
in the Right field. Next, place the insertion point in the Left
field. Type in your company's name, the book's title, or
copyright.

NOTE See Figure
3.23 for the
description of
each button.

Click on the page number button. Drag the cursor over the
inserted **[P#]** and then click the text attributes button. You'll
be presented with the Selected Text Attributes dialog.

I've chosen two attributes that need to be changed: size and
color. Change the Size field to **10 pt** as shown in Figure 3.25.
Click on Color then the More button in order to display the
Selected Text Color dialog (Figure 3.26).

Figure 3.26
Setting the color.

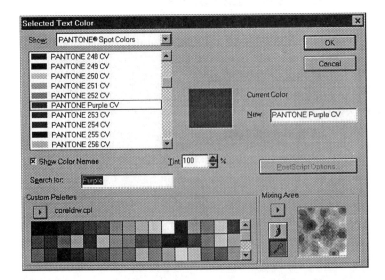

Figure 3.27
Select the header frame.

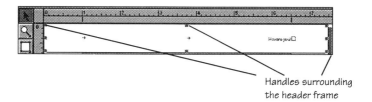

Handles surrounding
the header frame

Change the color model from RGB Color Model to PANTONE Spot Colors in the Show field. Click Show Color Names and type **Purple** in the Search for field.

NOTE There are many more color features you can play with.

Not only is the new color shown but the complete Pantone name is automatically matched and displayed in the New field. Click OK to return to the Selected Text Attributes dialog. Click OK again to return to the Header/Footer tab. The **[P#]** text in the Right field is now replaced with seemingly unintelligible text of:

NOTE The field may also have a font name included at the beginning.

<P10C1,3,0,228,100>[P#]<D>

Now, you could have typed this in yourself (sure!). Corel Ventura uses an internal text description language all its own to describe text attributes.

The **<P>** command actually sets the color to a 100% color tint. The **<D>** returns the text attributes to the footer's default. You really don't have to understand these special codes—just be aware that Corel Ventura uses them and they sometimes are revealed to you. Now, click Mirror to Facing Pages to verify. Select Left Page Footer and you'll see both fields reversed as you would expect. Click on OK to accept.

Creating the Chapter Tab

First, we must allow for chapter tabs to overlap the header and footer frames. What frames you ask? When you originally create page margins, Corel Ventura automatically creates frames the width of your document's target page but the height of the top (and bottom) margins.

Select the Pick tool and click in the header frame. As you can see in Figure 3.27, when the frame is selected, there are handles surrounding it. Right-click while the header frame is still selected, click on Format>General and then *un*check Flow Text Around Frame.

Figure 3.28
The Chapter tab
is created.

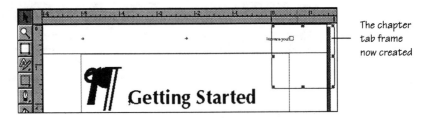

The chapter
tab frame
now created

Click OK to accept. Do the same with the footer frame.

Click on the entire page (don't just select the header or footer frame) and select the Frame tool.

To the right, draw a rectangle approximately 2"x2" on the upper-right corner of the target page. See Figure 3.28. The exact size isn't very important yet.

Using the Freehand Text tool, click in the frame. The insertion point should be at the upper left corner. Type:

1. Right-click and select Insert Special Item>Cross Reference.

2. Select the Chapter Number in the Reference Type field and click OK.

3. Press the **END** key and insert an em space by typing **CTRL**+**SHIFT**+M.

4. Type the name of the chapter title (like, **Getting Started**).

Using the Pick tool, select the frame, right-click and choose Format>General. See Figure 3.29.

1. Set the Rotation field to **90** degrees.

2. Set the Repeat on field to Right Pages.

3. Change the Width of **2.0"** and the Height to **.5"**.

4. Enter new Frame Origin values with the Horizontal field set to **7.0"** and Vertical set to **0"**.

5. Make certain that the Flow Text Around Frame is unchecked.

You've completed the chapter frame settings. Now, let's set up the frame's margins.

Figure 3.29
Setup the
chapter tag
frame.

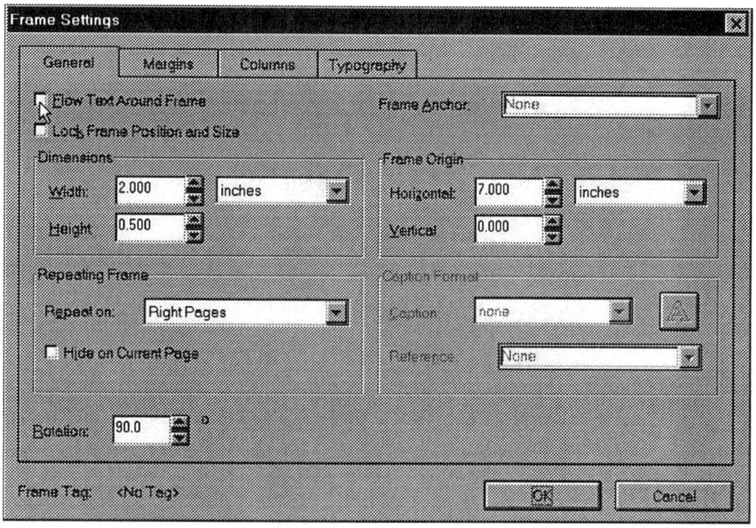

Click the Margins tab and change the Top field margin to
.125" and the Left field to **.25"**. This ensures that the chapter
tab text doesn't run into the leftmost frame's edge. Click OK
to accept the chapter tab frame settings.

NOTE This is the
same process as in
"Creating the
Footer," on page
79.

With the frame still selected, right-click and choose Uniform
Fill and choose the PANTONE Spot Colors. Type in **pur** in the
Search for field and when Corel Ventura displays **PANTONE
Purple CV** in the New field, click OK.

Your frame should now be completely filled with a spot
color. We'll do the final formatting in the next chapter but
your chapter tab is all ready to go.

For each chapter, you'll need to reposition this frame down
by two inches (see Figure 3.17, "The placement of chapter
tabs.," on page 73).

To reposition the chapter tab frame in other chapters of your
publication, you'll:

1. Temporarily set the frame's Repeat On field to No Other
   Pages (Figure 3.29).

2. Copy the frame to the clipboard (using Edit>Copy or
   CTRL+C).

3. In other chapters, simply Edit>Paste (**CTRL+V**) the frame
   to place the frame onto the page, reposition it to the right

vertical location, and set Repeat On field to Right Pages.

MANAGING A PUBLICATION

We'll show how to:

- Save a publication.
- Add chapters to a publication.
- Reorder a document in a publication.
- Remove a document from a publication.
- Reopen a publication.

Figure 3.30
The reference
page.

Pre-defined
borders to be
used with your
headers, footers,
and headings
(I don't use
them!)

Standard
callout formats
I use (the
line and the
associated
callout text is
grouped as one
object)

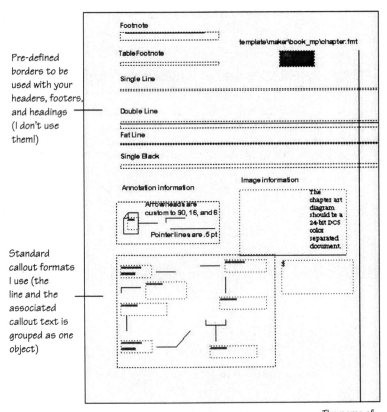

The name of
the template
and the version
of that template

Figure 3.31
Adding files to the
rest of the book.

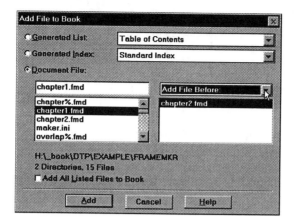

Figure 3.31
Adding files to the
rest of the book.

Using FrameMaker

Keeping Track of Publication Information

FrameMaker has a built-in mechanism for including
reference information, which will not be printed (sort of like
a scratchpad for notes). These are called reference pages.

I use these pages to hold information such as table formats,
notes on page design, standard line widths, and other
pertinent details. I store this in FrameMaker's reference pages
of a chapter's template file.

To understand how a reference page can be used, simply click
on View>Reference Pages.

On these pages, you can include almost anything you
want—they always remain with your document, but they are
never printed, and any item can be copied to the clipboard
and pasted onto your body or master page.

NOTE You can
create many ref-
erence pages.

For example, Figure 3.30 shows a reference page I created. As
noted, the reference page hides within your document.

FrameMaker itself makes use of tagged (named) objects in
reference pages in order to provide borders to paragraphs and
to format generated lists (like a table of contents or index).

Adding Chapter Files

To add chapters to a book, select File>Add File. To add
CHAPTER1.FMD to the publication, select File>Add File.

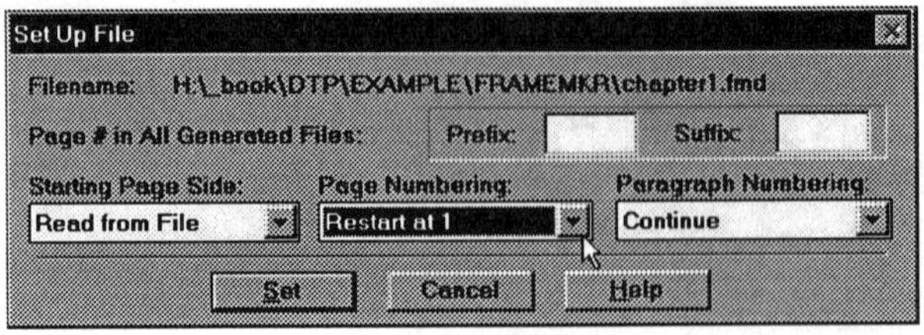

Figure 3.32
Start a chapter at
page 1.

Click on Document File and select the file CHAPTER1.FMD. See Figure 3.31.

Since we wish to place Chapter 1 before Chapter 2, click Add File Before: and then the Add button. Click Done to return.

The publication file PUB.FBK includes two chapters: CHAPTER1.FMD and CHAPTER2.FMD.

In order to set up the page numbering counter, you need to select the file in the publication file window and then click File>Set Up File. Do this for CHAPTER1.FMD (Figure 3.32). Click Set after setting the Page Numbering to Restart at 1.

Back in the publication window, select CHAPTER2.FMD and then File>Set Up File. Change the Page Numbering field to Continue and click Set.

This setting should be used for all other chapters. How do you ensure the format of page numbering? For prefaces and tables of contents, you will probably use lowercase roman numerals (i, ii, iii, and so on) and for chapters you'll probably use arabic numerics (1, 2, and so on).

These and other individual chapter document preferences are set within the Format>Document menu commands. You may wish to refer back to Figure 3.7, "Portion of the Document Properties dialog.," on page 64.

Rearranging Files

To rearrange files, select the book window (in our case, PUB.FMB). select a given chapter (like CHAPTER1.FMD) and click on either the Move Up, Move Down, or the Delete button. The Delete button does not delete the file, it simply removes the publication's reference to the file.

When you are done rearranging the file, click Done.

Verifying the Page Layout

Some of FrameMaker's menus have had some questionable organizational structure and where you would go to verify page attributes has been one of them. Well, starting with version 5, the menus have been improved dramatically.

Use the Format>Page Layout>Page Size menu command to verify the page size and pagination attribute of either single-sided or double-sided documents.

Use the Format>Page Layout>Column Layout menu command to validate number columns and margin settings.

Saving a Template

In the course of modifying a chapter you may change some properties that the entire publication ought to use. These changes should be placed into a chapter template. These are the steps:

1. Save the current chapter with a **CTRL+S**.

2. Perform a File>Save As to a chapter template file (I prefer a name like CHAPTER.FMT). Don't forget that this template file should be saved in a TEMPLATE subdirectory so that other publications can use the same template file.

3. Click on the Smart Selection tool then double-click in the text flow till the cursor changes to the insertion point.

4. Select the entire document's text flow with the menu command: Select All in Flow (or use **CTRL+A**).

5. Press the **DEL** key to remove all text.

6. Delete all of the pages except for the first page with the Special>Delete Pages.

7. Save the chapter template with a **CTRL+S**.

Using a Template to Change the Publication

Once you have created or modified a chapter template, you'll need to import its attributes to the rest of the publication.

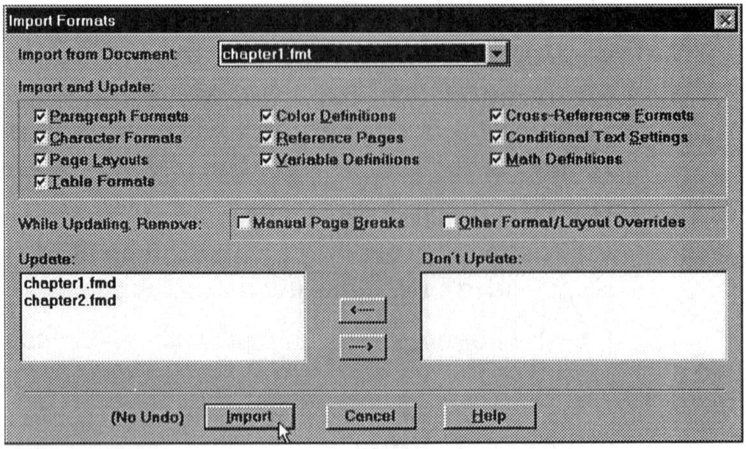

Figure 3.33
Import of formats
from a template
to the publication.

Here are the steps:

1. Make certain that the template file (CHAPTER.FMT) and the publication (PUB.FMB) are both opened. See Figure 3.33.

2. Click on the publication file so that it is currently viewed.

3. Select File>Import>Formats menu command. If not, you can highlight the file and press the left or right arrow buttons. Click Import when ready.

4. Save the publication file and any opened chapter files.

Using Corel Ventura

Keeping Track of Publication Information

NOTE Windows has a WordPad application that works great for keeping notes.

There is no hidden page capability for notes or other information in Corel Ventura. You should keep a separate text file for notes about each chapter. Include notes for caption line widths, arrow types, glossary terms, and so on. This is even more important if there are several writers working together on a single publication.

Verifying the Page Layout

Use the Pick tool ▮ to select the page frame. To view the chapter page size, right-click then select the Chapter>Layout menu. To view margin and column information, right-click then select the Frame>Margins or Frame>Columns menu.

Rearranging Files

To rearrange files with Corel Ventura, you simply:

1. Double-click the chapter name in the File>Publication Manager dialog.

2. Click on the File Operations radio button.

3. Select the chapter and drag it to its new position.

4. Choose Format>Renumber Publication.

PLACING FINISHING TOUCHES

Before we go on to the next chapter, there are several other items we need to cover, including:

- Setting a snap grid so that objects line up.

- Enabling typographer's quotation marks replacing straight marks with "curly" ones.

- Periodic saving of your publication.

DTP programs allow objects (text, graphics, and frames) to be placed in increments of .001".

I like aligning all objects horizontally and vertically to .1".

Using FrameMaker

Snapping a Page

You are using a desktop publishing package in order to achieve not only a great look but also to produce a page document, with perfectly placed objects.

You set this from the View>Options menu command (Figure 3.34). Edit the Grid Spacing field to **.1"**, check the Snap field, and click the Set button.

Figure 3.34
Setting the snap
guides.

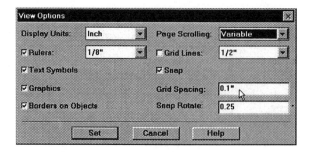

Using Typographic Quotation Marks

The Format>Document>Text Options menu allows you to
enable both Smart Quotes and Smart Spaces. This setting
should be consistent throughout your publication and ought
to be kept in your chapter template (file CHAPTER.FMT).

Typing Key Symbols

FrameMaker provides keyboard shortcuts to insert certain
symbols that are used in publications:

To insert symbol	Type
Trademark	**CTRL+Q** *
Registered trademark	**CTRL+Q** (
Copyright	**CTRL+Q**)
Em space	**ESC SPACEBAR** m
En space	**ESC SPACEBAR** n
Thin space	**ESC SPACEBAR** t
Nonbreaking space	**ESC SPACEBAR** h
Em dash	**CTRL+q SHIFT+q**
En dash	**CTRL+q SHIFT+p**
Discretionary hyphen	**ESC - d**
Nonbreaking hyphen	**ESC - h**
Forced return	**SHIFT+ENTER**
Left typographic quote	**CTRL+q SHIFT+r** (or ")
Right typographic quote	**CTRL+q SHIFT+s** (or ")

Planning for Automatic Saves and Backups

In order to save a document automatically, you can set
preferences with the File>Preferences menu command
below. Set Automatic Save at least every **10 Minutes**.

Figure 3.35
Saving opened
files automatically.

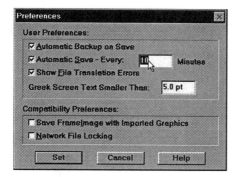

Redisplaying the Chapter

There are times when FrameMaker leaves graphics or "trash" on your monitor even though you know it should not be there. Don't worry. Type **CTRL+L** to refresh the display view.

Using Corel Ventura

Snapping a Page

With the Pick tool [icon] selected, click on the underlying frame for the entire page and either right-click and select the Grid Setup menu command or select Tools>Grid Setup (Figure 3.36).

Set both grid points per inch to **10**, check Snap To Grid, and then click OK. That sets up the grid for the text flow frame. You must also enable snap to take place by checking Snap To Grid under the View menu.

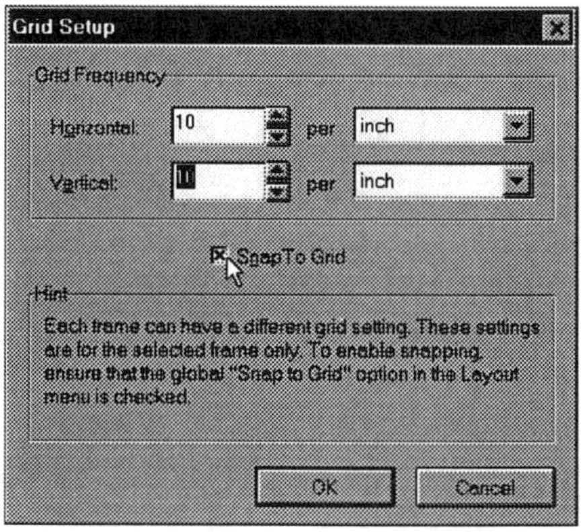

Figure 3.36
Setting the grid to
snap.

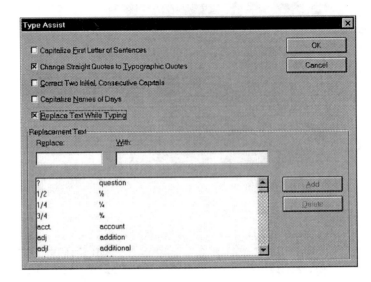

You can change grid settings for individual frames by selecting a frame and then changing the setup by right-clicking and selecting the Grid Setup menu command.

Using Typographic Quotation Marks

To replace straight quotes with typographic quotes, enable Change Straight Quotes to Typographic Quotes from the dialog displayed in the Tools>Type Assist menu (Figure 3.37). There are many other preferences that you can easily select in this dialog box, so experiment with them.

Typing Key Symbols

To insert special symbols in Corel Ventura, use the key combinations shown below:

To insert symbol	Type
Trademark	**CTRL**+**SHIFT**+2
Registered trademark	**CTRL**+**SHIFT**+R
Copyright	**CTRL**+**SHIFT**+C
Em space	**CTRL**+**SHIFT**+M
En space	**CTRL**+**SHIFT**+N
Thin space	**CTRL**+**SHIFT**+T
Nonbreaking space	not applicable
Em dash	**CTRL**+**ALT**+M
En dash	**CTRL**+**ALT**+N
Discretionary hyphen	**CTRL**+-
Nonbreaking hyphen	*not applicable*
Forced return	**SHIFT**+**ENTER**
Left typographic quote	**CTRL**+**ALT**+Q
Right typographic quote	**CTRL**+**ALT**+C

Planning for Automatic Saves and Backups

You can automatically save to a backup file when you save a chapter by checking the Make Backup on Save option within the Tools>Preferences menu (Figure 3.38).

This will save the current chapter with a file extension of .$HP instead of .CHP. If you need to restore a chapter, you'll have to rename the .$HP backup copy to the equivalent .CHP name outside of Corel Ventura.

Although Corel Ventura can automatically save a chapter, I prefer to check the Prompt to Save Chapter—just to be safe.

Click OK to exit the Preferences dialog.

Redisplaying the Chapter

There are times when Corel Ventura leaves graphics or "trash" on the display, even though you know it should not be there. Type **CTRL**+W to refresh the display view.

4 TEXT

The text layer can be confusing if you are not used to the idea of paragraph style definitions. This chapter explains all that, along with details about fonts and font management that I believe every writer ought to understand.

You can spend hours designing paragraph tag definitions so that they look right. This chapter should save you many hours of frustration by clarifying issues that are not explained well in most DTP program manuals.

We'll cover the following topics:

- Font technology and the administration of fonts.
- Foundations of a paragraph tag.
- The many faces of body text.
- Special paragraph tags.
- Run-ins and lists.
- Headings and sidehead concepts.
- Header and footer information.
- Indexing and cross-referencing.

FONTOGRAPHY

"What? You've bought another font? Aaggghhhhh!!!! They all look the same, don't they?"

Ever heard that?

There are folks who spend a lifetime studying the beauty and design of fonts. It can be fascinating and part of that fascination, probably has something to do with the fact that we spend a lot of our time reading books, reports, newspapers, billboards, and so on. The written word is everywhere and how those words look can make a big difference to a reader. Some fonts make reading easy—others are designed for impact only.

Of course, there are those who have no regard for font technology and have the view that a letter shape is just a shape—no big deal.

Using Text Characteristics to Advantage

Text is an element in all four hierarchical layers previously discussed that share characteristics such as:

- Font family (such as Times).

- Font weight and angle (such as bold, italic).

- Size (such as 12 points—a point (abbreviated as pt) is 1/72 of an inch).

- Color (normally black but can be anything).

- Kerning (the reduction of space between certain pairs of characters in display type, so that the result is more professional and pleasing to the eye).

I know of a documentation manager who actually left a company because they were so rigid on fonts and page design. The company insisted on Times Roman, she wanted Palatino. Hey, it happens!

Fonts used to be distributed in specific point sizes. Now, the mainstream font technologies provide fonts as algorithms that describe the curves and organization regardless of the printable or displayable size. This technique is scalable, hence, scalable fonts.

Although there have been several technologies that have come and gone over the years (Bitstream's SPEEDO, for example), there are two prevalent font technologies used in Windows today: Type 1 and Truetype.

Prior to Windows version 3, the only scalable font rendering technology was Adobe's Type Manager (ATM). ATM software controls the administration and display of Type 1 fonts. Type 1 technology is considered to be the standard for Postscript printer and imagesetters.

With the introduction of Windows version 3, Microsoft and Apple defined a competitive, font rendering technology called Truetype. Truetype font outlines, although not compatible with Type 1 font outlines, provide the same sort of information, while a separate type manager (like ATM) is not required.

Truetype fonts can be output on any printer or imagesetter through the Windows printer subsystem. In other words, Truetype fonts can be printed to a Postscript device with font outlines automatically converted to Type 1 outlines (or substituted by similar Type 1 fonts). This is accomplished through your Postscript printer driver's Advanced Options dialog (normally selected from Printer Setup menu).

Using Font Technologies

When to Use Type 1

Documents destined to be printed on a printer supporting Type 1 fonts implies that the printer is Postscript-compatible. So, all text and drawings with text must use Type 1 fonts. If you choose to circulate documents that use Type 1 fonts, make certain that users have ATM.

Adobe Type Manager is not included automatically with Windows, so don't assume your users will be able to use or view Type 1 fonts.

When To Use Truetype

Documents destined to be viewed or shared with other users

on-line must, however, always be Truetype. Generally, this is because every Windows system can support TrueType, and not every Windows system has ATM installed. Truetype fonts should be used in internal specifications, interactive help systems, and presentations.

Mixing Truetype with Type 1

Why not pick and choose fonts that are best for the job regardless of the font technology?

If the end user for your document is only you, then go right ahead! In general, however, I do not recommend creating any document that uses a mix of font technologies.

If Adobe is listening, why not make your Type 1 fonts (considered to be about the best in the font business) available as Truetype fonts? It would make sense! Other font vendors are beginning to put quality Truetype and Type 1 fonts in the same font package for one price. This trend certainly makes our lives easier.

Administrating Fonts

NOTE Rush out and buy any version of CorelDRAW if you want great fonts!

Chances are, you have access to several hundred high-quality fonts. If you installed them all you would have a great assortment of fonts to choose from. Unfortunately, your system's performance suffers because the font scaling technology must catalog these fonts every time most applications are loaded. This definitely applies to DTP programs.

Ares FontMinder provides a method of loading the Windows environment with the fonts that you desire. You should normally start FontMinder before you start your DTP program, although you can change your installed fonts at any time. FontMinder sports a very simple user interface. See Figure 4.1.

FontMinder searches your system for all of the available Truetype and Type 1 fonts. These form the master library.

You simply drag fonts from the Library into the Font Pack Fonts list box on the right. These fonts can be saved in a FontMinder font pack and named (lower left list box).

Figure 4.1
Basic FontMinder
user interface.

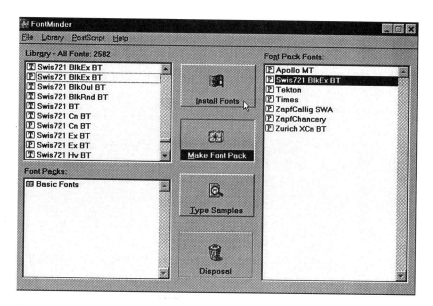

To load Windows with your selection of fonts, click the
Install Fonts button. That's all there is to it. FontMinder takes
care of all of the Windows and ATM initialization files that
we used to have to modify by hand. This utility program is
invaluable.

DEFINING PARAGRAPH TAGS

Basing One Tag on Another

All text should have a consistent style. And one way of
controlling styles is to group like text attributes into a named
paragraph tag. Your publication should have a couple of
dozen defined tag names that you can use to apply to
characteristics.

A couple dozen tags may sound like a lot, but they all
probably will stem from just a handful of basic style choices.

As an example, let's assume that all paragraph head styles
(so-named Heading 1, Heading 2, and so on) all use similar
style characteristics derived from a sans serif font like Utopia
(that's what I use in this book's headings).

Figure 4.2
Deriving
paragraph tags.

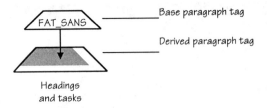

Base paragraph tag

Derived paragraph tag

Headings
and tasks

We could look at it as illustrated in Figure 4.2. The paragraph tag named FAT_SANS acts as a base tag. All derived styles (headings and tasks) inherit the same attributes and potentially could modify or enhance any of the attributes.

Before we go any further, I've mentioned the term sans serif. The term serif refers to a font whose letters have fine cross strokes across the ends of the ascenders and descenders. Most body text (as in this paragraph) uses serif fonts. Times (alias Times Roman or Roman) and Stone serif are good examples.

Sans serif refers to a font without these cross strokes. Helvetica is a good example of a sans serif font. Sans serif fonts are typically used in tables, section headings, headers, and chapter titles. Deciding when to use one or the other is based on the design style you wish to promote.

NOTE   Chapters and chapter numbers also share the same base paragraph style as headings.

We'll assign paragraph tags for the different headings. This book uses four of them: Heading 1, Heading 2, Heading 3, and Heading 4. In Figure 4.3, I've shown how three of the four heading styles are all based on one: FAT_SANS, which defines the font as a 12 pt., Optima bold (along with other attributes).

The actual heading fonts make minor modifications, yet each of the paragraph tags represent some variation of the FAT_SANS style attributes. What DTP programs support this powerful concept? Unfortunately, FrameMaker and Corel Ventura don't support the concept of a paragraph style derived from another style.

Regardless of the DTP program you use, you should think in derived styles.

Figure 4.3
Derived headings tags.

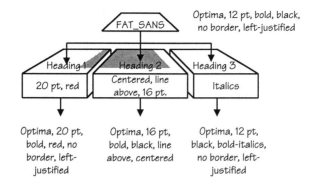

Use a piece of paper, WordPad, or FrameMaker's reference page in your document's template file to keep track of your base paragraph styles. If you don't write them down somewhere, you could eventually forget the relationship between paragraph styles!

I'll present a hierarchy of paragraph styles used in manual production and how each DTP program uses them.

Defining a Paragraph Tag

What is a tag?

NOTE Some common tag attributes are: font family, font size, line spacing (in other words, leading), color, justification, and so on.

A tag is a facility within DTP programs that allow you to assign formatting attributes to a paragraph. Rather than having to define attributes to every paragraph, you can assign a set of attributes a name.

This name can then be applied to a given paragraph so that it appears with the attributes assigned in the tag name.

Here are the reasons you should use tags in formatting your documents:

- Formatting a document with tags saves time (lots of time).

- Paragraph tags ensure consistency among chapters in a publication but also between writers working together on a project.

- If you need to change a tag's attributes, you change it once in the paragraph tag definition and it automatically is applied to all paragraphs using that tag name.

All paragraph tags should be assigned a name that is a combination of uppercase and lowercase characters. Spaces within a name are acceptable for readability. The name should be short (less than 12 characters).

Every DTP program defines tags slightly differently.

Using FrameMaker

Creating a Paragraph Tag
FrameMaker has a simple way of creating a tag. With a document chapter open, display the modeless Paragraph Designer dialog box. By modeless, I mean the dialog remains displayed until you close it (with **ALT+F4**).

You can display this dialog two ways:

- Press **CTRL+M**.

- Select the Format>Paragraphs>Designer menu command.

The Paragraph Designer dialog is displayed in Figure 4.4. This is actually a single dialog that has many faces (and I don't mean font faces). There are six of these properties.

Click on the Properties button and select Basic.

The Basic properties provide several components that are very important to any paragraph tag: tab stops, default next tag, line spacing (leading), space above and below the entire paragraph, indentation, and text alignment.

Figure 4.4
Basic properties in
the Paragraph
Designer.

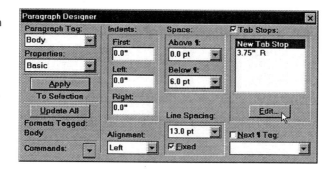

Figure 4.4 shows the attributes (again, FrameMaker calls them properties) of the paragraph tag named Body. Fill in the fields as shown.

You can also select a different tag by clicking the Paragraph Tag field and selecting another tag.

NOTE At any point, you can save a paragraph tag's definition by clicking Update All.

Once you have the Basic properties set the way you want them, you can set additional properties. Click on the Properties list button and on the next property: Default Font.

If you modified any of the tag's attributes, FrameMaker will prompt you to save the attributes. Figure 4.5 shows what will happen if you redefine an existing paragraph tag before you define another set of properties.

If you click on Apply Changes, the current settings are only applied to the selected paragraph. Clicking Update All will change all of the paragraph tags with the current name (Body, in this case) to the current tag settings.

Clicking Don't Apply or Cancel does not make the change. If you wish to define a new paragraph tag that doesn't exist yet, click on the Commands button and select New Format (Figure 4.6). You can enter in the tag name (like Body) and, like the previous figure, save the current attributes in the catalog or just apply the current formats to the selected paragraph.

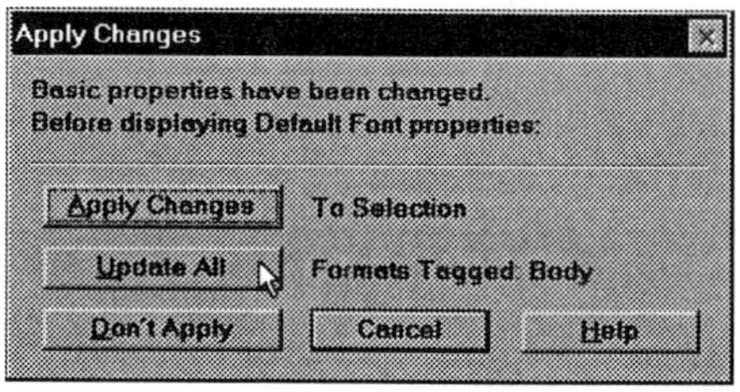

Figure 4.5
Apply changes to
the paragraph
tag.

Figure 4.6
Create a new
paragraph tag.

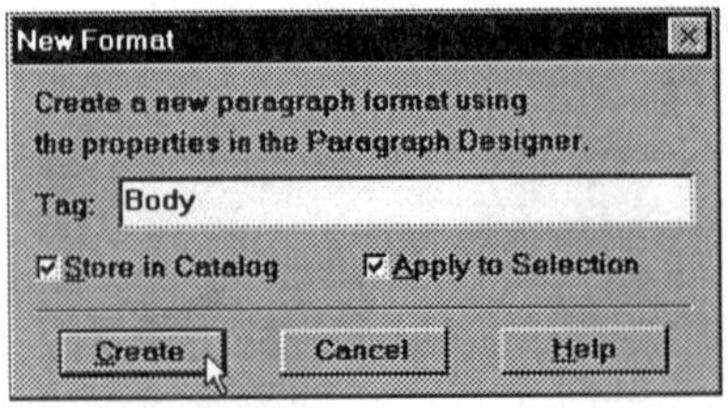

Click **Create**.

The **Default Font** properties dialog shows a whole new set of fields in the same dialog (Figure 4.7). They include the font family (the name of the font), size in points, angle (italics, normal), weight (normal or bold), color, kerning, and many line and baseline adjustment attributes.

Fill in the fields as shown then select **Properties** (and, of course, save these changes to the Paragraph tag catalog).

Another set of attributes is the **Pagination** properties. See Figure 4.8. You can specify where the paragraph starts (current position or top of page, for example) and if the paragraphs using this tag should remain with the next (or previous) paragraph.

The **Format** field is used to indicate whether the paragraph should align with the current flow settings.

I have reserved room for a sidehead area of 1.15" and a .1" gap on the left side of every page (see the description on page 62). This feature allows you to make room in the flow frame for sideheads, such as those used in this book.

Allocating a special column for sideheads does not just apply to this particular paragraph tag (in other words, **Body**). This effect applies to all paragraph tags in this flow.

Figure 4.7
Default Font
properties.

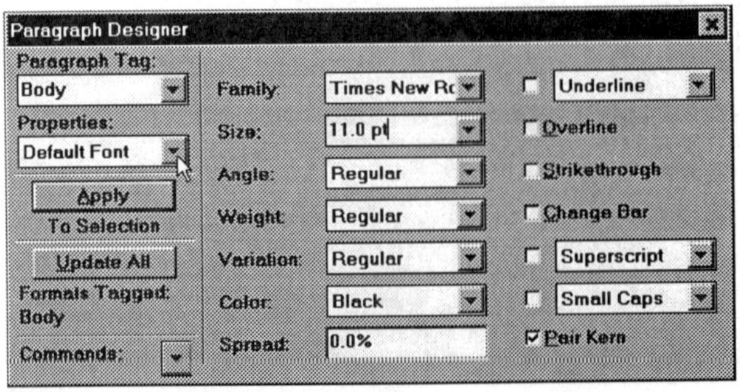

Figure 4.8
Setting the
paragraph
properties of a
tag.

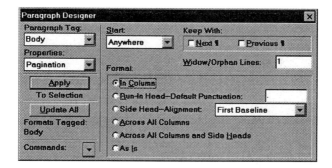

Let's look at this as a before and after diagram (Figure 4.9). When we originally created the text flow frame in the previous chapter, we reserved room for normal text flow occupying the entire width (5.5") as shown in the left.

When we created room for sideheads (a total of 1.25"), normal text flow is reduced to 4.25". Headings may cross both the sidehead and the normal body flow areas and some paragraph tags will only fit within this sidehead area (like figure captions and notes).

The Numbering properties (Figure 4.10) are used to create building blocks for automatic numbering of four sets of counters:

- Lists.
- Chapters.
- Figure captions.
- Table heads.

Figure 4.9
Making room for
a sidehead area.

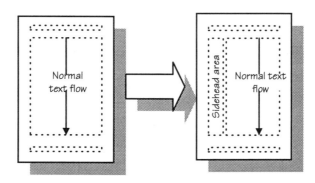

Figure 4.10
Setting the
numbering
properties in a
tag.

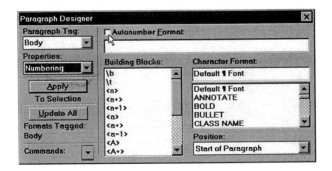

NOTE Although
rarely used, you
can place these
symbols at the
end of the para-
graph.

These properties also provide the ability to assign formatting features such as:

- Bullets.
- Task symbols (like the pointed finger, the right arrow, or whatever you want).
- Tabs.

In addition, these number counters or symbols can be assigned character attributes (we'll discuss them in Chapter 6). These character tags define text attributes (color, font, and so on) to selected text. You can see that I've assigned some already.

As an example, let's assign to the paragraph tag named Chapter the numbering property to increment the chapter number counter and to reset all of the other counters to 0.

Check Autonumber Format and enter in the field directly below it:

<n+>< =0>< =0>< =0>.

Figure 4.11
Using the
advanced tag
properties.

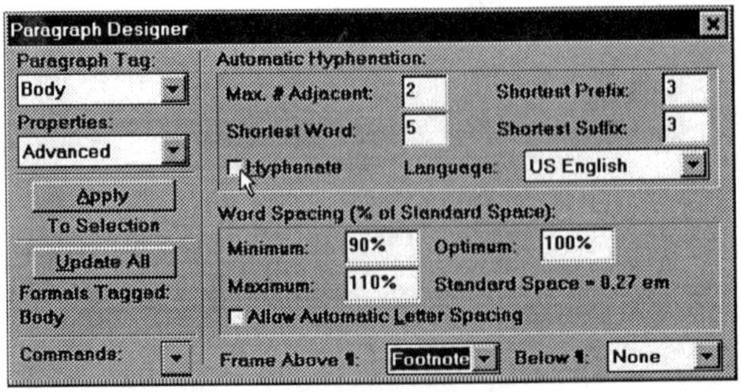

I've chosen to use the first counter (<n+>) to keep track of chapter numbers. The other three counters (figure, table, and list) are reset to 0 (< =0>) whenever the Chapter paragraph tag is encountered (which is only once at the beginning of each chapter).

For the paragraph tag named List No, the Numbering property is set to **< >< >< ><n+>\t**. This leaves the first three counters alone and increments the fourth counter (**<n+>**) by 1. Then it tabs over (**\t**). Pretty easy.

The Advanced properties dialog (Figure 4.11) takes care of hyphenation and word spacing. In FrameMaker you can specify hyphenation in individual paragraph tags. Additionally, you can define how to place a graphics frame above or below a paragraph. In the figure, I've shown a predefined graphics frame named Footnote. Our page design does not use any graphics borders on any paragraph.

This facility is sort of a primitive method of adding borders around paragraphs since it assumes that you have defined graphics frames with the type of border desired in a reference page.

Last but not least, the Table Cell properties instructs FrameMaker if the tag is placed in a table cell, how to adjust its placement. We'll just leave this one alone.

Creating a Tag from an Existing Paragraph
Let's say we have assigned to a paragraph the Body paragraph tag. You can change the attributes of the paragraph either by making changes in the Paragraph Designer dialog or by changing the ruler or the Formatting bar.

Let's modify the ruler above the page by clicking on the lower arrow and dragging it to the right .5": .

The name of the current paragraph tag is always displayed in the Status bar at the bottom of the FrameMaker window. Since you modified this specific paragraph, notice that the paragraph tag reflects that the Body paragraph has changed (with an asterisk): .

Click on New Format in the Commands field.

You'll be prompted to enter a new paragraph tag. Type in **Body Indented** (or whatever you want) and with Store in Catalog checked, click on Create.

You have just defined a new paragraph tag and the original paragraph tag (in this case, Body) remains unchanged.

Applying a Paragraph Tag to a Paragraph

Every paragraph must have an assigned paragraph tag. How do you apply a paragraph tag to a paragraph? You must first place the insertion point in the paragraph. Then you have several ways to apply the paragraph tag:

1. From the Formatting bar (you can display it by selecting View>Formatting Bar menu), pull down the list box and click on the paragraph tag name: Z_HalfLines.

2. You can select the Format>Paragraphs>Catalog menu command or click on the Paragraph Catalog button above the vertical scroll bar: .

   The Paragraph Catalog is then displayed (Figure 4.12). This is actually a modeless list box that stays around until you close it.

3. The third method is to use the keyboard shortcut of typing in the paragraph name till it is recognized. Type **F9** then type the first letters of the tag until it is recognized: ¶:Body . The text you type is underlined as you type in the Status bar. When your paragraph is recognized, press **ENTER** (or press **ESC** to cancel applying the paragraph tag).

Figure 4.12
Tag selection using the Paragraph Catalog.

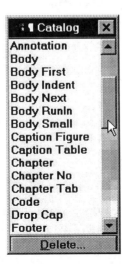

Figure 4.13
Delete a
paragraph tag.

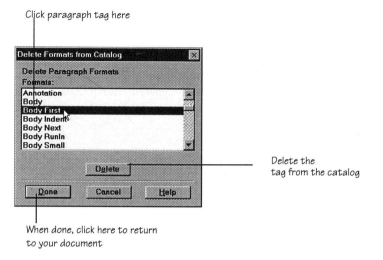

Click paragraph tag here

Delete the
tag from the catalog

When done, click here to return
to your document

Removing a Paragraph Tag There are two methods of removing a paragraph tag. The first is to click on the Delete button on the Paragraph Catalog.

The second is to click on the Delete Format command in the Paragraph Designer dialog Commands list.

In both cases, you'll be asked to select a paragraph tag to delete (Figure 4.13). You can delete several paragraph tags, one at a time, before clicking Done to return to your document.

Adding a Border If you wish to add line borders to headers or footers (this was common in documentation in the 1980s), you simply attach a frame to the appropriate paragraph style (see Figure 4.11 on page 106).

FrameMaker gives you the flexibility of placing any frame full of graphics/text above or below any paragraph tag. This is very useful for headers and footers where a line separation can be useful.

Using Corel Ventura

Creating a Tag The latest versions of Corel Ventura support a text editor capability originally popular with PageMaker. It allows you to quickly edit text without the benefit of the page layout, WYSIWYG (What You See Is What You Get) view. Working in text mode (Corel Ventura calls it the Copy Editor view) performs dramatically better than the page layout view.

Figure 4.14
Adding a new
paragraph tag.

We'll focus only on the page-oriented, WYSIWYG view. Make certain that you have View>Page Layout checked (you can quickly set it with the **ALT+F12** shortcut).

Every paragraph has a paragraph tag assigned to it. Paragraph tags use a name that may include spaces in it. Since we are going to be modifying some automatically generated paragraph tags (they all start with the letter Z), let's view them by checking the Generated Tags option in the Tools>Preferences dialog box.

Click the Tagged Text tool, [icon], and place the insertion point in the first paragraph. This paragraph will probably use the paragraph tag Body Text (you'll see that in the tag list below the menu bar as [Body Text]).

You'll know that you've enabled the correct tagged text mode because a tag symbol trails the cursor: [icon].

NOTE You can also type **SHIFT+F9** or click on the Format>Manage Tag List menu command then click Add Tag button.

Let's first create a new paragraph tag from the existing one (Body Text). Right-click and a pop-up menu will present paragraph formatting options (Figure 4.14).

Select Add New Tag to display the Add Paragraph Tag dialog (Figure 4.15).

Type the new paragraph tag **Body** in the Tag Name field. Browse through the Copy Attributes From list and select Body Text. The Tag Type field is used to define the basic attributes of the tag—we'll just leave it **Undefined**.

Finally, the Next Tag should be set to the new tag: Body.

Prior to version 5, Corel Ventura did not support the ability to define the next tag feature. When you are editing a paragraph and you press the **ENTER** key, the next paragraph can be tagged with a different tag automatically.

Figure 4.15
Create a paragraph tag from an existing tag.

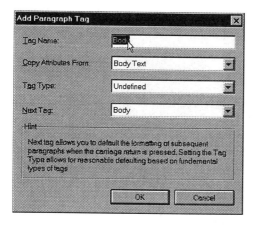

In this case, however, we'll define the default tag assigned to the next paragraph to be the same.

Click OK.

With the insertion point still in the current paragraph, Right-click. Click first on Format and then on the cascading Character menu.

Each of these submenu items represents some part of a paragraph tag's definition. Since each of these (starting with Character) can quickly lead to any of the others (like Typography), just click on one.

Click on the Character tab (Figure 4.16).

Figure 4.16
Define character settings in a paragraph tag.

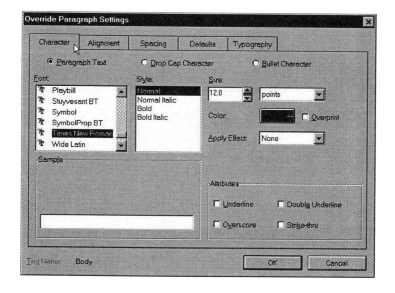

Figure 4.17
Set the alignment
definitions in a
paragraph tag.

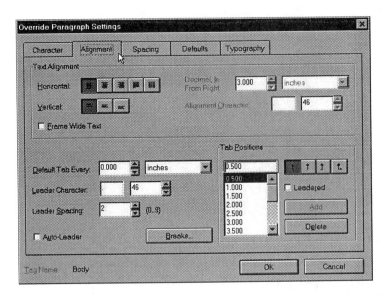

You can specify font attributes for the following by clicking
on them:

- Paragraph.
- Initial drop cap.
- Bullet.

In addition, you can specify underlining and other line
attributes common for legal publications (but not usually for
manuals).

Once you have specified the character attributes, click OK.
This assumes that you are creating a paragraph tag from one
that has been previously set correctly. In most cases, you'll
want to view and edit the other attributes.

Click on the Alignment tab (Figure 4.17). You can specify the
horizontal and vertical alignment, and tabs by assigning a
value in the Default Tab Every field or by individually
selecting a Tab Position value and indicating its alignment
and dot leaders. Click the Add button.

To delete a tab position, highlight it so that it appears in the
Tab Positions field and click Delete.

You can also click on the Breaks button.

Figure 4.18
Breaks definitions
in a paragraph
tag.

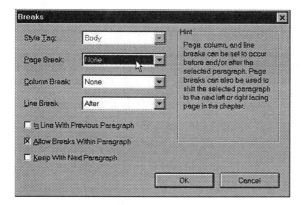

NOTE You can
also right-click at
the insertion point
and select Breaks.

This little gem is where you can do the magic of setting
sideheads and run-in paragraphs that most word processors
and other DTP programs can't (Figure 4.18).

For most paragraphs, the Breaks attributes will be set to the
default in the figure. Click OK to return. The Spacing tab
(Figure 4.19) is used to set the left and right margins of the
paragraph, line indentations, vertical spacing, and even text
rotation (which we'll use a little later).

You can always modify the indents in a paragraph tag by
moving the markers on the ruler. The Defaults tab (Figure
4.20) indicates the fine adjustments used for line
strikethrough types, superscripts, and subscripts.

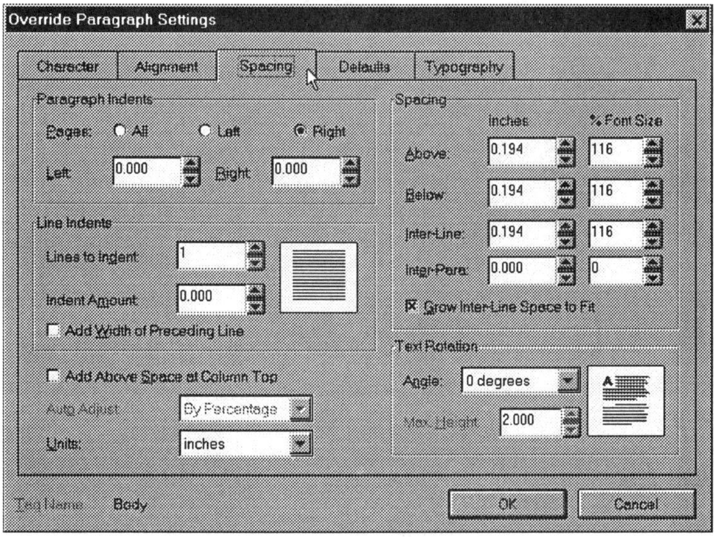

Figure 4.19
Setting the
spacing definitions
in a paragraph
tag.

Figure 4.20
Default definitions
in a paragraph
tag.

Figure 4.20
Default definitions
in a paragraph
tag.

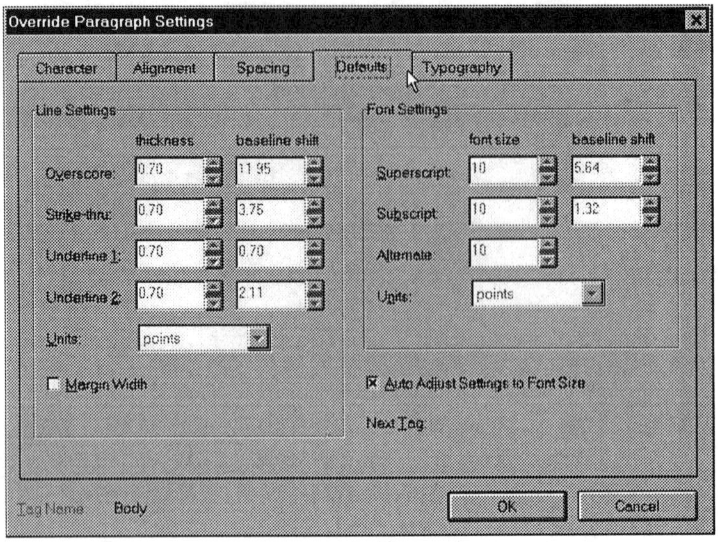

The most important field here is Next Tag (which is a new
feature starting with version 5). Finally, the Typography tab
(Figure 4.21) handles hyphenation, word spacing/kerning,
and character tracking.

Although I don't use border lines in our publication, the
Ruling Lines dialog can fill in this information in the
paragraph tag definition (Figure 4.22). Place the insertion
point in the paragraph to which you wish to add ruling lines,
right-click, and select Ruling Lines.

Figure 4.21
Setting the
typography
definitions in a
paragraph tag.

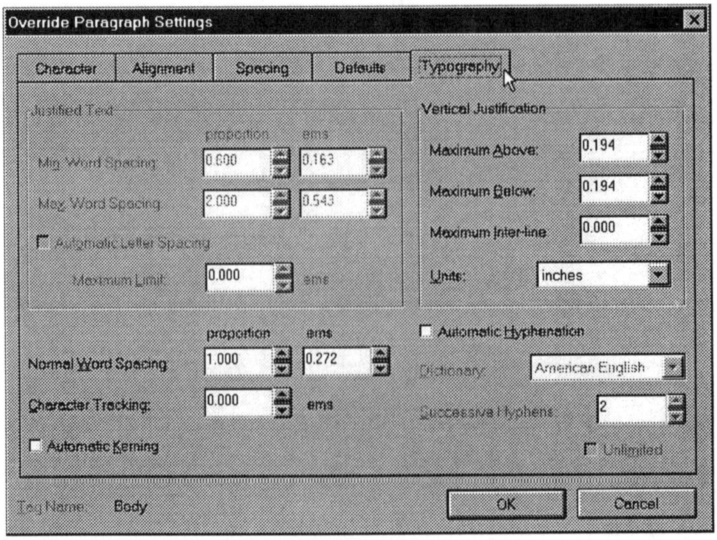

Figure 4.22
Filling in the Ruling Lines in the paragraph tag definition.

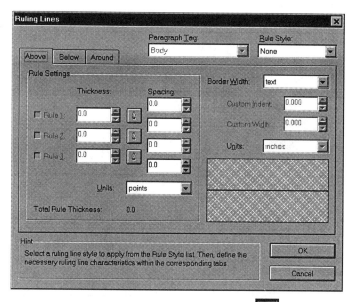

You must use the Tagged Text tool, to bring up the ability to assign ruling lines to a paragraph tag.

Not only can you select a Border Width matching the width of the frame, you can also set it to the width of the text in the paragraph. Wow! I don't know of any other DTP program that can currently boast that feature.

When you set the Rule Style to anything other than None, you can adjust the thickness of up to three ruling lines with independent spacing in between them. See Figure 4.23.

Not only that, you can set the color of each of these lines (make certain that if you check anything other than the black default that you choose a spot color). Click the Units to Points before you start. This appears to be the same line drawing technology used in CorelDRAW. Incredible!

As you edit the spacing and rule thickness, Corel Ventura calculates the total height in the Total Rule Thickness field so that you will always know the total rule height.

Removing a Paragraph Tag Click on the Format>Manage Tag List menu (or press **SHIFT+F9**). From the Manage Tag List dialog, select the paragraph tag you'd like to delete and click the Delete Tag button. You can repeat this process for other tags. When you are done, click on Close.

Figure 4.23
Modify a
paragraph tag's
ruling lines.

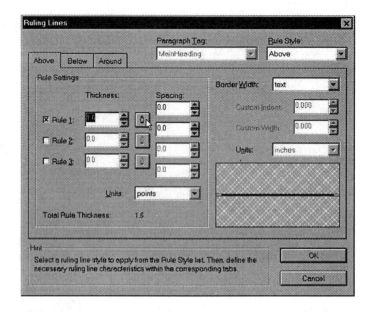

Saving
Paragraph Tag
Definitions in
a Style Sheet
Page attributes and paragraph tag definitions are stored in the chapter's style sheet file so don't forget to periodically save them. Initially, you'll need to create a style sheet with the Layout>Save Style Sheet As menu command. Within your publication's TEMPLATE subdirectory, save the file as CHAPTER.STY.

When you add another chapter, apply this same style sheet to the chapter file (using the Layout>Load Style Sheet menu command).

BODY TEXT PARAGRAPH TAGS

Body text is for mainstream paragraphs. We define different tags because there are minor attribute changes that make our life as writers easier instead of constantly overriding the basic Body paragraph tag.

Serif Font Paragraph Tags

The main body text is composed of several named paragraph definitions.

Style	Description
Body	Body text used for most normal paragraphs.
Body First	Body text that is the first in a chapter (this paragraph will typically move to the position following a chapter opening graphic image).
Body Indent	Body text with the left margin indented. This paragraph can stand alone or follow any of the List styles (such as List Body, List No, or List RunIn).
Body Next	Body text that remains with the next paragraph. This paragraph is critical to precede a numbered list since it resets the starting list number (paragraph tag List No discussed on page 124).
Body RunIn	Body text that is juxtapositioned to a RunIn paragraph list.

Here are some examples of what these paragraph tags should look like:

This is Body text. It is used for most normal typing purposes and doesn't have to be aligned with the next paragraph.

This is the Body First paragraph tag. It is similar to the Body paragraph tag, but it is moved down to stand out as the first paragraph of a chapter. Also, the first character is typically set as a drop cap (described in Chapter 6).

For quotes or text paragraphs that follow lists (where the text is indented), the Body Indent tag is used.

Body Next is exactly the same as Body paragraph tag except that it must stay with the next paragraph.

RunIn   This is a Body RunIn paragraph tag where the text follows a phrase. It is used mostly for terms or for feature descriptions.

The above indented paragraphs show the different types of tags that I use in manuals.

Sans Serif Font Tags

Style	Description
Body Small	Text that is set apart from normal text in a small, yet readable format.
Code	Monospaced text that demonstrates programming code or even command line text (prompts and user entries).

Body Small text is typically used in disclaimers or legal information. (I think it is small so that users won't read it!)

```
//      Here is an example of Code paragraph tag.
        main()          // Tabs are very important
        {
                        // Everything aligns perfectly!

        }
```

Using FrameMaker

NOTE I choose to use standard font styles for all paragraph tag descriptions.

Each paragraph tag's properties are defined as follows:

Body   Basic: All indents set to 0", spacing above set to 0 pt and below to 6 pt, line spacing 13 pt fixed, left alignment, and no next tag. Default font: StoneSerif 11 pt, pair kern. Pagination: starts anywhere, normal format, and leave room for sideheads in flow. Numbering, Advanced, and Table Cell: defaults used.

Body First   Same as Body except that spacing above is set to 26 pt.

Body Indent   Same as Body except that first and left indents are set to .25" (equal to first tab stop for lists).

Body Next   Same as Body except that paragraph stays with next paragraph. In addition, the Numbering property of Autonumber Format resets the list counter:
< >< >< >< =0>.

Body RunIn   Same as Body except that first line is indented .25" (this paragraph is an example) and the next tag is set to RunIn.

Body Small   Basic: All indents set to 0", spacing above set to 0 pt and below to 3 pt; line spacing 10 pt fixed, left alignment, and no next tag. Default font: Helvetica Neue (55) 8 pt, pair kern. Pagination: starts anywhere, normal format, and leave room for sideheads in flow. Numbering, Advanced; and Table Cell: defaults used.

Code   Basic: First and left indents set to .25"; spacing above and below to 0 pt; line spacing 12 pt fixed, left alignment, tab stops set every .25", and no next tag. Default font: Letter Gothic 10 pt, no kerning. Pagination: starts anywhere, normal format, and leave room for sideheads in flow. Numbering, Advanced; and Table Cell: defaults used.

Using Corel Ventura

NOTE Make certain that indents are set to All Pages.

Each paragraph tag's properties are discussed in the following:

Body   Character: Paragraph Text set to StoneSerif, Normal, 11 pt, black. Alignment: Left-justified horizontal. Spacing: All pages Left set to 1.25" and Right set to 0", Lines to Indent is 1 with Indent Amount set to 0". Spacing Above and Inter-Para set to 0", Below set to 6 pt, Inter-Line to 13 pt. Default: Next Tag set to Body. Breaks: set to default. Typography: set to default values with Automatic Kerning checked.

Body First   Same as Body except that Spacing Above is set to 26 pt.

Body Indent   Same as Body except that Left Indents are set to 1.25" (equal to first tab stop for lists) and the Right Indent set to 4".

Body Next   Same as Body except that Keeps With Next Paragraph is checked. This is the "magic" paragraph that is used to reset the list counter. We'll discuss this shortly.

Body RunIn   Same as Body except that Add Width of Preceding Line in Spacing tab is checked and the next tag is set to RunIn. (You may have to wait till you define RunIn—it is only a few pages away).

Body Small   Character: Paragraph Text set to Helvetica Neue (55) 8pt, black. Alignment: Left-justified horizontal. Spacing: All pages Left set to 1.25" and Right set to 0", Lines to Indent is set to 1 with Indent Amount set to 0". Spacing Above and Inter-Para set to 0", Below set to 3 pt, Inter-Line to

10 pt. Default: Next Tag set to Body Small. Breaks: set to default. Typography: set to default values with Automatic Kerning checked.

Code   Character: Paragraph Text set to Letter Gothic 10 pt, black. Alignment: Left-justified horizontal with left-justified tabs set every .25". Spacing: All pages Left set to 1.5" and Right set to 0"; Lines to Indent is 1 with Indent Amount set to 0". Spacing Above and Inter-Para set to 0", Below set to 0 pt, Inter-Line to 12 pt. Default: Next Tag set to Code. Breaks: set to default. Typography: set to default values with Automatic Kerning *un*checked.

SPECIAL PARAGRAPH TAGS

There are several special paragraph tags that I use to add some pizzazz to a publication. None of these is mandatory but they sure do help break the monotony for the reader.

Style	Description
Annotation	Smaller than body text tag that is used when annotating a figure—in fact, this is typically part of a graphics frame.
Caption Figure	Caption below a graphics frame (to be covered in Chapter 5)
Caption Table	Caption below a table (to be covered in Chapter 5)
Z_EndChap	A special character (usually a dingbat) that displays a special character (like a rose petal) at the end of the chapter.
Z_Figure	Paragraph that anchors a graphics frame (to be covered in Chapter 5)
Z_HalfLines	There are times when you really need a line between paragraphs that is half the line spacing.
Z_HalfLines Next	The same as Z_HalfLines except that this half line must go with the next paragraph. This paragraph should precede lists (paragraph tags List No, List Bullet, and List RunIn).
Z_Table	Paragraph that anchors a table (to be covered in Chapter 5)

Note that all the non-text paragraph styles all begin with Z_. The reason is that in a paragraph tag catalog list, they will appear at the bottom because they are less frequently used. I borrowed that naming convention from the old Ventura days (mid 1980s).

The following are samples of these special tags:

An annotation usually describes part of a drawing or a screen capture.

Figure 4.24 This is a sample of a Caption Figure style.

Table 4.1 This is a sample of a Caption Table style.

NOTE The next symbol represents the end of the chapter.

NOTE These two lines never have text on them.

This is a Z_HalfLines
And this is a Z_HalfLines Next paragraph.

Using FrameMaker

NOTE The Annotation paragraph tag is a great candidate for a spot color.

Annotation   Basic: All indents set to 0", spacing Above set to 0 pt and Below to 5 pt; line spacing 10 pt fixed, left alignment, and no next tag. Default font: Tekton 8 pt, pair kern. Pagination: starts anywhere, normal format, and leave room for sideheads in flow. Numbering, Advanced; and Table Cell: defaults used.

Caption Figure   Basic: All indents set to 0", spacing Above set to 0 pt and Below to 0 pt, line spacing 10 pt fixed, left alignment, and next tag set to Z_HalfLines. Default font: AvantGarde 8 pt, pair kern. Pagination: starts anywhere, normal format, keep with previous, and leave room for sideheads in flow. Numbering: Autonumber format checked with the field set to Figure <n>-<n+>< >< >. , Advanced; and Table Cell: defaults used.

Caption Table   Basic: All indents set to 0", spacing Above set to 0 pt and Below to 0 pt, line spacing 10 pt fixed, left alignment, and next tag set to Z_HalfLines. Default font: AvantGarde 8 pt, pair kern. Pagination: starts anywhere, normal format, keep with previous, and leave room for sideheads in flow. Numbering: Autonumber format checked with the field set to Table <n>-< ><n+>< >. , Advanced; and Table Cell: defaults used.

Z_EndChap   Basic: All indents set to 0", spacing Above set to 113 pt and Below to 0 pt, line spacing 29 pt fixed, Center alignment, and no next tag. Default font: StoneSerif 24 pt, pair kern. Numbering set to DINGBAT character tag: ß (which is actually the Zapf Dingbat font). Character tags are explained in Chapter 6.

Z_Figure   Basic: All indents set to 0", spacing Above set to 0 pt and Below to 2.5 pt, line spacing 6 pt fixed, left alignment, and next tag set to Caption Figure. Default font: StoneSerif 5 pt, pair kern (although it doesn't matter). Pagination: starts anywhere, normal format, keep with next paragraph, and leave room for sideheads in flow. Numbering, Advanced; and Table Cell: defaults used. There should never be text entered on this tag.

Z_HalfLines   Basic: All indents set to 0", spacing Above set to 0 pt and Below to 2.5pt, line spacing 6 pt fixed, left alignment, and next tag set to Body. Default font: StoneSerif 5 pt, pair kern (although it doesn't matter). Pagination: starts anywhere, normal format, keep with next paragraph, and leave room for side heads in flow. Numbering, Advanced; and Table Cell: defaults used. There should never be text entered on this tag.

Z_HalfLines Next   Same as Z_HalfLines but keep with next tag checked.

Z_Table   This is the same as Z_Figure with the next tag set to Caption Table.

Using Corel Ventura

Set all Spacing's Auto Adjust to By Addition.

NOTE This is the perfect paragraph tag in which to use spot color.

Annotation   Character: Paragraph Text set to Tekton, Normal, 8 pt, black. Alignment: Left-justified horizontal. Spacing: All pages Left and Right set to 0", Lines to Indent set to 1 with Indent Amount set to 0". Spacing Above and Inter-Para set to 0", Below set to 3 pt, Inter-Line to 10 pt. Default: Next Tag set to Annotation. Breaks: Set to default. Typography: set to default values with Automatic Kerning checked.

Caption Figure   Paragraph Text set to Tekton, Normal, 8 pt, black.

Caption Table   Paragraph Text set to Tekton, Normal, 8 pt, black.

Z_EndChap   Character: Bullet text set to your choice of Zapf Dingbat character, Normal, 24 pt, black, and bullet enabled. Alignment: Center-justified horizontal. Spacing: All pages Left and Right set to 0", Lines to Indent set to 1 with Indent Amount set to 0". Spacing Above set to 113 pt, Inter-Para set to 0", Below set to 0 pt, Inter-Line to 29 pt. Default: Next Tag set to Z_EndChap. Breaks: set to default. Typography: set to default values with Automatic Kerning unchecked.

Z_Figure   Character: Paragraph Text set to StoneSerif, Normal, 5 pt, black. Alignment: Left-justified horizontal. Spacing: All pages Left set to 1.25" and Right set to 0", Lines to Indent set to 1 with Indent Amount set to 0". Spacing Above and Inter-Para set to 0", Below set to 2.5 pt, Inter-Line to 6 pt. Default: Next Tag set to Z_HalfLines. Breaks: Keep With Next Paragraph checked. Typography: set to default values with Automatic Kerning checked. There should never be text entered on this tag.

Z_HalfLines   Character: Paragraph Text set to StoneSerif, Normal, 5 pt, black. Alignment: Left-justified horizontal. Spacing: All pages Left set to 1.25" and Right set to 0", Lines to Indent set to 1 with Indent Amount set to 0". Spacing Above and Inter-Para set to 0", Below set to 2.5 pt, Inter-Line to 6 pt. Default: Next Tag set to Body. Breaks: set to default. Typography: set to default values with Automatic Kerning checked. There should never be text entered on this tag.

Z_HalfLinesNext   Same as Z_HalfLines but with Keep With Next Paragraph checked. (There is no space between Lines and Next since Corel Ventura doesn't allow a paragraph tag that long).

Z_Table   This is the same as Z_Figure with the next tag set to Z_HalfLines.

DEFINING LISTS AND RUN-IN PARAGRAPHS

I believe in the adage, "If you can explain something in a table, USE a table!" The same applies to using lists. Lists are very useful mechanisms to explain related topics. The following tables give the details on commonly used lists and run-in paragraph styles.

Serif Font Paragraph Tags

Style	Description
List Bullet	Body text that is preceded with a bullet. The text is indented from the left.
List No	Body text that is preceded with a number. The text is indented from the left.

Sans Serif Font Tags

Style	Description
List RunIn	Paragraph that is bolded with a defined amount of spaces between it and subsequent body text (of Body RunIn tags). This tag is typically used in glossaries to identify terms. This and any Body RunIn tags associated with it are not indented.
List Small	Body text with smaller fonts are used to present a list typically of legal terms.
RunIn	A heading that runs into the body text immediately adjacent to it.

The following paragraphs show examples of lists and run-in paragraphs.

A paragraph that precedes a list should be tagged as Body Next tag. It will always stay with at least the first line of a list:

- This is a List Bullet paragraph.
- And another one.

This Body Next paragraph precedes a paragraphs of List No tags (the list counter is reset to 0; none of the other counters is affected).

1. This is the first entry of a List No paragraph tag.

2. The second.

3. And the third.

The following are examples of small font lists:

▶ This represents a list of List Small paragraph tags. Notice that we chose a different paragraph bullet code. (Looks kinda official, doesn't it?)

▶ And here's a second entry list.

The paragraph after a list is always tagged as Z_HalfLines to ensure some separation between lists and subsequent indented body text.

■ **List RunIn**   We use Body Indent in FrameMaker (don't use Body RunIn since there is no left indentation) and Body RunIn in Corel Ventura following run-ins.

■ **Glossary Term**   This is an example of a term set as a List RunIn. Notice that there is space between the run-in and the body text.

RunIn   This is a paragraph of Body RunIn that follows paragraph tagged as a RunIn. The run-in text is actually a different paragraph than the body following it.

Using FrameMaker

Although we don't explain character tags until Chapter 6, several of the following paragraph tag definitions reference character attributes by a character tag name.

List Bullet   Basic: Left indent set to .25", spacing Above set to 0 pt and Below to 6 pt; line spacing 13 pt fixed, left alignment, left tab stop .25", and no next tag. Default font: StoneSerif 11 pt, pair kern. Pagination: starts anywhere, normal format, and leave room for sideheads in flow. Numbering is set with Autonumber Format checked and field set to n\t (which is the bullet symbol of the DINGBAT character tag followed by a tab .25"). Advanced; and Table Cell: defaults used.

List No   Same as List Bullet except that the Autonumber Format is set to < >< >< ><n+>\t (which will increment the list number counter and tab .25").

List RunIn   Basic: Left indent set to .25", spacing Above set to 0 pt and Below to 6 pt, line spacing 13 pt fixed, left alignment, left tab stop .25", and no next tag. Default font: StoneSerif 11 pt, pair kern. Pagination: starts anywhere, Run-In Head-Default Punctuation set to an em space ( ); and leave room for sideheads in flow. Numbering is set to a n\t (which is set to the n character code of the DINGBAT character tag followed by a tab .25"). Advanced; and Table Cell: defaults used.

List Small   Basic: All indents set to 0"; spacing Above set to 0 pt and Below to 3 pt, line spacing 10 pt fixed, left alignment, left tab set to .25", and no next tag. Default font: Helvetica Neue (55) 8 pt, pair kern. Pagination: starts anywhere, normal format, and leave room for sideheads in flow. Numbering is set to a w\t (which is set to the w character code of the DINGBAT character tag followed by a tab .25"). Advanced, and Table Cell: defaults used.

NOTE   List Small is just a modified Body Small paragraph tag.

RunIn   The same as List RunIn but there is no Numbering, and the next paragraph is Body RunIn.

Using Corel Ventura

Don't forget to set all Spacing's Auto Adjust to By Addition.

List Bullet   Character: Paragraph Text set to StoneSerif, Normal, 11 pt, black. Bullet set to Zapf Dingbat, 7 pt, black (although you could set this to a spot color), Indent .25", and Shift up .013". Bullet is applied. Alignment: Left-justified horizontal. Spacing: All pages Left set to 1.25" and Right set to 0". Lines to Indent is 1 with Indent Amount set to 0". Spacing Above and Inter-Para set to 0", Below set to 6 pt, Inter-Line to 13 pt. Default: Next Tag set to List Bullet. Breaks: set to default. Typography: set to default values with Automatic Kerning checked.

List No   Same as Body except that the next tag is List No.

List RunIn   Character: Paragraph Text set to StoneSerif, Normal, 11 pt, black. Bullet set to Zapf Dingbat, 7 pt, black (although you could set this to a spot color), Indent .25", and

Shift up .013". Bullet is applied. Alignment: Left-justified horizontal. Spacing: All pages Left set to 1.25" and Right set to 0", Lines to Indent is 1 with Indent Amount set to 0". Spacing Above and Inter-Para set to 0", Below set to 6 pt, Inter-Line to 13 pt. Default: Next Tag set to Body RunIn (but, be careful—Body RunIn's next tag is RunIn and not List RunIn). Breaks: set to Line Break Before and Keep With Next Paragraph checked. Typography: set to default values with Automatic Kerning checked.

NOTE List Small is just a modified Body Small paragraph tag.

List Small Character: Paragraph Text set to Helvetica Neue (55) 8 points, black. Bullet set to Zapf Dingbat, 7 pt, black (although you could set this to a spot color), Indent .25", and Shift up .013". Bullet is applied. Should use the same symbol as that used in List Bullet. Alignment: Left-justified horizontal. Spacing: All pages Left set to 1.25" and Right set to 0"; Lines to Indent is set to 1 with Indent Amount set to 0". Spacing Above and Inter-Para set to 0", Below set to 3 pt, Inter-Line to 10 pt. Default: Next Tag set to List Bullet. Breaks: set to default. Typography: set to default values with Automatic Kerning checked.

RunIn Same as List RunIn without the Bullet applied (none needed). The Next Tag is set to Body RunIn. In order to add some space between the run-in and the paragraph text, insert an em space (**CTRL+SHIFT**+M) after the run-in phrase.

Z_SEC2 Same as List No except that the next tag is Z_SEC2, Left Indent is 1.25", and Right is 4". This is a great tag to apply a spot color (and to use a bold sans serif font).

Configuring for Automatic Numbering

Before going further, we need to set up the numbering so that whenever the Body Next paragraph tag is encountered, the bullet number counter is reset. Then, whenever the paragraph tag List No generates a new paragraph tag that precedes it (Z_SEC2) and increments the counter.

Select the page frame and right-click, and select Chapter>Numbering (Figure 4.25).

Figure 4.25
Setting the Auto-
Numbering levels
for lists.

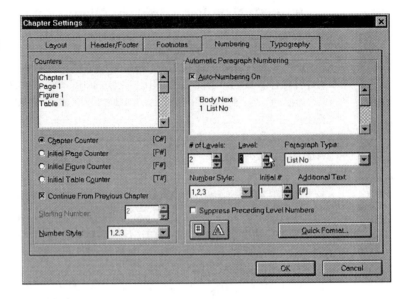

Click on **# of Levels** and set it to **2**, then set Level 1 to **Body Next**. Next, click Level to **2** and select **List No.** Set Number Style to **1,2,3** with Initial # to **1**, and Additional Text to **[#]**.

HEADINGS

Examples of Great Headings

Headings are designed to help the reader find information. Unlike a novel (which typically doesn't have headings), your readers may skip around in order to find critical information. I have yet to see a user's manual that doesn't have headings.

There are some conventions that are rapidly becoming the norm in generating headings that are readable. For starters, use terminology that is set in the active tense. For example, which heading is easier to understand?

Font Styles

Using Font Styles in Headings

Figure 4.26
Sans serif heading; serif body.

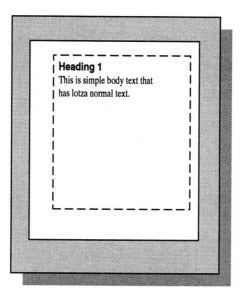

At the first level heading (as in "Headings," on page 128), it may be perfectly natural to have only a topic name. However, subheadings need to be a little more descriptive in order to entice the reader to read further.

Choosing Tags for Headings

Headings should be set in a font style that differs from normal body text.

Normally, a sans serif font (like Futura Bold or Helvetica Inserat) should be used for headings and serif fonts should be reserved for normal body text as shown in Figure 4.26.

I've seen body text in a sans serif font (like Helvetica) and headings in a serif font (like Times or Palatino). This is an unusual use of typefaces but it can look great. In fact, some of the earlier FrameMaker manuals used this style. This is shown in Figure 4.27.

From this point on, we'll use the tag Heading 1 to indicate heading level 1 which should be the topmost heading. Heading 1 is naturally followed by lesser subheadings I call Heading 2, Heading 3, and so on.

Figure 4.27
Serif heading, sans
serif body.

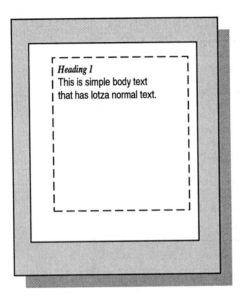

Although you may be compelled to have lots of levels of
headings, I would recommend that you limit the heading
hierarchy to at most three or four levels. These headings will
be used to automatically generate a table of contents.

There are no hard and fast rules with font sizes, but a good
rule of thumb is that point sizes should be 20% smaller with
each heading level (like Heading 2, Heading 3, and so on):

Figure 4.28
Basic font size
and inter-line
spacing.

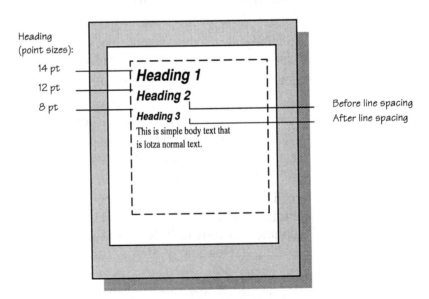

Figure 4.29
Font and spacing
between
heading levels.

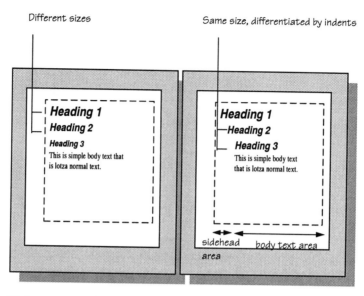

This means that if body text is 8 points then the Heading 3 should be 10 pt, Heading 2 would then be 12 pt, and Heading 1 is 14 pt. See Figure 4.28.

When headings are aligned the same (as on the left side of Figure 4.29), each level should be of a different font size.

If, on the other hand, headings are indented (as shown in the sample on the right side of Figure 4.29), then the indentation can be used to imply a hierarchy and the font sizes of Heading 2 and Heading 3 can be the same. Indenting the heading gives the impression that the body text is actually indented, leaving room on the left for headings and sideheads (comments).

The topmost heading level (Heading 1) should always be dramatically different so that your readers can easily distinguish major topics from subheadings. Make sure that it (Heading 1) really stands out in font size, spacing, and even spot color.

For some manuals, a fourth or fifth heading level may be required. An example would be a manual that describes programming APIs (Application Programming Interface) where descriptors are repeated for every function you are documenting as shown in Figure 4.30.

Figure 4.30
Using the
sidehead area for
heading
descriptors.

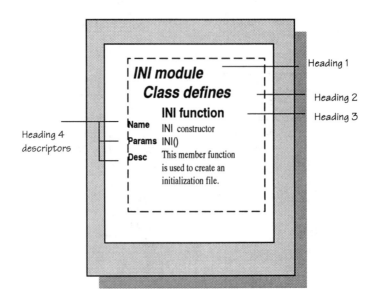

Although these less important descriptors are classified as headings, they can easily be placed in the sidehead area and can be optionally included in a table of contents (although they probably shouldn't be).

Using Color and Capitalization

Fonts and line spacing are not the only attributes that can be used to make headings stand out. Although there are varying views on capitalization of letters, the most important words are almost always capitalized.

Words that are not normally capitalized are conjunctions and short prepositions (typically fewer than four characters).

NOTE This table shows words that are not capital-ized.

Conjunctions and articles	Short prepositions
and	of
or	on
but	by
a	for
an	
the	

There are other words that you can add to this list—just be consistent with the list of words not capitalized.

Figure 4.31
Using rules in
headings.

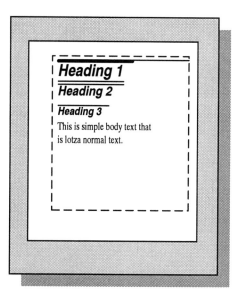

Using Rules in Headings

Borders (boxes around paragraphs or rules above or below a
heading) can be used to great appeal. Figure 4.31 shows
examples of rules that are pretty common in user manuals.

In Heading 1, a single line goes across the width of the
margin. Below the border, a thick line the width of the
heading extends below the thin line. (By the way, this is a
dead giveaway that you're using Corel Ventura!) This
technique is quite a trick! Otherwise, this heavy-thickness
border has little merit.

Heading 2 shows the double line technique (I've even seen
triple lines of varying line thicknesses). The double line
definitely stands out but it is being used much less these
days. Notice that the width sometimes matches the exact
width of the heading text (also, a Corel Ventura trick of the
trade).

The last technique shown, Heading 3, is a single rule that
spans across the entire column width or the width of the
heading (shown). It's simple, and if you must use a border, a
great choice. You can enhance it with the use of spot color
(instead of black) or even a gray (such as 50 percent black
which does not count as an extra color charge by a

printshop).

Heading border guidelines are as follows:

- Don't use border lines (or boxes around a paragraph) unless necessary.

- If your headers or footers have rules, do not use them in headings—your printed page will have too many lines!

- If you use border lines, only use them for one or at most two heading levels.

- Make certain that the imagesetter can successful print your rule lines if the style you have chosen is thin such as hairline.

Paginating Headings

What happens when headings must start at the top of a page or column? You must design heading styles so that if they are to start at the top of a page there is no space above—the page break is enough.

For example, if a heading is to have 14 pt of space above it, don't set it up so that 14 pt is automatically inserted. Corel Ventura lets you control both cases—most other DTP programs are designed so that if the heading falls at the top of a page the heading style's vertical spacing value is ignored.

One last important point: A heading must stay with the next paragraph (whether it is body text or another subheading). All DTP programs support the concept of keeping a paragraph style (such as Heading 1) with the next paragraph.

Defining Heading Tags

Let's go through the heading paragraph tags that add organization and structure to your document. The following tags are used in this book and can easily be used for your manuals:

Style	Description
Chapter	This is the paragraph tag used to denote the chapter text.
Chapter No	This paragraph increments the chapter number counter (sometimes this is a part of the Chapter paragraph tag).
Heading 1	First-level heading that is left-justified across both the sidehead area and the text flow area. This is normally included in a table of contents.
Heading 2	Second-level heading that is indented halfway between the sidehead area and the left margin of body text in the text flow area. This is normally included in a table of contents.
Heading 3	Third-level heading that is lined up in the left margin of the text flow area. This is normally included in a table of contents.
Heading 4	Fourth-level heading that is right-aligned in the sidehead area. This is not usually included in a table of contents.
Sidehead	Body text that is left-justified in the sidehead area to the left of the text flow area.
SubTitle	A subtitle that indicates what the publication is used for (such as "User's Manual").
Task	A paragraph tag that is used to make a task sentence stand out like a heading. I like preceding this with a special bullet at the right margin of the sidehead area.
Title	Only used for the title page which is frequently cross-referenced in running headers as the title of the publication. On the next page, the title tag text is shown as Publication Title.

The paragraphs on the next page illustrate the tags defined above.

CHAPTER TITLE

HEADING 1

Heading 2

Heading 3

Heading 4 The Heading 4 tag, like the Sidehead, runs parallel to the paragraph following it (this one).

NOTE This is a sidehead with a prefix that is fixed (NOTE).

The next paragraph following a sidehead should be one of the body paragraph tags. It exists in the text flow area.

USER'S MANUAL

⊃ **This is a task sentence.**

Publication Title

Using FrameMaker

Chapter   Basic: Indents are set to 0", spacing Above set to 0 pt and Below to 0 pt, line spacing 43 pt fixed, left alignment, and next tag set to Chapter. Default font: StoneInformal Italic 36 pt, pair kern. Pagination: starts anywhere, format anywhere, don't keep with next, and leave room for side heads in flow. Numbering, Advanced; and Table Cell: defaults used.

Chapter No   Basic: Indents are set to 0", spacing Above set to 0 pt and Below to 0 pt, line spacing 100 pt fixed, left alignment, and next tag set to Chapter. Default font: Times 100 pt, pair kern. Pagination: starts anywhere, Side Head-Top edge alignment format, keep with next, and leave room for side heads in flow. Numbering is set with Autonumber Format checked and field set to <n+>< =0>< =0>< =0> with the Default ¶ Font (which increments and displays the chapter counter while resetting all of the other counters to 0). Advanced, and Table Cell: defaults used.

NOTE Why set the space above to 44 points? Just in case you ever want to disable the top of page setting.

Heading 1   Basic: Indents are set to 0", spacing Above set to 44 pt and Below to 4 pt, line spacing 22 pt fixed, left alignment, and next tag set to Heading 2. Default font: Optima bold 20 pt, small Caps, pair kern. Pagination: starts top of page, format across Side Head and Normal Areas, keep with next, and leave room for side heads in flow. Numbering, Advanced; and Table Cell: defaults used.

If you are using color in your manual, this tag is usually set to a spot color.

Heading 2   Basic: All indents are set to .75", spacing Above set to 15 pt and 5 pt Below, line spacing to 20, left alignment, and next tag set to Body. Default font: Optima bold 18 pt, pair kern. Pagination: starts anywhere, format across Side Head and Normal Areas, keep with next, and leave room for side heads in flow. Numbering, Advanced; and Table Cell: defaults used.

Heading 3   Same as Heading 2 except that all indents set to .0", spacing Above set to 12 pt, 4 pt Below, 15 pt line spacing. Font is 14 pt.

Heading 4   Same as Heading 3 except that spacing Above set to 5 pt and line spacing set to 13 pt. Font is 11 pt and pagination set to Side Head Alignment to First Baseline. Since you will want to make certain that the entire heading stays together even across page breaks, set the Widow/Orphan lines to at least the maximum number of lines you expect (I set it to 4). Widows are lines of text that are left on a page and orphans are lines of text that are carried over to the next page.

Sidehead   Basic: Indents set to 0", spacing Above set to 0 pt and Below to 0 pt, line spacing 12 pt fixed, left alignment, and next tag set to Body. Default font: Tekton 8 pt, pair kern. Pagination: starts anywhere, format Side Head Alignment at Top Edge, keep with next, and leave room for side heads in flow. Numbering, Advanced, and Table Cell: defaults used.

Sideheads really need to stand out but be subdued—use spot color if you can.

NOTE   I like right justifying the title and subtitle.

SubTitle   Basic: Indents set to 0", spacing Above set to 20 pt and Below to 20 pt, line spacing 38 pt fixed, right alignment, and no next tag. Default font: Times 36 pt, pair kern, and Small caps (just because I like it). Pagination: starts anywhere, format across Side Head and Normal Areas, don't keep with next, and leave room for side heads in flow. Numbering, Advanced; and Table Cell: defaults used.

Task   Basic: Indent is set to 0" right, first to 1", left to 1.25", spacing Above set to 14 pt and Below to 0 pt, line spacing 14 pt fixed, left alignment, and next tag set to Body. Default font: Helvetica Neue (65) Bold 12 pt, pair kern. Pagination: starts anywhere, format Across Side Head and Normal Areas, keep with next, and leave room for side heads in flow. Numbering, Advanced; and Table Cell: defaults used.

Title   Basic: Indents is set to 0", spacing Above set to 0 pt and Below to 25 pt, line spacing 56 pt fixed, right alignment, and no next tag. Default font: Times 54 pt, pair kern, and Small caps (just cause I like it). Pagination: starts anywhere, format normal, don't keep with next, and leave room for side heads in flow. Numbering, Advanced; and Table Cell: defaults used.

Using Corel Ventura

Chapter   Character: Paragraph Text set to StoneInformal Semibold, 36 pt, black. Alignment: Right-justified horizontal. Spacing: All pages Left set to 1.25" and Right set to 0"; Lines to Indent is set to 1 with Indent Amount set to 0". Spacing Above and Inter-Para set to 0", Below set to 0 pt, Inter-Line to 43 pt. Default: Next Tag set to Body First. Breaks: set to In Line With Previous Paragraph and Line Break set to After. Typography: set to default values with Automatic Kerning checked.

Chapter No   Character: Paragraph Text set to Times, Italic, 100 points, black. Alignment: Right-justified horizontal. Spacing: All pages Left set to 1.25" and Right set to 4.85", Lines to Indent is 1 with Indent Amount set to 0". Spacing Above and Inter-Para set to 0", Below set to 0 pt, Inter-Line to 0 pt. Default: Next Tag set to Chapter. Breaks: set to None. Typography: set to default values.

Heading 1   Character: Paragraph Text set to Optima, Bold, 20 points, black (although this is the perfect candidate for a spot color). Alignment: Right-justified horizontal. Spacing: All pages Left set to 0" and Right set to 0", Lines to Indent is set to 1 with Indent Amount set to 0". Spacing Above set to 44 pt, Inter-Para set to 0", Below set to 4 pt, Inter-Line to 22 pt. Default: Next Tag is set to Heading 2. Breaks: set to default with Keep With Next Paragraph checked and Line Break set to After. Typography: set to default values.

Although I like the top heading level set all uppercase (with the first letter always a larger capital), there is no automatic way to do this with Corel Ventura.

Heading 2   Same as Heading 1 except that Left Indent is set to .75", spacing Above set to 15 pt, 5 pt Below, 20 pt Inter-Line. Font is 18 pt. Next Tag is Body.

Heading 3   Same as Heading 2 except that Left Indent is set to 1.25", spacing Above is set to 12 pt, 4 pt Below, and 15 pt Inter-Line. Font is 14 pt.

Heading 4   Same as Heading 3 except that spacing Above is set to 5 pt and line spacing is set to 13 pt. Alignment: horizontal justification is right-aligned. Font is 11 pt and breaks are set to Line Break to Before and Keep With Next Paragraph checked. Spacing is set so that Left is 0" and right is 4.350".

Sidehead   Same as Heading 4 except that alignment is left-aligned and font is Tekton 8 pt (spot color preferred). Spacing: Above and Below is 0 pt, Inter-Line is 12 pt. In order to precede the sidehead with an entry keyword (like NOTE), you need to enter the text along with an em space like: **NOTE CTRL+SHIFT+M.**

SubTitle   Character: Paragraph Text set to Times, 36 points, black. Alignment: Right-justified horizontal. Spacing: All pages Left set to 1.25" and Right set to 0"; Lines to Indent is set to 1 with Indent Amount is set to 0". Spacing Above set to 20 pt, and Inter-Para set to 0", Below set to 20 pt, Inter-Line to 38 pt. Default: No Next Tag set. Breaks: to default values with Line Break set to After. Typography: set to default values with Automatic Kerning checked.

Task   Character: Paragraph Text set to Helvetica 12 points, bold, black. Bullet set to 12 pt. Zapf Dingbat (notably spot color, right arrow), Indent set to .250", Bullet effect applied. Alignment: Left-justified horizontal. Spacing: All pages Left set to 1.0" and Right set to 0", Lines to Indent is 1 with Indent Amount set to 0". Spacing Above set to 14 pt, and Inter-Para set to 0", Below set to 0 pt, Inter-Line to 14 pt. Default: Next Tag set to **Body**. Breaks: to default values with Line Break set to After. Typography: set to default values with Automatic Kerning checked.

Title   Character: Paragraph Text set to Times, 54 pt, black. Alignment: Right-justified horizontal. Spacing: All pages Left set to 1.25" and Right set to 0", Lines to Indent is set to 1 with Indent Amount set to 0". Spacing Above set to 0 pt, and Inter-Para set to 0", Below set to 25 pt, Inter-Line to 56 pt. Default: No Next Tag set (well, actually to itself). Breaks: to default values with Line Break set to After. Typography: set to default values with Automatic Kerning checked.

SETTING HEADER AND FOOTER PARAGRAPH TAGS

When we discussed the layout layer in the previous chapter, we didn't use paragraph tags. These tags can be reapplied to the paragraphs in the layout.

Sans Serif Font Paragraph Tags

Style	Description
Chapter Tab	A paragraph tag used in the layout layer that defines the text in the chapter tab (normally white text).
Header	A paragraph tag that resides above the text frame. This normally includes text that is used to denote the title, page number, and current Heading 1 text.
Footer	This is text that usually presents less important information and frequently includes the name of your company.

This represents a typical Chapter Tab paragraph tag:

For most of you, the header and footer will have the exact same paragraph tag attributes. We've made the footer a little different by placing a small graphic in the footer thus reducing the footer width by .45". The following is the footer:

And the following is the header:

BreakOut4I User's Manual

Using FrameMaker

Chapter Tab Basic: Indents set to 0", spacing Above set to 6 pt and Below to 0 pt; line spacing 18 pt fixed, left alignment, and no next tag. Default font: Optima Bold 10 pt, pair kern, and white color. Pagination: starts anywhere, normal format, don't keep with next, and leave room for sideheads in flow. Numbering, Advanced; and Table Cell: defaults used.

For the following two tags, you should use spot color.

Footer Basic: Indents set to 0", spacing Above set to 0 pt and Below to 0 pt; line spacing 10 pt fixed, left alignment, right tab stop set to 5.5" (very important), and no next tag. You can, if you wish, add another centered tab stop at 2.75". Default font: AvantGarde 8 pt, and pair kern. Pagination: starts anywhere, normal format, don't keep with next, and leave room for sideheads in flow. Numbering, Advanced, and Table Cell: defaults used. You can, if you wish, add another centered tab stop at 2.75".

Header The same as the Footer paragraph tag except the right tab stop is set to 5.5" (the full width). You can, if you wish, add another centered tab stop at 2.75".

Using Corel Ventura

Finally, you can complete the chapter tab style the correct way. Once you set the paragraph tab definitions, you should select the chapter number and set the size to 24 pt. Note that there is an em space between the chapter number and the chapter text.

Chapter Tab Character: Paragraph Text set to Optima Bold, 10 pt, white. Alignment: Left-justified horizontal. Spacing: All pages Left set to .5" and Right set to .2"; Lines to Indent is set to 1 with Indent Amount set to 0". Spacing Above set to 5 pt, and Inter-Para set to 0", Below set to 0 pt, Inter-Line to 10 pt.

Default: No Next Tag set (well, actually to itself). Breaks: to default values (all breaks set to None). Typography: set to default values with Automatic Kerning checked.

Corel Ventura forces automatically generated paragraph tags for the header and footer (both beginning with Z_).

Z_FOOTER (*alias* **Footer)**   Character: Paragraph Text set to AvantGarde 8 pt, black (although I definitely prefer spot color here). Alignment: Left-justified horizontal, center tab set to 2.75", and right tab set to 5.5". Spacing: All pages Left set to 0" and Right set to 0"; Lines to Indent is set to 1 with Indent Amount set to 0". Spacing Above set to 0 pt, and Inter-Para set to 0 pt, Below set to 0 pt, Inter-Line to 10 pt. Default: No Next Tag set (well, actually to itself). Breaks: to default values (Line Break set to None). Typography: set to default values with Automatic Kerning checked.

Z_HEADER (*alias* **Header)**   The same as the Footer paragraph tag.

RULES FOR INDEXING AND REFERENCING

Let's spend a few minutes talking about indexing. There are several schools of thought on the subject. The sole purpose of indexes and cross-references is to make critical information easy to access. Indexes can be created by inserting an index marker within the text. The marker is a simple little "tick mark" shown at the position of the marker. The marker text is typically hidden from normal viewing but can be displayed or searched for using special DTP commands.

Referencing within Documents

There are times that you may have to cross-reference parts of a document from another location in the same document. Frequently, you cross-reference information with its page number as shown in Figure 4.32.

Figure 4.32
Insert a reference
marker and cross-
referencing a
page number.

Reference marker

Chapter 1 Communicating With A Modem

A modem is definitely one of the most sophisticated technologies that has gotten more powerful for less money.

...

See the description of a modem on page 21.

Cross-reference

A reference is created by inserting a reference marker somewhere in a paragraph. I suggest choosing a location that is consistent throughout your entire publication in case you wish to change them later. I prefer to place reference markers *after* the first word in the paragraph (after the first word A in Figure 4.32).

What if you need to make a cross-reference to the title of a publication? Titles are always set in italics (See Figure 4.33).

What if you need to indicate a chapter? Figure 4.34 shows some examples that use the correct punctuation.

Whenever you directly cross-reference a heading or chapter text, you should place quotation marks around it. Don't italicize headings or chapters (like you should with publication titles) since that could add to reader confusion.

I like placing a reference marker (and *See*, *See also* index entries) at the end of the first word in a paragraph. The cross-reference that "points" to the reference marker will be adjusted to reflect the exact page number at a later time (normally before you print).

Figure 4.33
Cross-
referencing a title.

The title of this book, *A Guide to Publishing User Manuals*, is self-explanatory.

Italicized title

Figure 4.34
Cross-
referencing a
heading.

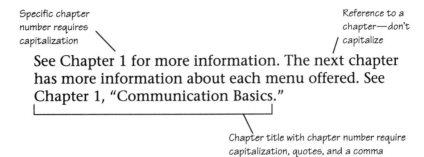

Specific chapter
number requires
capitalization

Reference to a
chapter—don't
capitalize

See Chapter 1 for more information. The next chapter has more information about each menu offered. See Chapter 1, "Communication Basics."

Chapter title with chapter number require
capitalization, quotes, and a comma

The following represents the way that an index would look after the DTP program generates it:

What about indexes? Most DTP programs don't visually distinguish the difference between reference markers and index entries.

Without any placement standards, these elements (indexes, references, and cross-references) would be difficult to find.

Type of marker	Placed
Cross-reference	After the first word in the sentence being referenced.
Reference	At the point where the DTP program substitutes the page number, figure number, table number, and so on.
Index entry	Preceding the first word where the index text appears.
Index See and See also	Directly after the first word of the index text.

I always place index markers at the beginning of the first word of the marker, as shown in Figure 4.35.

Figure 4.35
Index entry
marker.

Index entry

Chapter 1 Communicating With A Modem

A modem is definitely one of the most sophisticated technologies that has gotten more powerful for less money.

Figure 4.36
The generated
index.

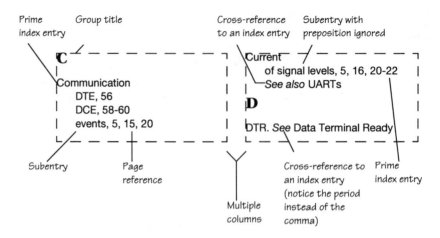

Figure 4.36 represents the way that an index would look after the DTP program generates it. The first word of the prime index entry should be capitalized. The first word of a subentry should be lowercase except for those words or acronyms that are always capitalized (DTE and DCE in the figure).

You may be saying at this point, "The prime index entries should also be lowercase!"

This is *your* choice since all index entries are typically lowercase. But, when you have tons of subentries and they span over one column, the reader may get lost trying to decipher the difference between prime index entries and corresponding subentries.

Look at any of Microsoft's documentation and you'll see exactly what I mean—some prime index entries occupy several pages.

A comma should follow an entry (or subentry) that has a page reference and between each page reference. Speaking of page references, they can be single or a range (like 20-22, in the figure) separated with a nonbreaking dash or an en dash.

You can use a cross-reference to another index entry in place of a page reference (*See* and *See also* keywords). In the case of an index entry that can refer the reader to another index entry in addition to the other index entries, use the *See also* keywords. Multiple cross-references should be separated with a semi-colon (;). *See also* index subentries should be alphabetized to appear at the end of all of the subentries.

When you are directing the reader to a specific index for a page reference, use the italicized *See* followed by the other index entry the reader should use. Use a period following the index entry instead of a comma.

Here are some basic rules to follow when generating indexes:

1. Group titles are automatically generated by DTP programs. The styles used could be something other than a bold version of a normal font. Each group title should be based on a sans serif style font (like Optima bold or Helvetica Inserat) and, preferably, in a different color.

2. Although you may find it time-consuming to insert, providing plenty of cross-references with *See* and *See also* entries will aid in the reader's enjoyment of your manual. *You can't expect users to know the exact term to use when looking up something!*

3. There are some fundamentals in index page design you should consider. Use sans serif fonts at a size smaller than normal body text and divide the index page into multiple columns (two columns will usually do). Although you can use a paragraph style for all subentries, the indented paragraph styles we use in this book are far superior in readability.

4. Ignore prepositions or conjunctions in the alphabetizing sequence (see the example of *signal levels*). Where index entries begin with numerics, alphabetize them as if they were spelled out (for example, *19* should be alphabetized under *nineteen*).

Who should create the indexing?

You should—the writer. Given some guidelines, every writer should take the responsibility to create index entries. Indexing is really important and should not be taken lightly or looked upon as "grunt work."

When should index creation take place?

As you write—maybe not in the first draft, but soon thereafter. Otherwise, when you are under a time crunch, the quality of the index suffers. Too many software manuals have unusable indexes.

Figure 4.37
Insert an index
marker.

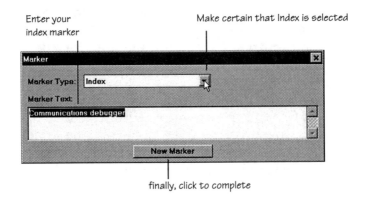

Using FrameMaker

Creating an Index Entry

The steps are very easy:

1. Place the insertion point where you would like the reference page to be included in your index.

2. Select Special>Marker and you'll see a special modeless (there's that term again!) dialog. See Figure 4.37.

3. Click New Marker to insert the index entry. A special symbol ⊺ is inserted at the marker.

   The Marker dialog does not "disappear." As a modeless dialog, it hangs around and can be used later just by clicking on it. To remove it, select it and enter **ALT+F4**.

Creating a Reference Marker

Creating a reference marker is almost the same as creating an index entry with a couple of minor exceptions.

- Reference markers should be placed at a different location in a paragraph than an index entry.

- Make certain that the Marker Type field is set to Cross-Ref.

Figure 4.38
Insert a cross-reference.

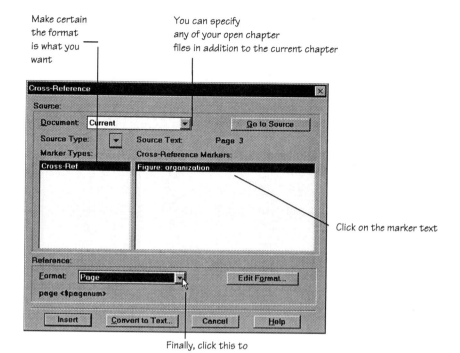

Make certain
the format
is what you
want

You can specify
any of your open chapter
files in addition to the current chapter

Click on the marker text

Finally, click this to
insert the marker

Referencing a Marker

It's easy to enter a reference to a predefined reference marker. In fact, FrameMaker wisely doesn't allow you to reference a nonexistent marker.

1. Place the insertion point where you want FrameMaker to insert the reference to a marker.

2. Select the Special>Cross-Reference menu command. A dialog will be displayed (see Figure 4.38). Click the correct reference source (the marker text description) and your format (the most frequent is Page).

3. To create a reference, click Insert. The reference is immediately displayed in your document.

Updating all Markers

With the introduction of version 5, a new menu command has been added to update all markers. Click on Edit>Update References. Check All Cross-References and click Update.

How to Handle Unresolved References

When you generate a book's table of contents and index (described in Chapter 7) or when you update the markers in your current chapter, you may be presented with a dialog that indicates that you have an unresolved reference.

Don't panic. FrameMaker makes the resolution very easy. Just, place your insertion point at the beginning of your document and click on Edit>Find/Change. Select Unresolved Cross-Reference from the Find list field and click Find. Once the unresolved reference is highlighted, correct it and click Find again until all unresolved references have been highlighted.

More Reference Formats

The following table shows the most common formats used for referencing text markers:

Format	Example
Page	Page 10
Chapter	Chapter 5
Heading	"Features"
Heading & Page	"Features" on Page 10

You can, of course, define your own with the Cross-Reference dialog. Click on the Format button. This will bring up another dialog shown in Figure 4.39.

Figure 4.39
Define a
cross-reference
format.

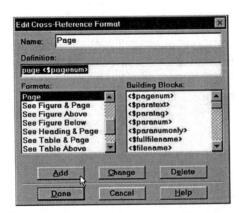

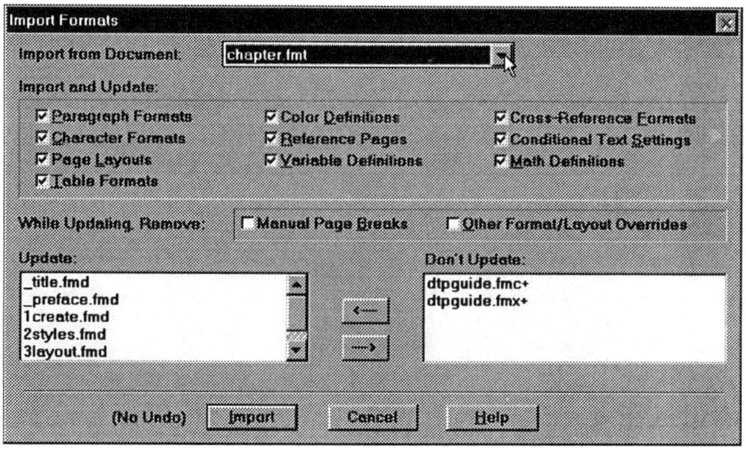

Figure 4.40
Import cross-reference formats to your entire publication.

Once you create a new format in your chapter, you'll need to import this to the rest of your publication's chapters. Open the publication file and select File>Import>Formats (Figure 4.40). Check the Cross-Reference Formats box. Click Import.

You'll notice in this sample that the table of contents (DTPGUIDE.FMC) and index document (DTPGUIDE.FMX) files are not modified. All other chapters in the publication are updated to the formats of the template (CHAPTER.FMT).

Using Corel Ventura

Creating an Index Entry

In order to create an index entry, follow our rules of marker placement. The steps are very easy:

1. Place the insertion point where you would like the reference page to be included in your index.

2. Right-click and select Insert Special Item>Index Entry or with the Index Entries Roll-Up displayed (with **ALT+F7**). Type in the Main Entry field entry **Alpha** (Figure 4.41).

3. Click on the Add to Index List button and click back into your document to continue. A small superscripted code (°) is inserted at that location. You can edit it later by placing the insertion point before the marker, right-clicking, and selecting Edit Special Item).

Figure 4.41
Adding an index
main entry.

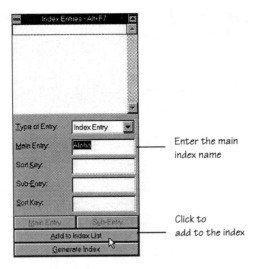

Figure 4.41
Adding an index
main entry.

Enter the main
index name

Click to
add to the index

Creating a Reference Marker

The easiest way to insert a reference marker is to bring up the Cross-Ref Roll-Up by selecting the Tools>Cross-Ref Roll-Up (or use the **ALT+F6** shortcut). See Figure 4.42.

The steps are very easy.

1. Place the insertion point at the position for your marker.

2. Right-click and select Insert Special Item>Marker or simply click the Insert Marker button in the Cross-Ref Roll-Up.

3. At the prompt, type your marker name (such as **Marker1**). Click OK.

Figure 4.42
The Cross-Ref
Roll-Up.

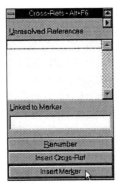

Figure 4.43
Insert the
reference.

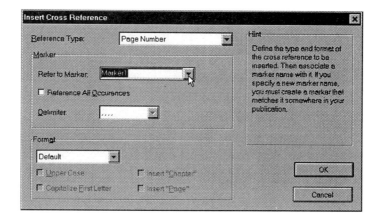

A small superscripted code (◦) will be inserted at that location (you can always edit it later by placing the insertion point before the marker, right-click, and select Edit Special Item).

Referencing a Marker

To refer to a marker, follow these steps:

1. Place the insertion point where you would like to reference your marker. Click the Insert Cross-Ref button in the Cross-Ref Roll-Up.

NOTE You can specify chapter, figure, or table formats.

2. Select the reference type as shown in (in our case this will be Page Number). See Figure 4.43. Select the marker by name from the list (in our case, Marker1).

3. Corel Ventura gives you is the ability to define multiple locations for a single marker name. You can check the Reference All Occurrences to allow multiple references. In addition, you can update the format to insert Chapter or Page prefaces, capitalize the first character, or capitalize the reference. We won't do any of that in this example.

4. Click OK.

Updating All References

To generate and update cross-references, click the Renumber button in the Cross-Ref Roll-Up. You will be asked questions about saving the chapter—answer them all affirmatively and watch Corel Ventura resolve the cross-references.

Figure 4.44
Insert a marker to
an unresolved
cross-reference.

Handling Unresolved References

References are not automatically generated, so you have to force a reconciliation. When you generate a table of contents, index, or update the markers in your current chapter, you may be presented with unresolved references (Figure 4.44).

You should periodically refresh the publication in order to reconnect cross-references to markers. From the Cross-Ref Roll-Up, click Renumber.

To insert an unresolved marker, place the insertion point at the location desired, select the marker (Unresolved Marker, in the example), and click Insert Marker.

Corel Ventura can take some time to traverse through all of the chapters in a publication. Make certain that you have enough available memory before you update all references. In addition, back up your chapter files regularly.

5 GRAPHICS AND TABLES

This is by far, my favorite layer to discuss. The use of graphics and tables in your manuals can help to communicate ease of use as well as providing a much-needed text break.

This chapter really tries to demystify graphics by focusing on practical topics that make a difference in publications.

- Organizing and setting file naming conventions.
- Creating great drawings.
- Working with images.
- Inserting graphics into your documents.
- Taking professional screen captures.
- Adding shadows behind graphics.
- Overlapping graphics for proper separation.
- Creating great looking tables.

ORGANIZING GRAPHICS

Once you construct a manual, the use of artwork (graphics, drawings, screen shots, and so on) can become difficult to organize. For example, management of images may become unruly in a hurry if you don't consider these issues:

- Which directory structure should I define in order to hold the different images?

- How should I classify images so that they are easy to find?

- When I use images in on-line help, must I use text fonts that are Truetype, and when I go directly to print, must I use Postscript Type 1? Help!

- When I work with images, the original image is modified several times before I actually use it in my documentation. Must I keep original artwork along with the resultant modified versions?

- I want to keep descriptions of images somewhere. Also some notes would help. Unless I use proprietary image file formats (as with CorelDRAW), is there no way to keep descriptions with images that can be viewed without going into CorelDRAW?

Although there are many different approaches, the following one may actually save you a lot of time once you realize that you'll need to reorganize everything.

In Chapter 1 we presented the disk organization of the entire publication. What I didn't present in any detail was the organization of drawings, bitmap images, and screen captures.

I classify artwork directories into the following subdirectories:

- Albums that catalog drawings
- Drawings
- Images
- Screen shots

Figure 5.1
Artwork as part of
a publication.

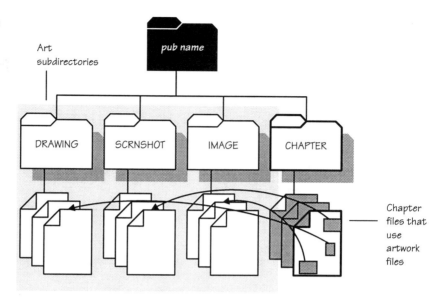

Structuring File Directories

It is recommended that you separate artwork into subdirectories based on file type (drawings, screen shots, and bitmap images) within the publication. See Figure 5.1 showing a publication that uses artwork files. Your publication's chapter files actually "point" to the art files.

Of course, if you plan on sharing this artwork with other publications or other uses, the artwork subdirectories could be "outside" of your publication's directory structure. See Figure 5.2 for example.

Albums

Artwork catalogs can keep track of each graphic used in a publication. If used for only one publication, it is a good idea to create a separate catalog for each chapter.

If artwork is used for more than one publication, you should set up a separate catalog for specific topics, or classify by drawing, image, or screen shot.

Figure 5.2
Artwork to be shared among multiple programs.

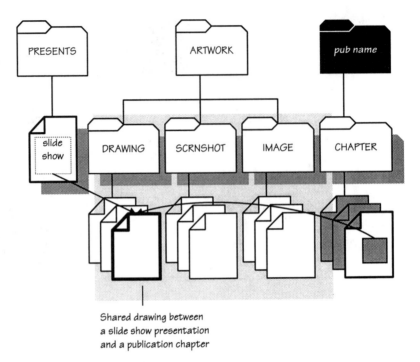

Shared drawing between
a slide show presentation
and a publication chapter

NOTE I know CorelDRAW gives you Mosaic. It just doesn't compare with ImagePals.

I have looked at various catalog programs and, in my opinion, the best is Ulead Systems' ImagePals Album program. It is easy to use, and the quality of thumbnail versions of the original artwork (minimized representations of the artwork) is outstanding.

What an Album Tracks

I have kept graphics used in the creation of this book in an album. Here are some of the thumbnail images that I maintained. There is a mixture of screen shots, drawings, and even bitmapped artwork. See Figure 5.3.

Graphics are inserted into a catalog by first selecting a catalog and then by clicking the **INS** key. Enter the filename(s) of the graphic you'd like to insert into the catalog album.

You can then select a graphic thumbnail, press **ALT+ENTER**, and fill in all sorts of information as shown in Figure 5.4, "The thumbnail properties associated with a graphic file in an album.," on page 160.

Figure 5.3
Thumbnail versions
of artwork using
ImagePals.

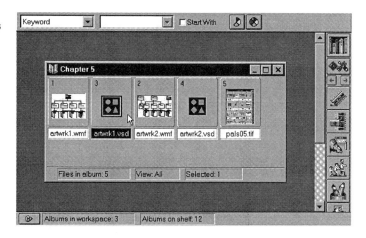

I'm not going to present a comprehensive tutorial on using the Album product, but a quick summary of key features should help to convince you of this product's importance for *all* DTP professionals:

- You can move a whole subdirectory full of supported graphic files into an album.

- It is closely integrated with the other ImagePals products (they are pals, right?).

- It enables you to sort on album thumbnails on almost any criteria.

- You can perform batch operations like full graphics file moves between directories without losing thumbnail properties, printing the entire album, and batch format conversions.

- The product works with a wide range of graphics file formats and always works reliably (in other words, it doesn't crash like some of the other image management software products on the market).

Sometimes you may need support for graphics files that are not recognized by Album. An example is the CorelDRAW format. In such a case, you'll need to export the proprietary file format to a file format that Album will understand (at least for its thumbnail). The same may be true for the DTP program you are using.

Figure 5.4
The thumbnail
properties
associated with a
graphic file in an
album.

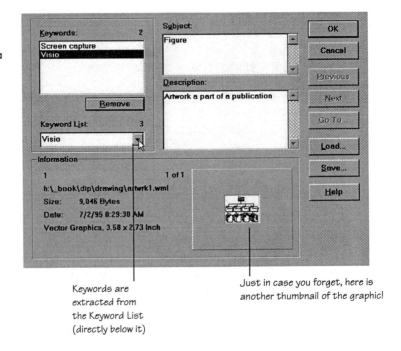

Keywords are
extracted from
the Keyword List
(directly below it)

Just in case you forget, here is
another thumbnail of the graphic!

I always create an ALBUM subdirectory that is a peer to the
SCRNSHOT (and other graphics) subdirectories. The album
files are placed there, "pointing" to files in the other
directories.

Choosing File-naming Conventions

If you don't come to grip with file-naming conventions
quickly, you and your team could easily become completely
confused keeping track of hundreds of graphics files from a
variety of different sources. The Windows file system does
not include descriptive information to indicate the programs
and methods used to create a graphic.

What kind of identification information do you need to keep
track of?

- Number of colors: four color, grayscale, RGB, and so on.

- Font information (TrueType or Type 1).

- Presence of drop shadows added to a graphic.

NOTE Windows releases post version 3.11 include long filenames, but the idea of naming conventions still applies.

You can use albums, as discussed in the previous section, to catalog this information but without some basic file-naming conventions, you'll still have a problem.

The convention that I use is:

<5/6-char-filename><2-char-ID><1/2-char-number>.<ext>

File naming suffix	Description
_4	Four-color (CYMK)
_1	Black and white
_3	RGB
_G	Grayscale
SH	Shadow (grayscale assumed)
_T	Truetype fonts in the graphics
_P	Postscript (and Type 1) graphics

Here are some examples:

IMAGE_4.TIF   Four-color (CYMK) separated TIF image (no incident numbering scheme).

MNMODSH.TIF   The fourth image of MNMOD with a shadow (grayscale shadows are assumed).

MAKING ARTISTIC DRAWINGS

Drawings are graphic files stored as objects, which have characteristics like curvature, position, color, and line width.

CGM   A Computer Graphics Metafile that has a .CGM file extension. Its popularity has decreased over the years since the early 2-CAD days. This is an ANSI standard (ISO 8632, ANSI X3.02-1986).

EPS   The Encapsulated Postscript format is a device-independent file format that, in its level 1 format, is used in both Windows and Mac. An EPS file normally uses an .EPS file extension and has preview information for screen display.

WMF   The Windows Metafile is a device-independent format for vector-based drawings. Although this format is newly supported, it has become the standard for all of the DTP programs I review here. WMF files use a file extension of .WMF. These files can also hold bitmapped image information.

There are more drawing file types, but these are the ones that are supported by major DTP programs and also generally print successfully. Once objects are drawn, you can usually edit them with a drawing product later. Each of the DTP programs provide limited drawing capability that we restrict only to basic logos or caption lines.

Of all of the formats presented, I endorse the EPS first and the WMF a close second. Use EPS drawing images when producing drawings for imagesetting output, and WMF for all other uses.

Drawing

Vector drawings (in either EPS or WMF format) are normally used for drawings and fonts that need to be sent to the printshop with high accuracy (and not in the dreaded pixelized form).

NOTE The only feature that Visio is currently missing is gradient color blending.

Typical drawings are those that show flow, relationships, or diagrams. Of all the diagramming packages I've used, the best is Visio. Every company that I've shown Visio to ends up standardizing on it. You can use high-end products (like CorelDRAW or Designer), but they carry so much file baggage that I would recommend using those packages only for the most complicated drawings.

This paragraph is extremely important (not that all of the others are *less* important). DTP products do not normally "understand" files produced by drawing products like Visio. In other words, FrameMaker can display Visio drawings only if you export the proprietary Visio drawings to a format like WMF that FrameMaker can import, or if you embed the Visio drawing using OLE.

Although embedding artwork into your DTP publication file may seem like the easiest thing to do, you'll regret it later. If you can link to the graphic file, you can change that artwork file without having to search in your publication for it.

Figure 5.5
The basic Visio
user interface.

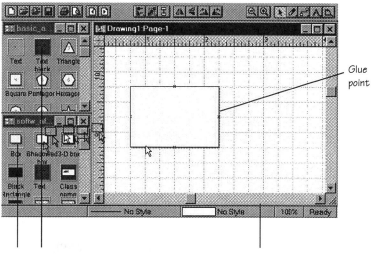

Glue
point

Two stencils of drawing symbols   The drawing workplace

Using DTP Drawing Tools

There is one more option that you should consider. Some of
the DTP programs (like FrameMaker) have their own drawing
tools (although minimal, they are really not bad). But what
happens if you wish to use these same drawings in other
documents, training material, presentations, online help, or
even in marketing material? Unfortunately, programs other
than your favorite DTP program (such as PowerPoint or
QuarkXPress) may be used, and drawings created using your
DTP program's drawing tools will not be usable.

I have chosen Shapeware Corporation's easy-to-use Visio
program as my drawing tool of choice. Let's run through a
simple overview. Typically, with publications, there is a need
to use a sophisticated drawing product like Visio. Did I say
sophisticated? But didn't I just say that Visio was easy-to-use?
Actually, Visio serves both purposes.

How Visio Works

Visio is a simple drawing product that outclasses the drawing
services of both Corel Ventura's and FrameMaker's built-in
drawing tools. If you don't have the creative juices to use
CorelDRAW to produce great looking art, Visio can make you
look good.

Figure 5.6
Creating a Visio
drawing.

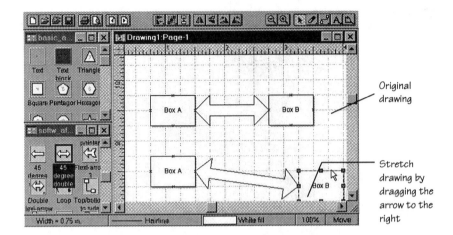

Original
drawing

Stretch
drawing by
dragging the
arrow to the
right

Its user interface provides for a stencil of symbols and a drawing workplace (that looks just like a piece of paper). See Figure 5.5.

By dragging drawing objects from the symbols onto your drawing workplace, you can construct a drawing easily. Shading is one click away. Color changes are almost as easy.

Visio's biggest accomplishment is its glue feature. You can combine drawings together and actually *glue* objects together (Figure 5.6). For example, if you move the box labeled Box B, the double-headed arrow will stretch with it and stay connected with the box labeled Box A.

Even adding text to drawings is easy. You simply select the drawing and start typing. Visio knows how to adjust the placement of text based on the geometry of the drawing object (in other words, the size of the box automatically influences how the text is positioned within the box).

There's another feature that I find exceptional. Shapeware Corporation has made the product *open* so that you can actually write custom Visual Basic programs to control Visio's operation. That capability is going to mean a lot more third-party add-ons in the future.

In addition, the company appears to be releasing new stencils every few months focused on specific industries. I have already purchased marketing, programming (flowcharting), technical, and home stencil packages that rival specialized products on the market.

In order for Visio drawings to be properly cataloged in the ImagePals Album product, you have to export the Visio drawing into a format that ImagePals understands: namely, WMF. This works fine, but I wish that Shapeware Corporation provided import converters so that Visio proprietary drawing formats could be directly referenced by the DTP products (FrameMaker and Corel Ventura) and the major graphics cataloging programs like Ulead Systems Album.

By the way, Visio does provide the ability to use the Windows clipboard and OLE integration—but we'll see later in this chapter why that shouldn't be counted on with DTP publishing.

CREATING AND WORKING WITH IMAGES

Brief Overview of Image Files

Bitmapped images are used for high-resolution artwork. The use of these images should be restricted to fancy chapter art and never for technical drawings that need to retain font and object clarity. Bitmapped images do not maintain line or curve information like drawing files do. Every pixel (dot) has color information.

We'll talk about CMYK bitmapped images which are nothing more than cyan, magenta, yellow, and black images (one "plane" or view per color). CMYK represents the four-color artwork you hear so much about from imagesetters.

CMYK is the basis for color printing. RGB is the bitmap representation in three planes: red, green, and blue. RGB is the representation of bitmapped images on your video monitor. In fact, all visual information is converted to RGB planes by Windows before being displayed. RGB has little bearing on an imagesetter.

Grayscale images are those in which each dot in the image has a corresponding lightness and darkness. Grayscale image formats usually support up to 256 shades of gray per dot.

And finally, true color is a 24-bit, very high-quality representation of bitmaps with each RGB components represented by values ranging from 0 to 256. More and more video graphics cards are supporting true color displays.

BMP　This is the Windows and OS/2 format that has been used ever since I can remember. It is the format used for copying bitmaps to the Windows clipboard. It is a good format but fairly limited in color information and compression. I would avoid saving files in this format.

DCS　An extension to EPS by Quark, Incorporated (the makers of QuarkXPress) that separates colors into color planes suitable for imagesetter color separation.

EPS　Didn't know that EPS could also hold bitmap information? It sure can. EPS files describe every color as an ASCII-readable numeric code. It takes a lot of space, but it is still the standard output format used by imagesetters today.

JPEG　Developed by the Joint Photographic Experts Group, this format has tremendous file compression capability supporting grayscale, true color, and CMYK images.

PCX　Originally created by ZSoft Corporation (you know, the makers of PC Paintbrush) this format describes a wide range of bitmapped images. It is used seriously on PC systems, but not taken too seriously outside of that domain (like on Macs).

TIFF　The Tagged Image Format jointly developed by Aldus and Microsoft has become the cross-platform (Mac and UNIX systems alike) bitmapped format of choice. It supports practically every bitmap format in existence and uses some pretty innovative compression techniques to minimize the amount of disk storage your files need without loss of quality.

WMF　The WMF format is pretty robust in that it also can represent drawings and bitmaps in 16, 256, and RGB true color images.

Of all the formats presented, I endorse the TIFF (file extension .TIF) as the best choice.

Figure 5.7
The Capture user
interface.

The type of visual
object that will be
captured next

The keyboard sequence
that invokes Capture

Quick buttons that are used
to control the next capture

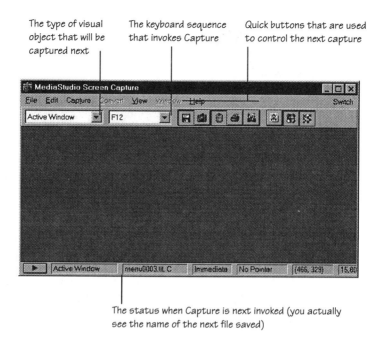

The status when Capture is next invoked (you actually
see the name of the next file saved)

Taking Screen Captures

I have looked at many screen capture programs (practically
all of them, I think) and I have settled on the one that is
spectacular: Ulead Systems Incorporated's ImagePals Capture
program. The main reasons are:

- It works reliably at any Windows-support video
  resolution (other screen capture utilities have trouble).

- It captures both Windows and MS-DOS screens.

- The assortment of Windows objects (menus, areas,
  windows, and so on) is the best.

- It fully automates capturing with post-processing, which
  saves steps (color to grayscale conversion, adding a
  shadow or border, and so on).

- Files captured can be auto-numbered and automatically
  saved into a Ulead Systems' Album catalog of your
  choosing.

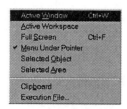

Screen Capturing Options

I will show you the highlights and some hints (learned the hard way) to guarantee spectacular screen capture results every time.

When you invoke Capture, you are greeted with a typical Windows application screen (Figure 5.7). Or is it?

The Capture screen is full of helpful information and one-button shortcuts to control the capture activity. If you pulled down the Capture menu, you'd see all of the Windows' visual elements that can be captured.

There are many features that will save you significant amounts of time and frustration, such as saving captures to automatically numbered files, saving files into an album catalog (see page 159), and even the ability to wait a number of seconds before capturing after the special Capture hotkey is depressed.

To top that off, you can set up post-processing (Figure 5.9) to convert the file type to a different resolution, expand or add a shadow around the image, and (my favorite) even change the resolution to more closely match your fonts and style demands. I use 180 pixels/inch for captures.

It couldn't be any easier.

Figure 5.9
Processing a capture before saving the file.

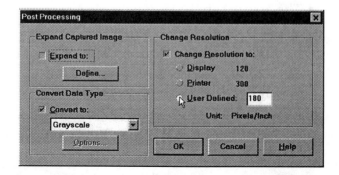

In Summary

Screen captures are best captured as:

- 8-bit grayscale TIFF images (only one channel should be saved).

- LZW compressed, 8K strip size, with preview information enabled.

- Do not enable horizontal differentiation since that will approximate the bitmap image and could produce less than perfect screen capture images.

- For highest dot density, create screen captures and associated shadows at 180 pixels (or dots) per inch even though your screen may be at 72 or 96 pixels per inch.

- Shadows should be generated from a blurred (or feathered) shadow (see page 196).

NOTE In order to preserve memory and resources, you do not need to keep the ImagePals Album program open.

Just a word of warning. If ImagePals capture fails with a message box like:

```
Invalid parameter
```

you are probably running out of available memory. Shut down one of the applications to free some needed valuable memory resources and try again.

INSERTING GRAPHICS INTO YOUR APPLICATION

NOTE I use the terms *graphics* and *figure* to refer to the same things: drawings and images.

I will present two methods of integrating graphics (drawings and images) into your publication.

- Placing a graphic into your base as a repeatable object.

- Anchoring a graphic into your text with a figure caption. We'll also discuss how to reference these graphics.

Let's define several new paragraph tags used for graphics:

- **Z_Figure**   You must set this as the paragraph that holds the anchor to the figure.
- **Caption Figure**   This paragraph is where you enter the caption.

Don't forget to precede every figure with the **Body Next** paragraph style. This will ensure that the figure has some text preceding it.

The Wrong Way to Copy Graphics to Your Publication

Copying the artwork from the drawing application (like Visio) and then copying it into a DTP program's chapter file is as easy as:

1. Selecting all objects in your drawing application.
2. Copying the drawing to the Windows clipboard using **CTRL+C**.
3. Pasting the clipboard contents into your DTP application using **CTRL+V** (or **SHIFT+INS**).

Don't do it!

Why not? Chances are you have inserted an OLE image into your chapter that may cause the following problems:

- When you send your publication files to your printshop, it may result in problems with embedded objects (in other words, your drawing).
- If you need to change the original drawing later, the changes are not automatically updated (unless you did a Paste Link).
- If any of your images are to be four-color separated, embedded objects are not automatically rendered as separations in four-color EPS or four-color TIFF.

The Right Way to Copy Drawings to Your Publication

I recommend you keep *two* versions of graphics: one in the proprietary graphics program format; and the other version should be exported to some standard file format supported by DTP programs such as WMF, TIFF, or even EPS.

These exported files are now in a format that any application could import (presentation graphic programs, word processors, DTP programs, and even other graphics programs).

Placing Graphics as Repeatable Objects

Let's put a logo onto every page of a document. I am assuming that you have created a graphics object that can be placed into the corner of every footer (we'll only put it on the even-numbered pages).

The same technique applies to any type of graphics object. Our example will be a logo drawing created using Visio filename: LOGO.WMF.

Using FrameMaker

Here are the steps to place a graphic (drawing or bitmap image) on a given page throughout a chapter.

1. In one of your chapter files, select the Right Master page by clicking View>Master Pages menu. **PAGE DOWN** (or **PAGE UP**) to a page that the Status bar indicates as Left. This is how you traverse between master pages.

2. Select the Right master page. Click the outside of the text frames with the Object Selection tool.

3. Select File>Import>File. Enter the name of the file you wish to insert (Figure 5.10).

4. The graphic is automatically placed by FrameMaker in the middle of the frame (which is actually the entire page since you did not select one of the text frames). Thus, the graphic is floating on the page (Figure 5.11).

Figure 5.10
Selecting the file
to import.

Click on the
graphics file
you wish to
import

Refer to
the file always

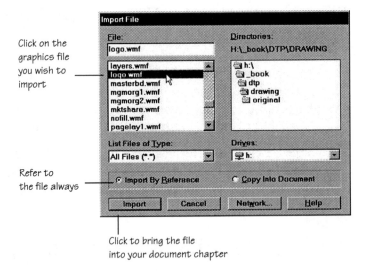

Click to bring the file
into your document chapter

5. Optionally, scale the graphic to suit your needs by selecting the Graphics>Scale dialog (Figure 5.12). Click on Scale and the logo is centered at the correct size.

6. However, the graphic needs to be repositioned. Drag it down to the leftmost corner of the master page as shown in Figure 5.13.

7. Switch back to the Body Pages view and you'll see how the odd-numbered (or pages on the right) pages will show that graphic.

Figure 5.11
FrameMaker has
placed the
graphic.

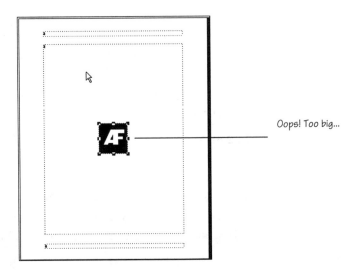

Oops! Too big...

Figure 5.12
Scale the graphic.

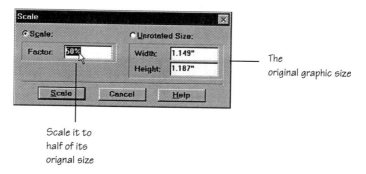

The
original graphic size

Scale it to
half of its
orignal size

8. Switch back to the Right Master page and select the graphic. Copy it to the FrameMaker clipboard (menu command Edit>Copy), switch to the Left Master page and paste it to the page with Edit>Paste. Reposition it to the right side of the footer.

There are *no* restrictions on the number of graphics you can place on master pages.

Repositioning Graphics

You can reposition the graphics frame by changing the location (left and right) positions in the Graphics>Object Properties dialog, or you can simply drag the frame to the position desired.

You can change the position of the graphics within the frame by clicking on the graphic and dragging it to a new position within the frame (you can also modify the position with the Graphics>Object Properties dialog).

The Graphics>Object Properties dialog works for both graphics and for frames. You can also use the Graphics>Object Properties command to adjust the angle of the frame or the object. Graphics objects can be rotated to any angle, but frames can only be rotated in 90° angles.

Updating Your Publication

Don't forget to reselect the entire publication file and import the Page Layouts with the Import Formats dialog (menu command File>Import>Formats).

If you don't want a repeatable graphic on all pages but only on a few select pages, simply add another master page with a unique name (menu command Special>Add Master Page while in the master page view). Then, you can insert graphics on that page. The master page First Page usually has a unique graphic that is only applied on the first page of a chapter.

Figure 5.13
Positioning the graphic.

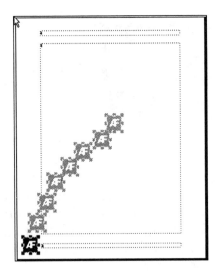

Using Corel Ventura

There are two unique ways to insert graphics into a Corel Ventura publication:

NOTE These techniques are the basis for anchored graphic insertion.

- Create a frame then paste the graphics in the frame. This is the technique we'll use.

- Use Corel Corporation's Mosaic drag-and-drop feature.

Inserting Graphics into Frames

There are several steps to inserting graphics on a page.

1. First, select the page frame with the Pick tool.

2. Create a frame by selecting the Frame tool and then, somewhere in the page, create a frame rectangle (Figure 5.14). If existing text shifts around this frame, don't worry. The default is that other objects on a page can be displaced by a frame.

NOTE Frames in FrameMaker can hold *multiple* graphic images.

3. Click on the Pick tool and select this new frame. A graphic image must reside in a frame—it cannot "live" without a frame, and a frame can hold no more than one graphic.

4. Select File>Load Graphic (or press the shortcut key **F10**) and browse through your directory for the desired graphics file.

Figure 5.14
Creating a frame
for graphics.

Select the
Frame tool

Click,...

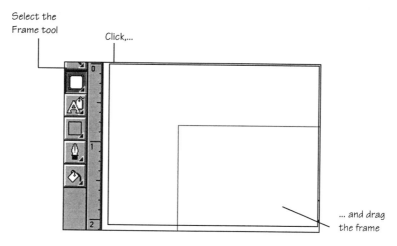

... and drag
the frame

In our case, we'll use a sample logo (LOGO.WMF). Once you have selected the file, click OK.

5. What happened? The graphic in Figure 5.15 is huge! Corel Ventura assumes that you wanted to fill the entire frame with the graphic, so the original graphic is resized to fill the frame's dimensions automatically.

Right-click (with the frame still selected) and choose Format>Graphic. See Figure 5.16.

Uncheck Fit in Frame and click OK.

Figure 5.15
Initially loading a
graphic.

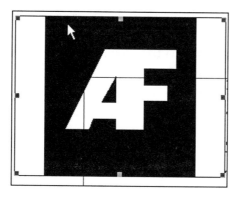

Figure 5.16
Setting the
graphic to its
original size.

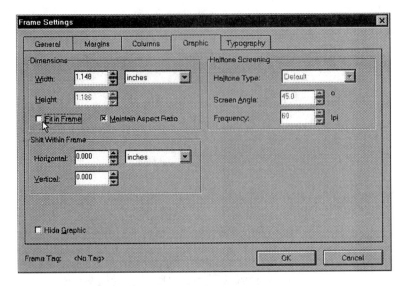

6. The graphic reverts to its normal size (Figure 5.17) even though the surrounding frame doesn't change. Corel Ventura never really did this very well in the past—resizing a graphic back to its original size used to be a difficult and frustrating chore.

7. Let's scale the graphic to 50 percent of its original size. There is no scale function, so you need to bring back the Graphics tab (in the Frame Settings dialog). Change the Dimensions width to pt, and enter a new width half of the original size. Make certain that the Maintain Aspect Ratio remains checked, and click OK.

8. Resize the surrounding frame to a size just a little larger than the graphic (otherwise, you'll clip the edges) and drag the frame to the lower left-hand corner of the page (Figure 5.18).

Figure 5.17
The graphic
returns to its
original size.

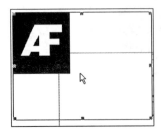

Figure 5.18
Positioning the
repeated frame
in the footer area.

**Using the
Mosaic Roll-
Up**

The Mosaic Roll-Up provides a subset of features found in the Mosaic utility provided with CorelDRAW.

A second method of easily loading a graphic onto a page is to use Corel Ventura's Mosaic Roll-Up. With the introduction of version 5, Mosaic provides a simple method of inserting a supported graphics image into your document without presetting a frame. In other words, the Mosaic Roll-Up displays the graphics collections as a floating thumbnail viewer.

NOTE   Mosaic currently does not recognize *all* file types that Corel Ventura recognizes (like WMF).

You display the Mosaic Roll-Up by selecting File>Mosaic Roll-Up (or **ALT+F1**). You can browse in a subdirectory by clicking on the file folder icon at the top left. By clicking on the folder symbol at the upper right you can select a graphics format (like TIFF) or a Mosaic collection (which is similar to a Ulead Systems' Album we discussed earlier).

Pick your graphic and drag it onto your document's page (Figure 5.20) or into an existing frame (the previous frame's image is automatically replaced).

With Corel Ventura sharing some of the same characteristics as CorelDRAW, you can now use the pasteboard area outside of the page to drop graphic frames. This way, you can move them later onto the page.

The beauty of Mosaic is that if you drop the graphic onto your page, a frame that is sized correctly around the original graphic's size is automatically created for you. You can always change the frame's size and attributes later, but that feature alone is worth its weight in gold.

To make it repeating, you'll need to right-click with the graphics frame selected and choose Frame>General. Select Right Page in the Repeat on field.

Figure 5.19
Selecting the
image from
Mosaic.

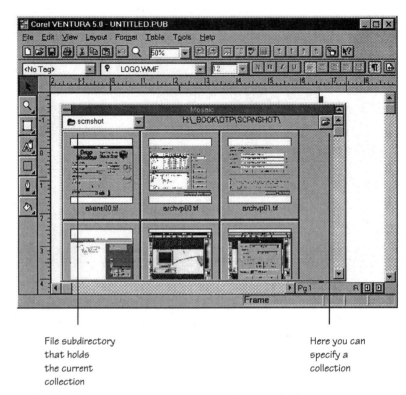

File subdirectory
that holds
the current
collection

Here you can
specify a
collection

If you have selected the overall chapter's format to use
mirrored pages, the graphic can be mirrored on opposite
sides of the page if you set Repeat on to All Pages. To remove
a repeated graphic, set the Repeat on field to No Other Pages.

*Corel Ventura restricts the number of repeated frames to six per
chapter.*

**Repositioning
the Graphic** What if you want to reposition the graphics frame later?
There are several ways:

- You can reposition the graphics frame by modifying the
  position in the Format>Frame General tab dialog.

- You can reposition the graphics frame with the
  Placement Roll-Up (**ALT+F8**) which actually provides a
  quick way to change the dimensions (or even rotation of
  any angle) of a frame.

- You can select the frame and simply drag it to the
  location desired.

Figure 5.20
Image dragged
onto the page.

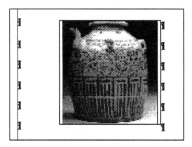

To reposition the graphics image within the frame, drag the image around the frame by holding down the **CTRL** key while the frame is selected.

Updating the Publication Once you have created the repeating frame, you should save your sample chapter to a template chapter file and use it to construct new chapters. There is currently no automatic way to use one chapter's style sheet as the basis for other chapters.

Anchoring Graphics

Captions

A caption is used to provide identification of some object (like a figure, drawing, table, and so on) both numerically and with descriptive text.

A caption includes a figure (or table) number that is sequentially incremented along with descriptive text. If the figure (or table) moves, so should the caption.

A caption should be used to add optional explanatory information to the figure. I'm not saying that you should use captions as a publication standard—it is a lot of work, but it does make the connection between a table or figure to body text much more clear to the reader.

Bad Design Examples

Let's look at some examples that I've noticed from several user manuals. Unfortunately, most manuals don't use captions at all.

Figure 5.21
No caption at all.

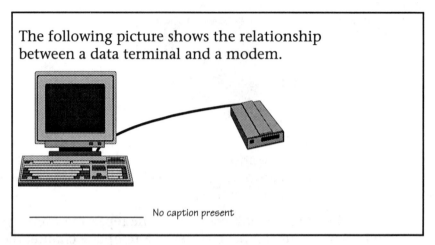

That's the easy way out.

Captions can be too large. Figure 5.22 is a representative example I have found in several manuals.

Not only does the caption overpower the figure itself, the fact that it precedes the figure almost takes away from the caption's purpose of adding optional explanatory information. It practically forces you to read it before looking at the diagram.

Although captions on the sidehead area work fine and can be treated like annotation (or as a sidehead), often a caption explains too much—the figure (or table) should be doing the explaining in simple terms. Leave the detailed explanations to body text.

Figure 5.22
An overly large figure caption.

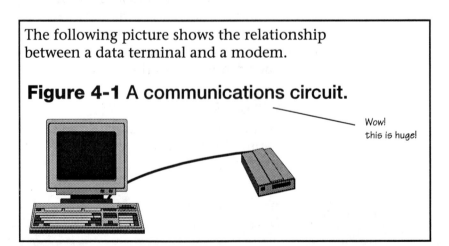

Figure 5.23
Basic
communications
circuit with too
much information.

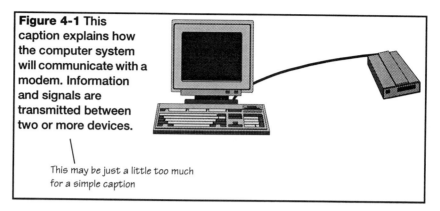

Figure 4-1 This caption explains how the computer system will communicate with a modem. Information and signals are transmitted between two or more devices.

This may be just a little too much for a simple caption

Good Design Example

Figure 5.24 shows the method that I use throughout this manual (as if you haven't noticed).

The caption follows the figure (or table), flows inline or in the sidehead margin with the body text along with a simple caption. The font is a sans serif much like what is used in the header and is slightly smaller than normal body text.

Now, for the most important part: you must keep preceding paragraphs together with figures (and tables). This book is very careful about placing figures and tables at either the top or bottom of pages. However, most manuals place figures and tables inline with body text.

With inline figures and tables, figures should be kept with associated text. I can't tell you how many times I've seen manuals where the concept of keeping paragraphs together have been misused (and not caught by an editor before the final manual printing).

Figure 5.24
The right way to
present a figure
caption.

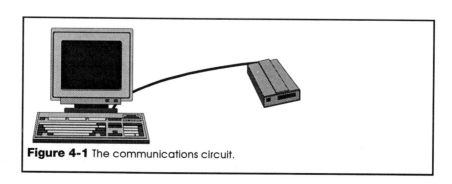

Figure 4-1 The communications circuit.

Figure 5.25
Positioning of
body text with
figure.

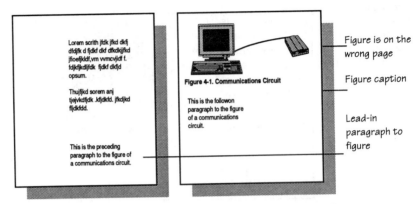

Lead-in paragraph references the figure (but it is on the next page)

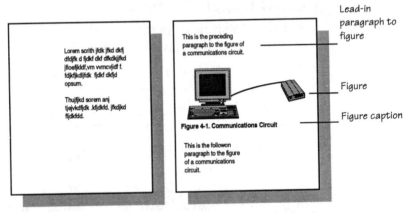

Lead-in paragraph references the figure that directly follows it

NOTE The text of
the sample has
been changed to
protect the ven-
dor!

Figure 5.25 is a sample from a manual in which the lead-in text describes a figure that is on the following page. It also shows the corresponding text that explains the figure. The lead-in paragraph and the figure should stay with each other and not cross page boundaries.

Using FrameMaker

You are going to need to define a special sequence of paragraph tags for anchoring graphics. In order to insert graphics into your publication, you must perform several steps.

Creating the
Lead-In
Paragraph

Create a paragraph tag entitled **Z_Figure** (enter the name in the Paragraph Tag field in the Paragraph Designer dialog). This paragraph should have the basic attributes shown in Figure 5.26.

Figure 5.26
Setting the
lead-in graphics
paragraph tag.

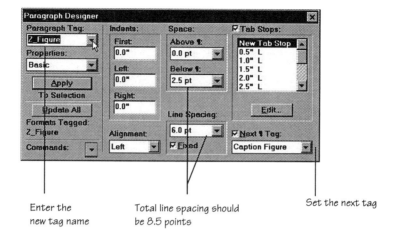

Enter the
new tag name

Total line spacing should
be 8.5 points

Set the next tag

Also, check the Keep with Next field in the Pagination properties.

Click New Format under Commands, and make certain you indicate that the paragraph tag is saved in the catalog. (You may not wish to apply it to the selected paragraph.)

Setting an Anchor Click on the Smart Selection tool and place the insertion point in a paragraph right above where the graphics is to be placed. Apply the Z_Figure paragraph tag to this paragraph.

Inserting the Graphic Select File>Import>File and select one of the supported graphics files (I like DCE_DTE.WMF). See Figure 5.27. Notice that I leave Import By Reference selected. Click Import.

If you were importing an image (TIFF or BMP, for example), FrameMaker would ask you for the resolution you would like to specify with the dialog shown in Figure 5.28.

Figure 5.27
Selecting a file to
import.

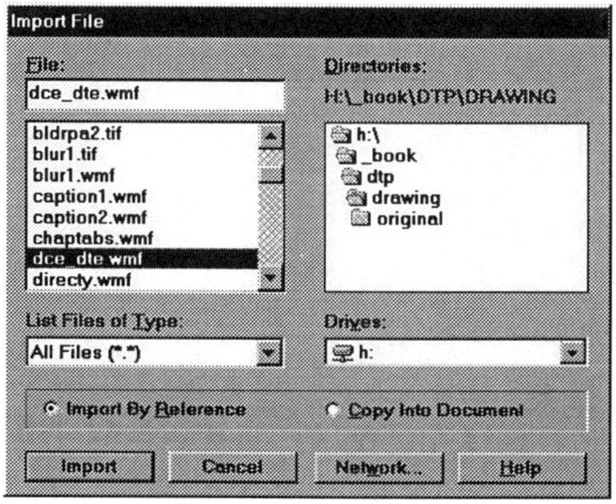

Figure 5.28
Bitmap images may be scaled before being imported.

You could choose to fill the entire frame

But this dpi gives us the best clarity and the right size

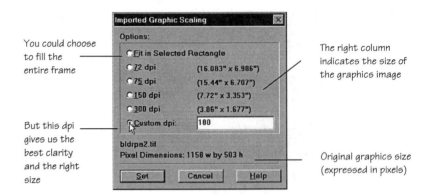

The right column indicates the size of the graphics image

Original graphics size (expressed in pixels)

NOTE The frame marker is nonprint-able!

In any event, the graphic file (DCE_DTE.WMF, remember?) is inserted below the anchor marker (where your insertion point was located prior to the file selection). See Figure 5.29.

The graphic frame (denoted by the black square handles around the rectangular frame) is anchored to the preceding paragraph. As you insert or remove text preceding this paragraph, the frame moves accordingly.

Let's position it so that the drawing is located in the left margin below the text (which is 2.25" from the page edge). By extending the size of the frame around the graphic, we can add some annotations to the figure.

Making Room for Annotations

We'll add annotations to the frame and even on top of the graphic. Let's expand the frame to the width of the body frame. Select Graphics>Object Properties. Change the Width to **5.5"** and click Set. Now, the frame has filled the entire width of the text flow. Click on the graphic and move the frame to the right, approximately to the position that you desire. Let's make more space available at the bottom of the frame. Select the graphics frame.

Figure 5.29
The drawing is centered below the text frame.

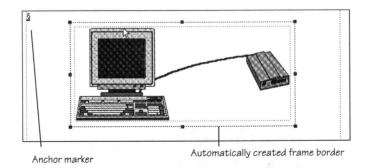

Anchor marker

Automatically created frame border

Figure 5.30
Extending the
height of a
graphics frame.

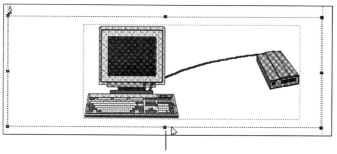

Drag the border downward

Although you can use the Object Properties menu to resize the frame, just grab the lower frame's middle handle and drag it down (Figure 5.30).

Changing the size of the outer graphics frame does not change the size of the graphic (although you can do that by either scaling or by dragging the graphic's handles).

Annotating the Graphic

For annotations to line up correctly, you should enable the snapping grid (this is set with the dialog accessed via the View>Options menu). Set a snap that gives you enough flexibility for aligning annotation text and lines.

Click on the Line tool and draw a line in the frame (as shown in Figure 5.31). Next, click on the Text Frame tool, drag to create a small text frame, and type in **A note**.

When you add text, lines, or other objects from the Tools palette, you should *always* have the graphics frame selected. FrameMaker is smart enough to know that any objects positioned within the frame must belong to the frame.

Select the annotation text with the Object Selection tool (Figure 5.32). Create a paragraph tag that uses the Tekton font (or another sans serif font) of 8 pt and call it **Annotation**.

Figure 5.31
Type an
annotation to the
graphic.

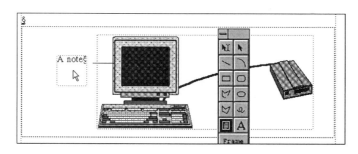

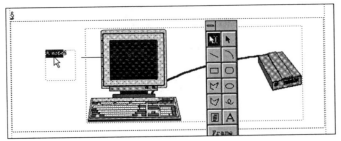

Of course, you can move any of the objects within a frame by selecting them and dragging them to new locations within the frame (Figure 5.33). You can also copy them to other frames. With the objects selected, press **CTRL+C** to copy to the clipboard, select another frame in your publication, and then paste (**CTRL+V**).

If you wish to just delete the graphic within a frame, select the graphic and press **DEL**.

Deleting a Graphics Frame

If at any time, you wish to remove a graphics frame, select the surrounding frame and press **DEL**. The frame, the graphic, and the anchor marker all disappear!

Adding Figure Captions

FrameMaker uses a hierarchical numbering system where a series of number counters are defined in a paragraph tag.

In FrameMaker, the caption is part of paragraph tag: Caption Figure. We'll define it using a Numbering format:
Figure <n>-<n+>< >< >. (with a trailing period and space for your caption).

This counting formula is the key for FrameMaker to keep track of counters and to properly substitute numbers corresponding to four distinct counters.

Each bracket serves a unique purpose. The first <n> references the current chapter number and will be displayed.

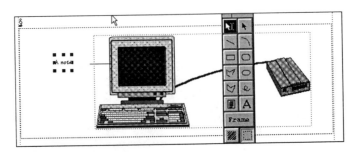

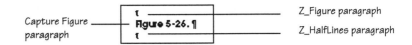

The dash separator follows the chapter number. Note that in this book, a period (.) would be used instead. The next figure counter <n+> is incremented. The next two brackets do not include any reference to numeric counters and are ignored. They actually represent the table and the bullet list numbered counter, respectively. The counter sequence finally ends with a period and a space. The table caption numbering sequence would be:

Table <n>-<><n+>< >.

Like the Z_Figure paragraph tag, Caption Figure should be created with a total vertical space that is relatively small with space below set to 6.0 pt and Fixed Line Spacing set at 2.5 pt.

Unfortunately, there is currently no FrameMaker mechanism that enables you to create a graphics tag that defines the attributes of a graphics frame and its corresponding frame caption paragraph. The solution is to modify the paragraph tags so that they create the correct next paragraph tag when you press **ENTER**.

If you haven't already, modify the Basic Properties of the Z_Figure paragraph tag in the Paragraph Designer dialog. Set the Next ¶ Paragraph tag to Caption Figure. Click Update All.

NOTE In the previous chapter we already set Z_HalfLine's next tag to Body.

Select the Capture Figure paragraph tag (again in the Paragraph Designer dialog) and set the Next ¶ Paragraph tag to Z_HalfLines. Click Update All.

Next time you anchor a graphic to a Z_Figure paragraph tag, press **ENTER** three times and you'll create the paragraphs shown in Figure 5.34. Place the insertion point back to the Z_Figure tagged paragraph and follow the steps listed in the section "Inserting the Graphic," on page 183.

Referencing Figure Captions

How do you reference figures from other parts of your publication? As with any other FrameMaker cross-reference we've discussed, you can reference a caption by first defining a reference marker then later inserting a cross-reference.

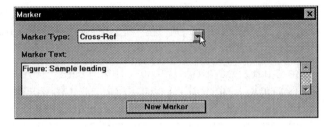

To insert a reference marker, do the following:

1. Place the insertion point at the end of the caption. Type in your caption description.

2. Press **HOME** and place a marker (Figure 5.35) with a unique name that is inserted (as hidden text—it is not displayed or printed). I like preceding table markers with **Figure:**.

Notice that FrameMaker's odd-shaped ^T represents a reference marker: **Figure 5-26.** Sample leading. ¶ ·

At some other location in the publication, you may wish to reference a marker by following these steps:

1. Position the insertion point at the point at which you wish to insert the cross-reference.

2. Select the Special>Cross-Reference menu and select the Source Type, Reference Source fields to the appropriate reference marker.

3. Click on Insert to create a reference.

FrameMaker supplies a variety of formats that can be modified or you can add new formats. The example shown in Figure 5.36 inserts a figure's number at the insertion point. To change formats, all you have to do is click on Format.

Format	Example
Page	Page 10
Figure	Figure 5-2
Figure & Page	Figure 5-2, "Features Revisited," on Page 10
See Figure Above	See Figure 5-2 above

Figure 5.36
Insert the figure
cross-reference.

Make certain that
Cross-Ref type is selected

You can select reference markers
from this chapter or from others currently open

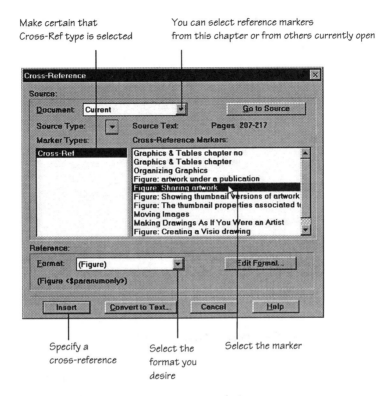

Specify a
cross-reference

Select the
format you
desire

Select the marker

Inserting In-Line Graphics

You can always insert a graphics frame at the insertion point without a figure caption. To do this, follow the same instructions for anchored frames with the exception that you don't create a paragraph with the Z_Figure tag.

Follow the instructions starting with the section "Inserting the Graphic," on page 183 up to "Making Room for Annotations," on page 184.

Select Special>Anchored Frame to display the dialog in Figure 5.37. Normally, FrameMaker assumes that the anchoring position is set to Below Current Line. We'll set At Insertion Point and play with the offset until it looks correct. I set the sample to **-10 pt** —it is all dependent on the size of the graphic and the text line spacing of the paragraph.

Figure 5.37
Insert a graphic
in-line with text.

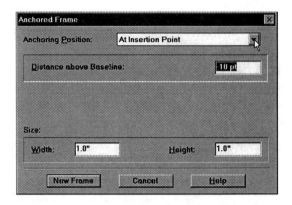

As the text preceding the image grows (and shrinks), the graphics frame moves accordingly.

In Case You Didn't Know...

There are several additional FrameMaker key features concerning graphic files that are important to be aware of.

Relative File Placement   As long as the requested file is in the path of your document, graphics files are considered to be stored relative to your chapter. This allows you to move the entire publication (chapters and graphic files) to another directory without re-linking file references to the document.

Multiple graphics files in a single frame   You can perform multiple file imports into a *single* frame. I'll show you an application of this capability starting on page 209.

Adding frame attributes to a frame   Just like any other object, you can apply a background color or set the outside of the frame to a lined border of almost any width.

Using Corel Ventura

Creating the Lead-In Paragraph   There are two paragraphs that should precede a graphics frame. The Body Next paragraph should lead with the text introducing the graphics.

The next paragraph is Z_Figure. This provides the necessary space between the graphics and the preceding paragraph. The Z_Figure paragraph tag is defined exactly the same as Z_HalfLinesNext except that the Next Tag field should be set to **Z_HalfLines**.

Figure 5.38
The graphics frame has been inserted.

Inserting the Graphic

Using one of the techniques discussed starting on page 174, insert your graphics image (I've chosen, in this example, the immortal vase that has been used in Corel Ventura examples since the mid-80s). It should look something like that shown in Figure 5.38.

Notice that the graphics frame has actually offset paragraph tags to the right of the frame boundaries. We'll get rid of that in a moment.

Setting an Anchor

We'll need to name the frame since a name will help us associate the frame with its anchor point. Right-click and select Frame>General (Figure 5.39).

Assuming you are happy with the dimensions of the frame (I know I am), make certain that Flow Text Around Frame is checked, enter an anchor name (I choose **Vase**), select Caption to below and select the Figure Reference.

Figure 5.39
Setting up the frame to be anchored.

Frame Settings

| General | Margins | Columns | Graphic | Typography |

☒ Flow Text Around Frame   Frame Anchor: Vase

☐ Lock Frame Position and Size

Dimensions
Width: 2.183 inches
Height: 2.196

Frame Origin
Horizontal: 1.917 inches
Vertical: 1.717

Repeating Frame
Repeat on: No Other Pages
☐ Hide on Current Page

Caption Format
Caption: below
Reference: Figure [C#]-[F#]

Rotation: 0.0 °

Frame Tag: <No Tag>

OK   Cancel

Figure 5.40
Select the
graphics frame
anchor method.

Click OK. With the Freehand Text tool or the Tagged Text tool selected, click at an empty paragraph where you wish to place the graphic. Apply the Z_Figure paragraph tag to it. Right-click and select Insert Special Item>Frame Anchor (Figure 5.40). Pull down the Name list and click on Vase and set the Below Anchor Line radio button. Click OK.

As with all Corel Ventura special items, a little ° symbol is inserted to mark the anchor, and the frame is positioned below the current line with a caption.

Adding the Caption Stretch the frame across the entire margin. Corel Ventura automatically creates a paragraph tag named Z_LABEL FIG that provides the attributes for the figure number. Set the Z_LABEL FIG paragraph tag as AvantGarde Bold 8 pt, black, and left-justified to 1.25". All other paragraph properties can be left to their default values.

As you can see in Figure 5.41, click past the generated figure number and type in your caption (example, **This is the vase.**). You can apply a different tag to the caption (instead of Z_CAPTION) but, I choose to use Ventura's tag name.

Figure 5.41
Typing the figure
caption.

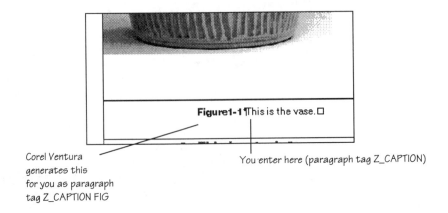

Corel Ventura
generates this
for you as paragraph
tag Z_CAPTION FIG

You enter here (paragraph tag Z_CAPTION)

Figure 5.42
Reference
another figure.

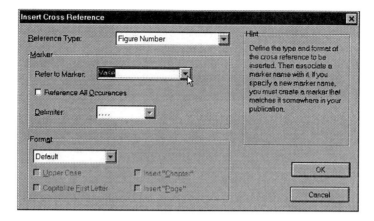

The paragraph tag attributes for Z_CAPTION should be set to AvantGarde 8 pt, black, and left-justified at 0" (since it is offset "magically" past the figure number tag). Keep the text to one line.

Referencing the Caption To reference the caption, place the insertion point at the location where you wish to reference the anchor marker. Right-click and choose Insert Special Item>Cross-Reference.

Choose the Refer to Marker field (in our case, Vase), select the Reference Type (there are many to choose from, but we'll choose Figure Number), and the Format as Default (Figure 5.42). Click OK.

Whenever you want the figure number to be "evaluated" and replace the little marker ° symbol, just select Layout>Renumber Publication.

Annotating the Graphics To annotate the graphic, we'll need to bring out the drawing tool flyout from the Toolbox. See Figure 5.43.

By holding down the mouse on the Drawing tool, you will be shown five drawing tools (left to right): Rectangle tool, Line tool, Round Rectangle tool, Ellipse tool, and Box Text tool. We'll use two of them: the Line and Box Text.

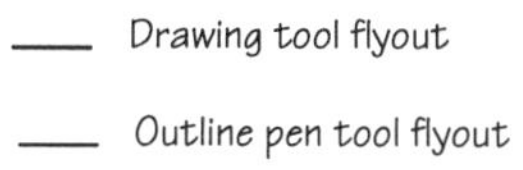

Figure 5.43
Annotation tools
from the Toolbox.

_____ Drawing tool flyout

_____ Outline pen tool flyout

Figure 5.44
Setting the callout
line attributes.

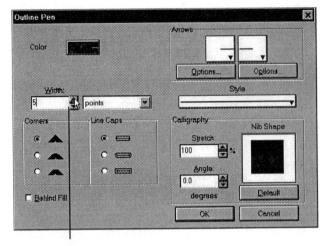

Select the width
of the callout

NOTE Without
snap to grid capa-
bility, it is next to
impossible to get
line and text
objects to line up
correctly.

Each frame can have its own grid alignment. With the frame selected, select Tools>Grid Setup and set both the Horizontal and Vertical (I like .1" or even .05"). Click on Snap to Grid, then click OK.

Select the graphics frame and then click on the Line tool ▨. Click in the frame, and with the **CTRL** key depressed (this keeps the lines straight), drag the line to form a callout. Right-click and select Outline Pen menu command.

Set the pen Width field to .5 pt and click OK. You have many, many more pen options—experiment with them if you like.

With the frame still selected, choose the Box Text tool ▨. Drag a rectangle, click the Freehand Text tool in the mini-text frame, and type **The vase** (the callout's text). Apply the Annotation paragraph tag. Your sample callout and annotation should look something like: ▭ .

Chances are your mini-text frame that includes the phrase **The vase** will have a box outline around it. You'll want to remove that, but there doesn't appear to be any way to select the box and to set the outline width to 0" (Corel Ventura won't let you). With the box around your text selected with the Pick tool, click on the ▨ Outline tool to bring out the flyout options:

Click on the Remove Line button (the one with the cursor over it) with the huge **X** on it to remove the outline.

An important warning: Make certain that the frame is always selected when inserting drawing objects, otherwise the objects will be connected to the page frame and not to the graphics frame. You'll know that you have misplaced objects outside the frame when box text or callout lines remain after a page's graphic frames have been reanchored.

Deleting a Graphics Frame
Place the cursor to the immediate left of the anchor and press the **DEL** key. The anchor and the frame disappear.

Inserting In-Line Graphics
This process is similar to that described in "Setting an Anchor," on page 191, the only difference is that you set the At Anchor radio button in the Insert Frame Anchor dialog.

Updating the Display
Corel Ventura sometimes has trouble when you add more objects (text or graphics frames) into a document that either adjusts figure numbering or even appears to lose track of anchored frames.

Save your publication (always do that first!), select Re-Anchor Frames, and then Renumber Publication to get everything recalculated and properly redisplayed.

You may see a warning box displayed indicating that the frame has text that won't fit on a page. This is not catastrophic, but it does mean that you have a frame that has run outside of the page boundaries or overlaps another graphics frame incorrectly.

Sometimes it is very difficult to find the offending graphics frame, and you may actually have to temporarily cut out other frames or even surrounding text to expose the problematic frame.

If you use many graphics frames, make frequent backups of your document, and make certain that there are no problems by frequently executing the Re-anchor Frames command.

Assigning a Tag to a Frame
One of the most innovative features of Corel Ventura (starting with version 4) has been the concept of a frame tag. If you want all frames to have the same dimensions, captions, and aspect ratio, Corel Ventura has the ability to assign a tag to a frame.

To create a tag based on an existing frame that you have set correctly, do the following:

1. Select the frame with the Pick tool.

2. Choose Format>Manage Tag List and then select the Frame Tags tab.

3. Click on Add Frame Tag.

4. Type a tag name (like you would a paragraph tag) and click OK.

To apply a frame tag, follow these steps:

1. Select the frame or frames you wish to tag with the Pick tool (hold down **SHIFT** to select multiple frames).

2. Click the frame tag desired from the Frame Tags list in the toolbar.

There are currently two *small* problems. As long as your graphics are exactly the same size (like DOS screen shots), you will be overriding named frame tags with just about every frame (which defeats the purpose of a frame tag).

The other problem is that frame tags are saved in a special file based on the chapter filename. It is not saved as a style sheet shared by all chapter documents in a given publication.

To get around that problem, open a new chapter and merge frame tags from another chapter's frame tag file. Not elegant, but it works.

ADDING SHADOWS TO GRAPHICS

Figure 5.45 shows two versions of a graphic. Which of the two screen shot versions do you like? I bet you like the shadowed one. Neither FrameMaker or Corel Ventura provide the capability to add the blurred shadow look so common these days with computer art in brochures and advertisements. With the assistance of some great image editors, we can do it!

Figure 5.45
Figure with and
without shadows.

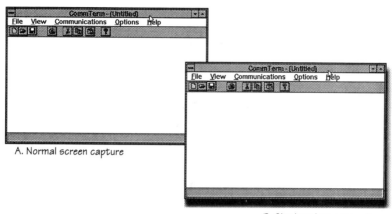

A. Normal screen capture

B. Shadowed screen capture

Shadows are created as a bitmap image with the following properties:

- They should be saved as 8-bit grayscale TIFF images (only one channel should be saved, although Photoshop can sometimes add additional masking channels).

- They should be LZW compressed, 8K strip size, with preview information enabled.

- Do not enable horizontal differentiation since that will approximate the bitmap image and could produce less than perfect screen capture images.

- For highest dot density, create screen captures and associated shadows at 120 or 180 (my preference) dpi.

- Shadows should be generated from a blurred (or feathered) shadowed filter.

- Although I show how to blur a background color based on pure black, you can choose something lighter like 50 percent gray (represented as either R=144, G=144, B=144 or C=0, M=0, Y=0, K=50 percent).

You should always keep the shadow image separate from the drawing or image to which you are adding the shadow. That way, if most of your screen capture shots are the same size, you can share one shadow image with all of the images.

Using FrameMaker

FrameMaker allows a graphic and a shadow bitmapped file to

coexist in a single anchored frame. Perfect!

Using Corel Ventura

Uh, oh. Unfortunately, you cannot combine two or more graphics files into a single anchored frame. The only way to keep a graphic close to a shadow bitmap file is to anchor two frames right next to each other.

A simple solution (although this requires a couple more steps) is to combine the shadow file with the graphics file to produce a single graphics file to import into Corel Ventura.

Adding a Shadow to a Screen Capture

NOTE This also applies to any bit-mapped image.

With the clarity of screen capture images taken by ImagePals, you may not need the shadowed look. But, if you wish to take screen captures from your manual and use them in presentations or brochures, it adds depth and professionalism.

Unfortunately, it is not easy to learn how to achieve professional results. I will show you two different image editor tools that can be used for combining a shadow with a bitmap image.

Using Photoshop to Create a Shadow

In order to properly create a good looking shadow, you'll need an image editor of the calibre of Photoshop from Adobe Systems Incorporated. Your image editor should be able to:

- Create selection masks.
- Feather the image (or blur may work just fine).
- Expand the dimensions of the image without rescaling.

Let's take the necessary steps to add a shadow behind a screen capture:

1. Expand the size of the image by 20 pixels and properly position the shadow image.

2. Select the screen capture image and save the selection marquee.

3. Feather the shadow image and fill with black.

4. Paste the original selection into the original location.

For this exercise to work properly, the screen shot image (or any image for that matter) must have a well-defined border.

As mentioned earlier in this chapter, the ImagePals screen capture program can be automatically expanded with a border of 1 pixel. Our screen capture image is assumed to be a gray-scaled TIFF image. Let's perform each of the steps.

➲ **Open the screen capture image.**
Open your screen shot file (I'll open mine entitled BLURIM1.TIF).

➲ **Expand the size of the image.**
Select the Image>Canvas Size menu command and add 20 pixels to the width and the height. Before pressing the OK button, click on the placement square at the upper, left corner (Figure 5.46).

NOTE The image is *not* scaled to fit in the new expanded size.

This tells Photoshop where to position the current image, thus making room for the shadow at the lower right corner of the image.

➲ **Select the screen capture image.**
Select the white space outside of the screen shot with the magic wand (Figure 5.47).

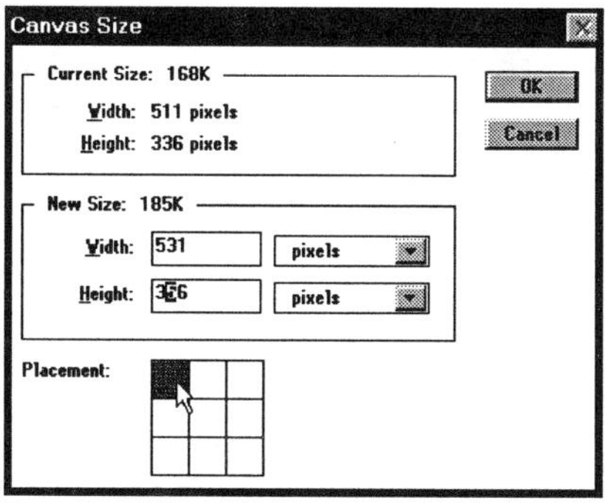

Figure 5.46
The image is expanded.

Figure 5.47
Select the white
space outside the
screen shot
image.

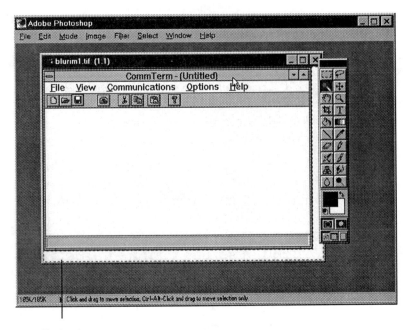

Notice the marquee

Click on Select>Inverse to select only the original screen
capture image (Figure 5.48). After you've selected the image
(the screen shot image should have a scrolling marquee
rotating around it), copy the image to the clipboard
(**CTRL**+C).

⊃ **Save the selection marquee.**
Copy the selection to a mask channel (Select>Save Selection
in Figure 5.49).

Figure 5.48
Select the original
screen shot
image.

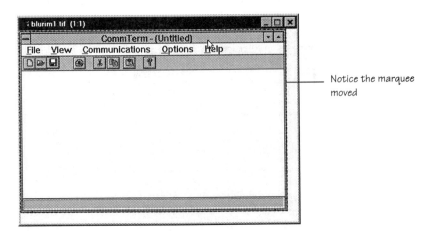

Notice the marquee
moved

Figure 5.49
Save the original image's selection marquee.

Accept the defaults with the Save Selection dialog to a Channel called New. You can always change the name at a later time.

↻ **Feather the shadow image and fill.**
While holding **ALT** and **CTRL**, drag the image to the lower right, making sure that you leave some space to the right and bottom edge of the newly expanded image (Figure 5.50).

NOTE The original screen image should remain after you've dragged the selection marquee.

Choose Select>Feather and, at the prompt, specify a feather radius of **5**. The corners of the marquee will become rounded.

Make sure that the default colors are set with black as the foreground color and white as the background color. Press **ALT+DEL** to fill the selected image with the foreground color (which happens to be black with the image feathered). See Figure 5.51.

Figure 5.50
Adjust the selection marquee for the shadow.

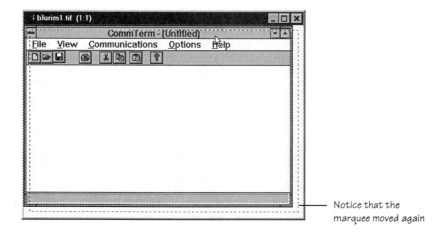

Notice that the marquee moved again

Figure 5.51
Create the
shadow.

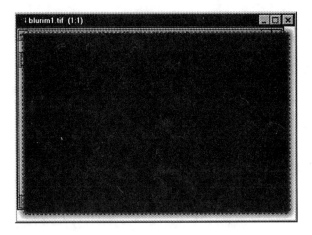

○ **Paste the original selection.**

NOTE The
shadow selection
channel is named
#2 by Photoshop.

The selection is now the feathered image you just created.
You can load the previous selection by clicking on
Select>Load Selection.

The original screen shot image's selection marquee magically
appears. Now, copy the clipboard contents (which, by the
way, still haven't changed) into the selection marquee. Press
SHIFT+INS (or **CTRL**+V), and you now have a combined image
and shadow (Figure 5.52).

Unselect the marquee (Select>None) and save your image. I
saved it as BLURIM2.TIF. Photoshop may give you a warning
message that the alpha channels cannot be saved. That is
okay; you shouldn't need the selection mask channels.

Figure 5.52
The image with a
shadow.

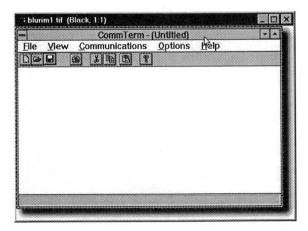

Using ImagePals to Create a Shadow

Photoshop does a spectacular job of creating a well-defined shadowed image. We can accomplish a shadow using the amazing ImagePals Image Editor. Let's take the necessary steps to add a shadow behind a screen capture:

1. Expand the size of the image by 20 pixels and properly position the shadow image.

2. Select the screen capture image and save the selection marquee.

3. Feather the shadow image and fill with black.

4. Paste the original selection in the original location.

⊃ **Open the screen capture image.**
In Image Editor, open file BLURIM1.TIF.

⊃ **Expand the size of the image.**
Copy the entire image to the clipboard by pressing **CTRL+L** (this selects the entire image), then **CTRL+C** (this copies the selected image to the clipboard), then click on File>New, and finally click on Active Image.

But, don't click OK yet, because this will change the width and height to the exact size of the image copied to the clipboard and change the data type to Grayscale (8-bit).

Instead, click User Defined and change the width and height by increasing both by **20** pixels. Click OK and you will have a new image big enough to hold the shadow and the original image. Press **CTRL+V** to paste the clipboard image as the new selection.

⊃ **Feather the shadow image and fill.**
While holding **ALT** and **CTRL**, drag the marquee image to the lower right making sure that you leave some space to the right and bottom edge of the newly expanded image.

The original image automatically floats with the move. Now, fill in the marquee with Edit>Fill and click on Black.

Figure 5.53
Visio drawing without and with a shadow.

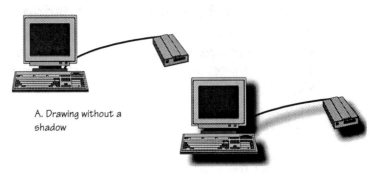

A. Drawing without a shadow

B. Drawing with a shadow

You can always select a gradient fill or even change the foreground or background colors to a gray (instead of black). Click on OK. The screen shot image is black.

At this point, deselect the marquee with a **CTRL+N** and choose Effect> Blur>Heavily about five times to get the desired effect. Press **CTRL+V** to repaste the original image. Save as a TIFF file. The final results look as good as Figure 5.52.

Final Note on Image Shadows

If you use the same size screen shot, you will really only have to have one shadow mask that can be placed behind all of your screen shots and images.

Adding a Shadow to a Drawing

Okay, you've just drawn a stupendous diagram using Visio. Looking at Figure 5.53, which looks better? The shadowed drawing looks really dramatic.

NOTE The same technique works for CorelDRAW or almost any other drawing program.

This is a little tricky, but actually a little simpler to create than bitmapped image shadows. (It is just a more difficult to insert into your DTP document.) These are the steps to create a shadow for a drawing:

1. Expand the size of the image to accommodate a shadow.

2. Select the screen capture image and save the marquee.

3. Feather the shadow image and fill with black.

4. Save the shadow image to be combined with the drawing.

Figure 5.54
Select the
drawing and copy
to the clipboard.

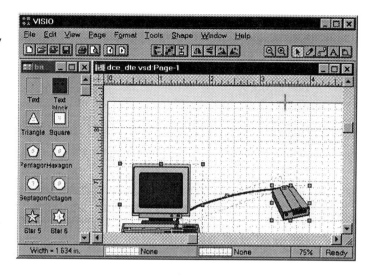

⊃ **Create the shadow image file.**

Let's look at a drawing that we use in our sample manual
(Figure 5.54).

Within Visio, select all of the drawing's objects (**CTRL+A**) and
then copy to the clipboard as a Windows metafile with
CTRL+C. No drawing program that I'm aware of can really
add decent shadows with the feather style, so we'll have to
bring up an image editor (again, let's use Photoshop).

From Photoshop, open a new image (menu command
File>New)—it will automatically have the metafile's pixel
dimensions in the clipboard. Leave the dimensions,
resolution, and mode alone. Click OK.

You can always import the file directly rather than use the
clipboard.

Press **CTRL+V** to insert the drawing from the clipboard into
Photoshop. See Figure 5.55.

Figure 5.55 Paste
the drawing from
the clipboard.

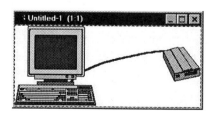

Figure 5.56
Collecting white
space into
marquee.

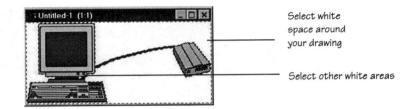

Select white
space around
your drawing

Select other white areas

⊃ Expand the size of the image to accommodate a shadow.

NOTE Once a
drawing is pasted
into an image edi-
tor, the drawing is
a bitmapped
image.

Expand the original image by 20 pixels horizontally and vertically with the Image>Canvas Size as we did before. Don't forget that you must not scale the image larger—leave the image the *same* size.

Using the drawing in our example, increase the canvas size to a width of **374** pixels, and a height of **170** pixels.

⊃ Select the screen capture image.

Select the white space around the entire image by clicking the magic wand tool in the white space. You'll need to hold down the **SHIFT** key to click to add other nondrawing areas (Figure 5.56).

You may be asking, "Why select the white areas and not the drawing itself?" The answer is that it is really difficult to place marquees around a drawing object that is not as distinct as a rectangle screen shot. We'll place marquees around everything other than the drawing and then simply invert the marquees to the drawing.

Once all of the nonimage drawing is selected, choose Select>Inverse in order to select the drawing. This effectively reverses the marquee so that the drawing is selected.

⊃ Save the selection marquee.

We'll feather the shadow image and fill with black foreground color. Copy the selection marquee (it should be circulating around the drawing by now) to a mask channel with Select>Save Selection.

Before we insert the shadow, let's clear the entire image. Select the entire image by pressing **CTRL+A**.

Figure 5.57
Switch
foreground color
to white.

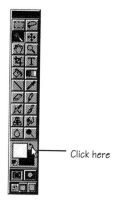

Click here

Before going further, make certain that the foreground color is now white, as shown in Figure 5.57.

Press **ALT+DEL** to fill the selection with the foreground color (which is white) and then switch the foreground to black. See Figure 5.58.

⊃ Create and save the shadow image.

NOTE Leave some white space between the dragged marquee and the edge of the workspace.

Reload the original marquee selection with Select>Load Selection. Hold **ALT** and **CTRL** while you drag the marquee to the lower right of the workspace. See Figure 5.59.

Now, set Select>Feather to **5** pixels. You'll notice that the selection marquee rounds out to a less-defined shape. Don't worry if the marquee doesn't show everything that should be selected—it's most likely there.

You may wish to feather more than 5 pixels. Don't do it— you risk making the shadow more pronounced than your drawing.

Figure 5.58
Clear the entire
image and then
set the foreground
to black.

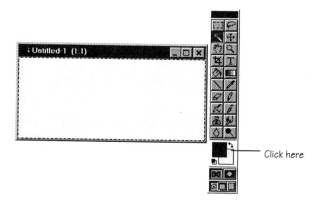

Untitled-1 (1:1)

Click here

Figure 5.59
Drag the shadow
marquee
downward to the
right then fill with
black.

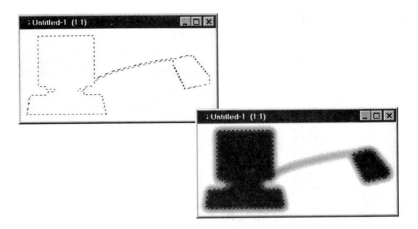

You are ready to create the shadow. Press **ALT+DEL**, which will delete the selected feathered marquee with the foreground color (which is now black).

NOTE The cable shadow reappears. Super!

Save the shadow file and use it in combination with your original drawing file within your final DTP document. The filename I'll use to save the shadow TIFF image is BLURDSH.TIF—remember my file naming conventions earlier in the chapter?

Using the ImagePals Image Editor

Let's select the drawing. Use the magic wand and click in the outer white space surrounding the actual drawing. Hold the **SHIFT** key and click on other holes that may also need to be selected.

Next invert the selection to select only the drawing (Edit>Select>Invert menu command), then copy the image to the clipboard (**CTRL+C**). Select File>New and click Active Image before clicking OK.

Clicking the Active Image sets up the Width and Height to the image dimensions. Then, click User Defined and adjust the Width and Height by an additional **20** pixels.

Click OK. Paste the image with Edit>Paste>As Selection (**CTRL+V**). Click the White button under the Edit>Fill menu in order to clear the selected drawing.

With the selection still enabled, click on Effects>Blur>Heavy several times, then Edit>Fill, and click the Black button.

Figure 5.60
The finished
drawing and
shadow.

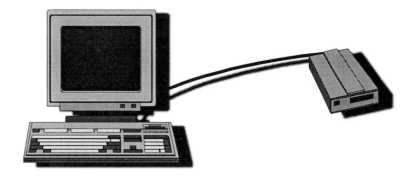

The final result superimposes the drawing frame on top of
the shadow (Figure 5.60). Wow!

Preparing Your Drawing

It is common to draw boxes with text in them so that you
can place a shadow or other background color.

Examples

A shadow TIFF file is used behind the drawing (or screen
capture image). You must ensure that all objects have a color
fill *even if it is white*. Otherwise, if you want to place a
backdrop shade behind a drawing, it may not work. See
Figure 5.61.

Using FrameMaker

FrameMaker allows you to place multiple graphics files in
one frame. This makes placing both a drawing and a shadow
TIFF background shadow image in one frame extremely easy.

The steps to incorporating a shadow TIFF file into a
FrameMaker document are these:

1. Import the shadow TIFF file.

2. Expand the image's anchored frame.

3. Select the frame and import the drawing file.

4. Make the drawing's fill background empty.

5. Stretch the shadow TIFF file until it fits appropriately
   behind the drawing.

Figure 5.61
A drawing should always have a white fill (rather than a transparent one).

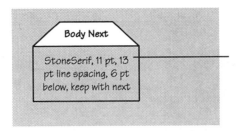

Oops! The drawing behind Body Next has a white background but the rectangle below was created without a color (white)

At the location desired in your FrameMaker document (usually an anchored frame), perform a File>Import>File menu command with the TIFF shadow file **BLURDW2.TIF** (Figure 5.62).

FrameMaker creates a frame that is a little bit larger than the imported file. Expand the handles of the frame and shift the shadow image to the lower right.

Select the frame again and import the drawing file DCE_DTE.WMF.

What happened? Notice that the selected drawing has a default white background. Make certain that the drawing is still selected and then click the Fill tool and set to **None** by clicking in the Fill popup in the Tools palette. See Figure 5.63.

Figure 5.62
Import the shadow, then the drawing file.

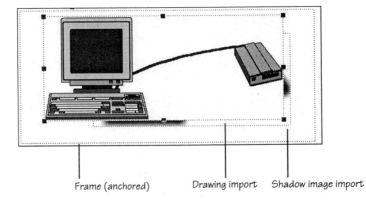

Frame (anchored)   Drawing import   Shadow image import

Figure 5.63
Make the
drawing's
background
frame transparent.

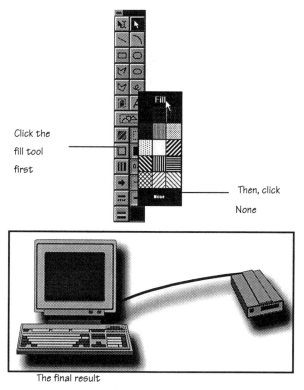

Click the
fill tool
first

Then, click
None

The final result

Stretch the background shadow as desired.

Do Shadows Have to Be This Difficult?

I've shown the traditional method of adding shadows. There are, however, a couple of innovative techniques that you should consider.

Using Painter to Add a Shadow

Fractal Design's outstanding bitmap imaging product, Painter, is an artist's dream. In version 3.1, Fractal has added an effect called drop shadow. To use it, follow these steps:

1. File>Open the bitmap file (for example, BLURIM1.TIF).

2. Select the image to have a shadow by pressing **CTRL+A** (or Edit>Select All).

3. Extend the size of the canvas from the Canvas>Canvas Size dialog by adding **20** to top, bottom, left, and right.

Click OK.

4. Make the still-selected image a floating object. Click on the floating tool 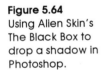, then on the object.

5. Select Effects>Objects>Create Drop Shadow and set up the Drop Shadow values to your liking; then click OK.

6. Now, save the result as a TIFF file.

Using Alien Skin's Drop Shadow Plug-In

And if that wasn't simple enough, how about a generic plug-in to your favorite image editing program?

Alien Skin Software (I know, *weird* name) has released a set of Photoshop-compatible filters called The Black Box. Start Photoshop. Follow these simple steps:

1. Select File>Open and select the image file (in my case, BLURIM1.TIF).

2. Extend the canvas with Image>Canvas Size by **20** pixels on all sides (make certain the image stays in the middle).

3. With the Wand tool, click the white space surrounding the image, then choose Select>Inverse to select the original image.

4. Click Filter>Alien Skin>Drop Shadow (Figure 5.64) and set the Blur—I dragged the control to **5**. Then click OK.

5. Save the image as a TIFF file.

It couldn't be any easier.

Figure 5.64
Using Alien Skin's
The Black Box to
drop a shadow in
Photoshop.

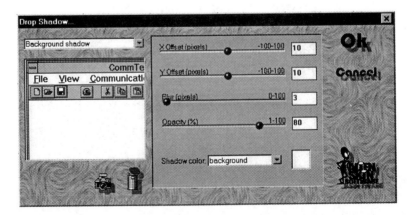

Figure 5.65
The master image.

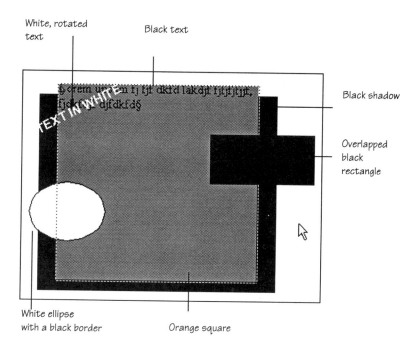

White, rotated text

Black text

Black shadow

Overlapped black rectangle

White ellipse with a black border

Orange square

HANDLING OVERLAPPED IMAGE OBJECTS

Consider the graphics in Figure 5.65, which are composed of overlapping drawing and text objects created using a DTP application. We have created a graphic in two colors: black and orange (there is actually a third color: white).

I will cover color separation in more detail in Chapter 7, but you can't wait until the final publication stages to think about color separation. You need to consider how to handle it correctly before you construct a lot of graphics incorrectly.

Although the content shown here may not look interesting, the intent is to show how to properly organize graphics objects (including bitmapped images, vector drawings, and even text) so that they color separate properly.

These graphics issues are sometimes confusing and will hit you time and time again if you don't understand what the DTP program can and cannot do.

This image represents the following objects in reverse order (back to front).

- Black shadow.
- Orange spot color primarily on top of the shadow, but with the top edge extended beyond the shadow.
- Black text on top of orange square with the second line on top of both the orange square and the black shadow.
- White, rotated text on top of the three objects (shadow, square, and black text).
- White ellipse with a black border on top of the orange rectangle and the shadow.
- Black rectangle on top of the orange rectangle and the shadow.

As long as you are printing to a device that will take care of color (like a color plotter or color laser printer) and you don't have to color separate, you can skip this section.

If, like most of us, you want to add one spot color to a publication to add a little pizzazz, please follow along. In fact, sometimes a spot color in a manual doesn't cost that much, so you may as well design it in.

A Quick Overview of Color Separation

When you print color-separated publications, you always print the spot color(s) first. Spot colors provide accents where black objects (like text or border lines) are destined to overlap all spot colors.

If you examine the image in Figure 5.65, notice some interesting things. We actually have a spot color object overprint black, and we have black objects overlap the spot color. *All in one graphic!*

NOTE Newsletter and marketing brochures do this all of the time.

You'd never do that, you say? Consider the title of a book that you want in a spot color, with a TIFF shadow (in black) underneath it. This is exactly the opposite to our example tables where we use a spot color (although a tint of a spot color) underneath black text. How do you direct the DTP program to handle the graphic?

Choosing the Right Printer

The selection of the correct printer for color separation is important—printing to a Postscript printer is different than to an HP LaserJet 4. Always choose a Postscript printer for color separation—your print shop will use one. It is the only way to verify separated output.

Non-Postscript printers may not handle knockouts and overprints correctly—especially when it comes to text (as shown in our example).

Printing the Spot Color Plate First

Printing color-separated output requires that a separate plate is printed for each color. Since most publications keep the number of color plates to a minimum, I assume that four-color plates are not used except for perhaps the cover of your publication.

NOTE You can always apply a tint that is less than 100 percent solid color.

The spot color plate is printed first. It would look like Figure 5.66. Notice that the angled white text is knocked out from the orange spot color.

Why is the spot color square black? Because when it is printed, that black represents 100 percent of the spot color (which will be ultimately printed as 100 percent orange color).

Figure 5.66
The correct spot color plate.

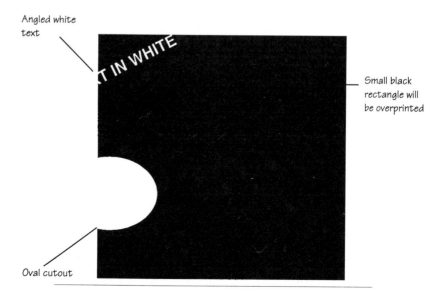

Angled white text

T IN WHITE

Small black rectangle will be overprinted

Oval cutout

Figure 5.67
The black plate.

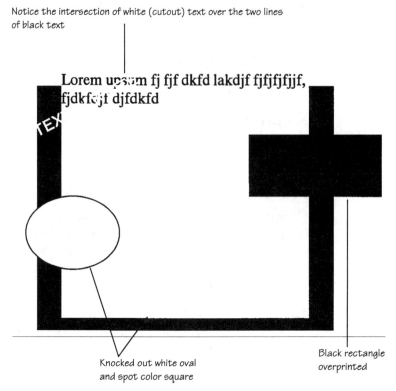

Notice the intersection of white (cutout) text over the two lines of black text

Lorem upsum fj fjf dkfd lakdjf fjfjfjfjjf, fjdkfojt djfdkfd

Knocked out white oval and spot color square

Black rectangle overprinted

Notice that the two lines of black text are not knocked out, but are overprinted on top of the orange spot color square. You usually do not want the topmost color to overprint colors underneath. This applies to both color spots or white objects. But, there is one exception: Black usually overprints on any or all other spot colors.

Printing the Black Plate Last

The black plate is printed last. This plate (Figure 5.67) shows the graphics objects that are black. Let's see how the DTP programs support the proper creation of overlapped graphics objects.

Color Separating Drawings

Those of you who have tried to color separate drawings (WMF, EPS, and so on) have probably been a little frustrated. The example shown on the previous pages appears to not work with standard imported drawing files.

Figure 5.68
Figure with shadows behind various graphics and text objects.

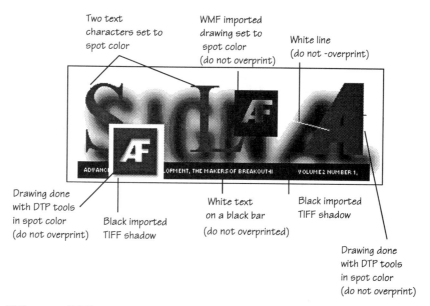

Two text characters set to spot color

WMF imported drawing set to spot color (do not overprint)

White line (do not -overprint)

Drawing done with DTP tools in spot color (do not overprint)

Black imported TIFF shadow

White text on a black bar (do not overprinted)

Black imported TIFF shadow

Drawing done with DTP tools in spot color (do not overprint)

Why not? The DTP program displays the other formats as drawings, and there are instructions on how to render (in other words, display) the drawings in the file format and its dimensions. Color information is displayed, and if you print to a color printer, it should print just fine.

Unfortunately, if you attempt to treat these drawings with color separation and overprint information, the DTP program doesn't know what to do.

The Sample Graphics

Let's use FrameMaker and Visio for an example that applies to all of our DTP and drawing programs. The choice of an output printer is also significant. We need to provide a shadowed look for the title of our product. The following frame has a combination of text, drawing, and bitmap images (Figure 5.68).

The leftmost AF drawing was constructed using the DTP's internal drawing tools. It is set to not overprint the shadow TIFF image under it. The rightmost AF drawing was created using Visio and exported as a WMF file. FrameMaker gives you the ability to assign the drawing object to a spot color (which is what I've done) as a non-printed knockout. The AF is transparent and shows the TIFF shadow underneath.

Figure 5.69
Select overprint
characteristics.

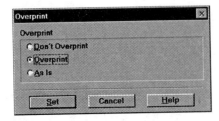

To assign overprint status to a graphics or text object, you click on the object using the Object Selection tool and bring up the dialog shown in Figure 5.69 by selecting Graphics>Overprint.

If you printed this graphic to a laser printer without regard for color separation, it would print as you see it. The trouble begins once we try to color separate this drawing into two colors: black and the color spot (I chose Pantone Purple CV).

Viewing the Color Plates

FrameMaker has an interesting feature that allows you to view your document based on colors that you can select whether you overprint, ignore, or cut out (or not overprint— a knockout).

If you select the View>Color>Views menu, the View 1 button shows the standard view where all colors are displayed and white is cut out (this means the same as nonoverprint or knocked out). Click on View 2 and move the colors to select only the spot color Figure 5.70.

Figure 5.70
Setting color view
2.

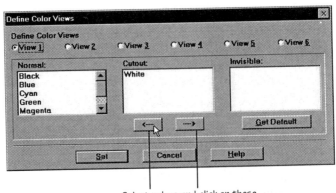

Select colors and click on these
arrow keys to move to Cutout or Invisible

Figure 5.71
The spot color
view.

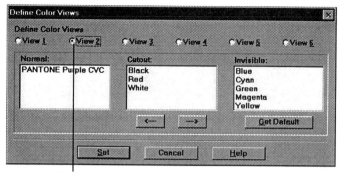

View 2 selected (only spot color is viewed)

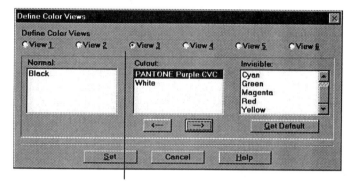

View 3 selected (only black is viewed)

Click Set and some of your graphic disappears. What you see is the purple spot color components of your graphic (just like it should print). See Figure 5.71.

You'll notice that the white diagonal line is correctly cut out of the rightmost A drawing. The two AF drawings and the two text characters appear to be displayed correctly.

Let's look at the black view. Set View 3 to display Black with the white and color spot cutout. Click Set. Figure 5.72 is what you'll see.

The diagonal white line is correctly cut out even over the TIFF shadow. The two text characters and the A (on the right) drawn with the DTP's drawing tool is correctly cut out.

The DTP-drawn AF is knocked out of from the TIFF shadow correctly. And, of course, the white text on the black bar is cut out correctly.

Figure 5.72
The black spot
plate.

Where did it go?

There's something wrong. The AF that was imported as a WMF file is not cut out and we set it to not overprint. FrameMaker, like the other DTP programs, can really only knock out drawing objects that it understands: fonts and internally drawn objects.

The answer? If you want spot colors and you need to overlap and cut out objects, you need to make certain that spot color drawing objects are created in tools that your DTP program understands.

As an example, I redrew the AF symbol using FrameMaker's drawing tools (even though I did the original in Visio). It wasn't easy, but it worked.

Another choice is to create complex drawings like ours only in a newsletter or on a title page for your publication. You may choose to create that one page using a drawing program and color separate it in the drawing program (like CorelDRAW).

Printers Can Produce Different Results

I have two HP laser printers. I printed this graphic to each and I was surprised at the results. First, I printed the spot color (purple, remember?) and the result is as shown in Figure 5.73.

Figure 5.73
The printed spot
color plate.

Figure 5.74
Black plate on a
Postscript printer.

All of the objects look just fine. I printed this on an HP LaserJet 4L, 4, and a Postscript printer. By printing color-separated objects to a laser printer, you should catch most problems before the actual final production phase (covered in Chapter 7). You'll notice that all spot color art prints as black since the printshop applies the color to the black images to print 100 percent spot color.

NOTE Postscript output always works correctly.

Let's print the black plate (Figure 5.74). It looks great on an HP LaserJet 4 and a Postscript printer. The leftmost AF drawing is cut out properly over the TIFF background shadow image. The A and the white line are cut out as expected.

But, note that the WMF-imported AF symbol didn't print. As we discussed, if the drawing isn't drawn using the DTP program's internal drawing tools, imported drawings don't properly knock out.

The DTP-drawn AF symbol is not cut out.

You've probably noticed the same phenomenon on the HP LaserJet Series II whenever you try to print white text on a black background. It just doesn't print correctly.

Let's print the black plate to an HP LaserJet 4L (Figure 5.75).

Figure 5.75
Black plate on an
HP LaserJet 4L
printer.

What happened? Oops!

Figure 5.76
Define a spot
color.

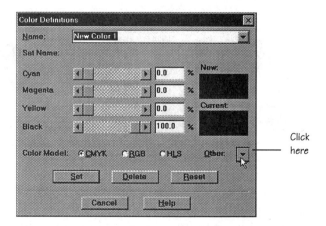

Click
here

The answer? The only true method to guarantee great results is to print to a Postscript printer—that is what your printshop will use.

Color Separating Images

Bitmapped image files need to be separated into four plates (CYMK) to print correctly. Not only is it expensive, but you need to make certain that images are saved in four-color format. I mentioned earlier that there are different bitmapped image file formats. In particular, there are two common formats that already provide their images color separated.

Both CYMK TIFF and CYMK EPS provide bitmapped images already separated. In order for the DTP program to properly view them, these files provide a combined full-color plate view. Therefore, a CYMK file actually includes five images.

The four images corresponding to each color do not become important until the image is printed as separated process color.

Using FrameMaker

Creating a Spot Color

In FrameMaker, you must construct a spot color before you can actually use it (it must become part of your palette).

Figure 5.77
Select the
Pantone color.

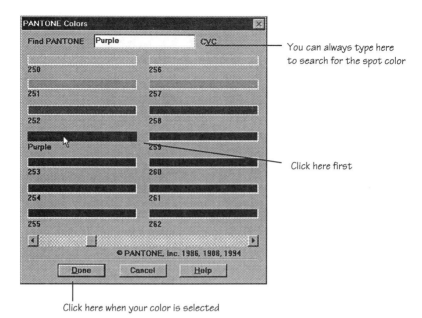

You can always type here
to search for the spot color

Click here first

Click here when your color is selected

1. Create a spot color by selecting View>Colors>Definitions.
   You'll be presented with the dialog shown in Figure 5.76.

2. Select the Other button and then select Pantone. Another
   dialog (Figure 5.77) will be displayed that shows the
   Pantone spot color choices. You can page down through
   the hundreds (actually thousands) of choices. Let's just
   click on Orange, then click Done.

3. Your spot color is defined (Figure 5.78). Click Set.

Figure 5.78
Last step in
defining a spot
color.

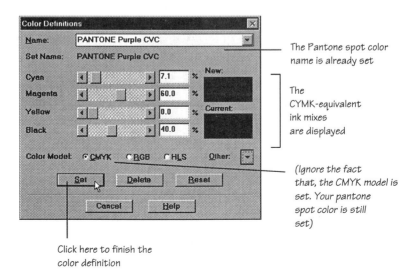

The Pantone spot color
name is already set

The
CYMK-equivalent
ink mixes
are displayed

(Ignore the fact
that, the CMYK model is
set. Your pantone
spot color is still
set)

Click here to finish the
color definition

Figure 5.79
Using drawing
objects.

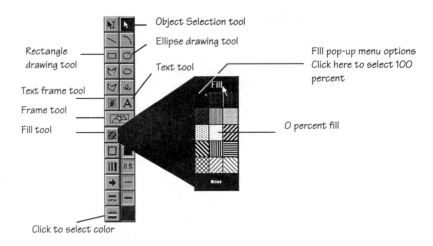

Object Selection tool

Ellipse drawing tool

Rectangle
drawing tool

Text tool

Fill pop-up menu options
Click here to select 100
percent

Text frame tool

Frame tool

Fill tool

0 percent fill

Click to select color

Creating the Drawing

Here are the steps we'll use:

1. You'll need to use the Graphics Frame tool (Figure 5.79) to create the frame that will hold your drawing. Make it the width of your flow inside the margins (our example uses 5.5").

2. Create a black shadow with the drawing tool and fill it with 100 percent black. Holding the **SHIFT** key, create a square and click on the Color tool. Select the Orange spot color you just defined.

3. Create another rectangle to the right and fill with 100 percent black. Create an oval using the Ellipse drawing tool and fill set the fill to 0 percent black (the outline should still be black).

4. Click on the Text frame tool and type in some text. Click on the Text tool and type **TEXT IN WHITE**. Click on the text object with the Object Selection tool and rotate it about 20 percent with the Graphics>Rotate menu command.

Figure 5.80 shows the percentage tints of the nonhatched fill shades available to you using the Fill pattern pop-up menu.

Figure 5.80
Fill tints.

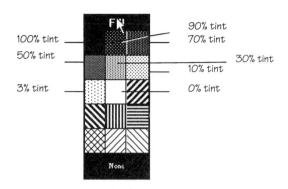

100% tint
50% tint
3% tint
90% tint
70% tint
30% tint
10% tint
0% tint

Setting Overprint and Knockouts

FrameMaker assumes that all objects (text and graphics) are knocked out. The only change you have to make is to select the small black rectangle as an overprinted object.

1. Click on the black rectangle. Click Graphics>Overprint and set Overprint, then apply by pressing Set (Figure 5.81).

NOTE In order to overprint the text, I created both a spot color rectangle and a text frame.

2. But wait! We're not done. Remember I said that FrameMaker assumes that all objects (both graphics and text) don't overprint. The two lines of black text will look horrible if you don't overprint them since FrameMaker would normally produce a cutout of text onto the spot color plate and black text on the black plate.

Select the black text frame and set the text to overprint using the same technique as we did in the previous step for the small black rectangle.

Figure 5.81
Selecting an object to overprint.

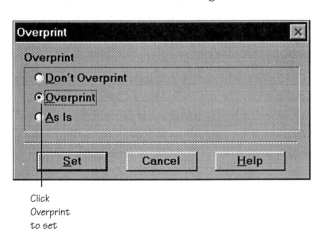

Click
Overprint
to set

Figure 5.82
Apply a spot
color to a drawing
object.

Select the color system   You are not limited to 100 percent

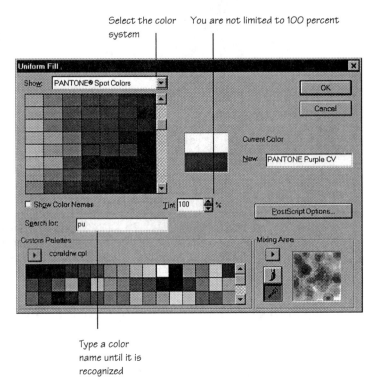

Type a color
name until it is
recognized

Using Corel Ventura

NOTE There are
many more
options available
when selecting a
color, so please
experiment.

Corel Ventura does not require you to preselect a spot color
in order for you to apply it to frame or to drawing objects. To
select the coloring system (Corel Ventura gives you the same
selections available on CorelDRAW), select the object.
Right-click and select Uniform Fill. See Figure 5.82. Clicking
Show Color Names will present spot colors by name rather
than by color rectangle.

By default, Corel Ventura treats any object in the background
of another object as a knockout. You can select objects to
overprint, first by selecting the object using the Pick tool.
Then, set the Overprint check box in either the Frame
Settings, Paragraph Settings, and Selected Text dialog boxes.

Unfortunately, there is no method to view a document's spot
color (to verify that when you go to print that the spots are
properly knocked out) nor can you apply a spot color to a
graphics image—it is either black or already color separated.

GENERATING "KILLER" TABLES

We could write a whole book on tables and their many styles. Nothing communicates complex subjects better than tables.

⊃ **Feature checklists**

I considered placing a checklist with every feature I discuss in this book. Here is an example:

Feature	FM	VP
Paragraph tags	■	■
Character tags	■	
Table tags	■	

Table 5.1 Features Supported by Leading

Although we could create boring tables, I really like to use a white bold sans serif table heading on a gray or black background. Each *table cell* is bounded by a line.

⊃ **Programming Function Tables**

Wouldn't it be great to have a predefined table that is all set for defining a programming table of functions?

Member Function	Returns	Description
INI(int *arg*)	void	Constructor
~INI()	void	Destructor
GetValue(*void***)**	int	Returns the current integer value 0 through 25
SetValue(*int, int***)**	int	Sets the number of times the class should loop

Table 5.2 Programmer's Function Table

In this table, I use the concept of alternating tint shading per row. I also could have used tints per column.

⊃ **Regular Table**

A normal table should have simple border lines per row with a header that stands out. Note that there is not even a table caption:

Column A	Column B	Column C
Line 1 of column A	Line 1 of column B	Line 1 of column C
Line 2 of column A	Line 2 of column B	Line 2 of column C
Line 3 of column A	Line 3 of column B	Line 3 of column C

Necessary Table Features

Critical features that I believe should be available when creating a table are:

- Ability to define a table's attributes with tags like a paragraph's attributes.
- Ability to handle continuations over multiple pages *gracefully*.
- Paragraph tags applied to cells automatically.
- Automatic table captions that stay with their corresponding tables and automatically increment the reference counter.
- An easy method to reference either the caption's text and the caption's table reference counter.
- Ability to insert a graphic in a table cell.
- Ability to merge cells to form a new, larger cell.

Although there are many more table features we could discuss, we'll concentrate on the main ones that you should use.

New Paragraph Tags

Let's create a few more paragraph tags:

Caption Table   Similar to Caption Figure, this paragraph tag keeps track of the caption numbering as well as the table's caption text.

Table Body   Body text that isn't indented like Body and one point smaller than the normal body paragraph tags.

Table Bullet   Bullet, centered in the table cell using a dingbat character (alphabetic Dingbat n).

Table Checkmark   Left-justified check mark (Symbol decimal code 0214) used for tables used to simulate a menu (each vertical cell is a menu command).

Table Code   Containing the same attributes as Code, except that it is not indented and it is, like Table Body, one point size smaller than normal Code text.

Table Entry   Text that is entered from the user's keyboard. Although not used much, this tag provides the ability to list keyboard commands in a table in a size that is one point smaller than normal body text.

Table Header   Contains the attributes used for headers (white bold sans font like Helvetica Neue 65 bold) that is very noticeable, with a gray, spot color, or black background.

Z_Table   The lead-in paragraph to a table (described in the next section).

Don't forget to precede every table with the **Body Next** paragraph style. This will ensure that the table has some text preceding it.

We'll talk about how you can use character formatting overrides within individual table cells in Chapter 6.

Using FrameMaker

Creating a Table Lead-In Paragraph

We'll have to create a special paragraph tag to which we'll anchor a table. We'll call it Z_Table. This paragraph tag will have attributes set in the Paragraph Designer dialog shown in Figure 5.83.

Make certain that the Keep With Next is properly checked in the Pagination tab of the Paragraph Designer dialog.

Figure 5.83
The lead-in
paragraph to a
table.

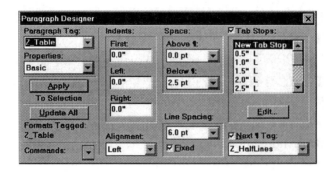

Click on the New Format command button. You can select Apply to Selection to the current paragraph if you wish, but make certain that this paragraph doesn't have any text in it.

The paragraph spacing should be small—8.5 pt (line spacing plus space below) will do. The paragraph tag following after the table is Z_HalfLines which provides space after the table and the automatic caption.

Defining the Table Caption

FrameMaker uses a hierarchical numbering system where a series of numbers are defined in a paragraph tag.

In FrameMaker, the caption is part of the table tag definition. We'll define it using a Numbering format:

> **Table <n>-< ><n+>< >.**

This formula is the key for FrameMaker to keep track of counters and to properly substitute counters corresponding to, in our case, four distinct counters.

The Table prefix text is displayed followed by the counter(s) and caption (optional).

Defining a Table Tag

With the insertion point, create a paragraph to lead into a table. Select Table>Insert Table menu command.

We won't use these default table formats except to get started. Click Insert and a table is placed at the insertion point along with the table caption.

Figure 5.84
Insert a table with
standard table
formats.

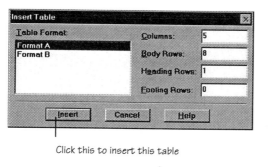

Click this to insert this table

The table
anchor

The table caption

Pretty dull looking. As with all DTP programs, FrameMaker gives you the ability to add table rows or columns by selecting Table>Add Rows or Columns.

Select the entire table with the Smart Selection tool and reshape the table design as follows:

NOTE Press
CTRL+T to display
Table Designer.

1. Enter **Boxed** in the Table Tag field (Figure 5.85). Be sure to reposition the Title Position field to **Below Table**.

Figure 5.85
Set the basic
attributes of the
new table design.

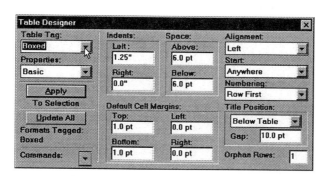

Figure 5.86
Set ruling and
shading borders
for the table.

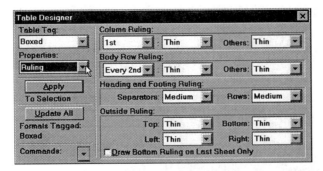

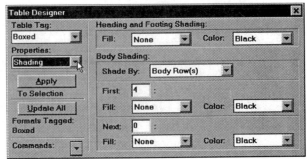

2. Click the Ruling Properties button and set the values as presented in Figure 5.86.

3. Click the Shading Properties field and set the fields. Don't forget to set the Heading to color **Gray 50%** (a color I defined) or **Black**.

   If you wanted to alternate a 3 percent tint with every column, the Shading Properties would look something like Figure 5.87.

4. All ready to go. Click on the New Format Command and you'll be asked if you really want to create a new table formatting tag.

Figure 5.87
Set up alternating
columns shaded
with a 3 percent
black tint (very
light gray).

Figure 5.88
Apply a
paragraph tag to
a table column.

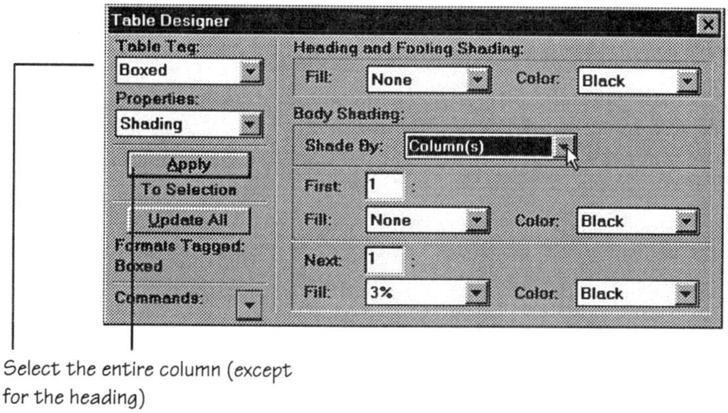

*Select the entire column (except
for the heading)*

NOTE Make certain that the entire table and the table caption are selected.

Make certain that Store in Catalog is checked (and you can optionally apply it to the current table selected). The table tag is now in the catalog!

I can use the Smart Selection tool to select multiple cells and apply a paragraph tag to them. An easy method to enable a bullet list (as in Figure 5.88), is to select the cells and then apply the paragraph Table Bullet to them.

Inserting Tables

I've made other table tags that simplify my life using FrameMaker's table tag mechanism. To insert a Boxed table tag, do the following:

1. Place the insertion point on an empty paragraph.

2. Apply the Z_Table format to it.

3. Select the Table>Insert Table menu command.

4. As in Figure 5.84, select the table tag desired and enter the number of columns, headings, and rows.

5. Press Insert and the table is placed.

FrameMaker, unlike most other DTP applications, automatically displays the updated counter without requiring you to update all counters manually.

Changing a Table's Tag Format

You can change a table's tag format by selecting the entire table, bringing up the Table Designer dialog, selecting the

Table Tag field desired, and finally clicking on the Apply button.

That's all there is to it!

Multipage Tables

FrameMaker will continue a long table onto another page and will carry the caption with it automatically. In addition, if you insert the system variable Table Continuation in the table's caption, the content of that variable is automatically placed in the subsequent pages that the table occupies. You would usually define (Continued) in that system variable.

Referencing Table Captions

On page 230, I showed you how FrameMaker creates captions as part of a paragraph's tag definition. But, how do you reference them from other parts of your publication?

As with any FrameMaker cross-reference we've discussed, you can reference a caption by first defining a reference marker, then later inserting a cross-reference.

To insert a reference marker, do the following:

1. Enter a caption after your table's table caption (you can't edit the table counter since it is automatically presented for you).

2. Place the insertion point at the end of the caption. Type in your caption description.

3. Press **HOME** and insert a marker with a unique name that is inserted as hidden text—it is not displayed or printed. I like preceding table reference markers with **Table:**. See Figure 5.89.

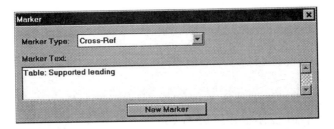

Figure 5.89
Insert a table
reference marker.

Figure 5.90
Insert the
cross-reference.

Make certain that
this is selected

You can select reference markers
from this chapter or from others currently open

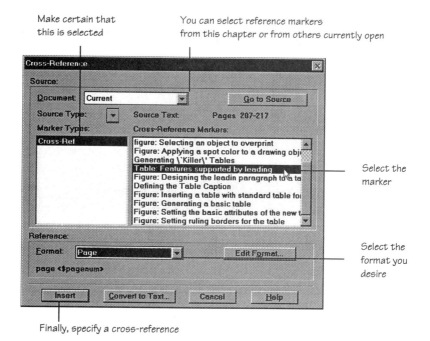

Select the
marker

Select the
format you
desire

Finally, specify a cross-reference

You'll notice that the ^{T} symbol represents a reference marker: Table 5.2 Features supported by leading §.

At some other location in the publication, you may wish to reference a marker by following these steps:

1. Position the insertion point where you wish to insert the cross-reference.

2. Select the Special>Cross-Reference menu (Figure 5.90) and select the Source Type, Reference Source fields to the appropriate reference marker.

3. Click on Insert to place the reference.

FrameMaker supplies a variety of formats that can be modified or you can add new formats. The example shown in Figure 5.90 places a table's page number at the insertion point.

To change formats, all you have to do is click on Format.

Some of the formats that have immediate significance to tables and example definitions are shown in the next table.

Format	Example
Page	Page 10
Table	Table 5.2
Table & Page	Table 5.2, "Features supported by leading" on Page 10
See Table Above	See Table 5-2 above

Correcting a Table Problem

When a FrameMaker table crosses a page, sometimes the table's caption overlaps in the table (Figure 5.91).

To correct this, select the entire table caption text and click Edit>Cut. The table caption magically readjusts below the table. Place the insertion point on the captionless line and replace the cut caption with Edit>Paste.

Spot Color with Tables

If you use a spot color tint in a table, black text will not overprint correctly. Select the text frame (**CTRL**+click) on the page and select Overprint with the Graphics>Object Properties menu command.

The better method to enable black text overprint for body text and table text is to set all text frames to overprint in the Master pages.

Using Corel Ventura

Creating a Table Lead-In

Create a new paragraph tag that has the same attributes as Z_Figure. Call it Z_Table and make certain that the Keep With Next Paragraph is checked in the Breaks dialog.

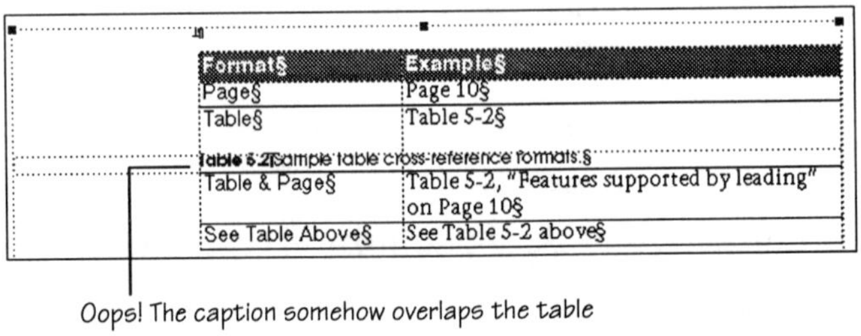

Figure 5.91
A FrameMaker's table caption problem.

Oops! The caption somehow overlaps the table

The total spacing of the paragraph should be about 8.5 pt in total vertical space. Place the insertion point on this paragraph.

Defining a Table Tag

Currently, Corel Ventura does not support the concept of table tags (assigning table attributes to a name). That is a little odd since it provides tags for graphic frames. Oh well.

Inserting Tables

NOTE You can also select Table>Create Table.

With the insertion point on the Z_Table tagged paragraph, click on the table button ▦, and you will be presented with a Table dialog with three tabs: General, Positioning, and Cell Borders.

The first General tab (Figure 5.92) provides the positioning and basic table "geometry" (number of rows, headers, and columns) information.

First, set the Rows to **3** (or whatever you like), Columns to **3**, and Number of Header Rows to **1**. Set the Table Border fields as shown. In addition, for each Column Number use the thumbwheel to select each column from 1 to the number of columns you specified.

Figure 5.92
Set up the general table settings.

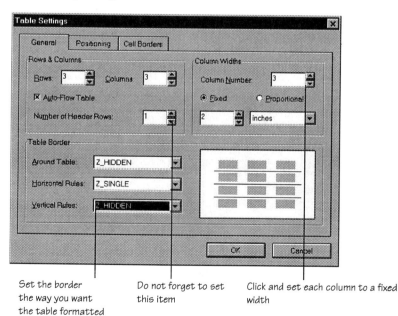

Set the border
the way you want
the table formatted

Do not forget to set
this item

Click and set each column to a fixed
width

Figure 5.93
Set up the table
positioning.

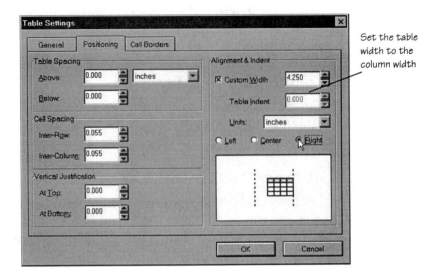

*Set the table
width to the
column width*

Make absolutely certain that you set each column to **Fixed**. In this example, I set the columns to **.75"**, **1.5"**, and **2"**, respectively.

You may wish to use proportional widths if you want the table to be adjusted automatically across the entire text frame. On the other hand, most tables fit neatly below text (and, in our case, 1.25″ into the table flow frame). Setting any column to proportional makes alignment extremely difficult. Click on the Positioning tab. See Figure 5.93. Don't worry about the spacing and justification settings. Check Custom Width to 4.25", Table Indent to 0", and set the table to be right-justified in the text flow frame.

Figure 5.94
Set up the pen
drawing
characteristics for
cell borders.

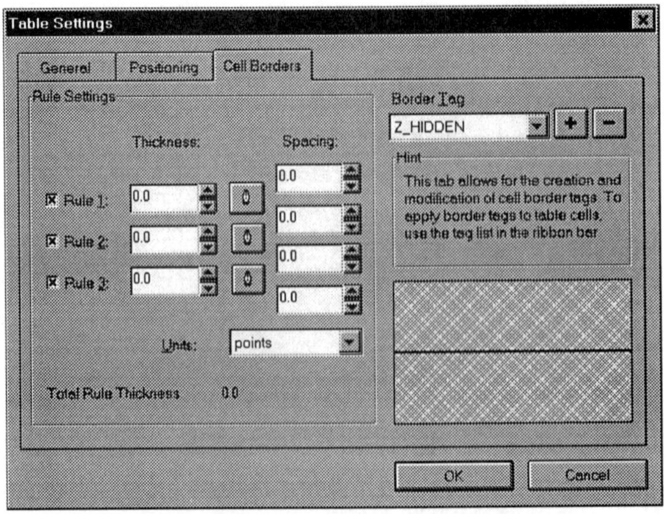

The total of all column widths you specified in the General tab should add up to the width specified in the Custom Width field.

Click the Cell Borders tab. Figure 5.94 shows the options available for the cell borders. You can select line borders (color, thickness, and spacing) as you can around the frame and paragraph tags. In our case, we won't modify the table ruling lines.

Click OK. The table is positioned to the right as planned above the Z_Table paragraph tag.

Select the entire header, right-click, and choose Cell Color. Although we'll set the color to 100 percent Black, you can also set the table heading color to your spot color (my preference).

Defining the Table Caption

What about table captions? If you choose not to use table counting schemes, then you don't really have to concern yourself with these.

Supporting a table caption is done with the use of anchored frames. In other words, you create an anchored frame as we did earlier for graphics figure frames. Place the insertion point in the frame and follow the table creation instructions presented in the last section.

Figure 5.95
Set up the table
caption using
frames.

Figure 5.96
Select the format to quickly apply to an existing table.

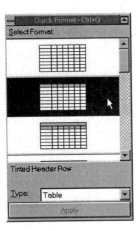

With the frame selected, right-click, choose, Format>General, and set the caption as shown in Figure 5.95.

Select the Reference field to the Table [C#]-[T#] format presented in the figure. The biggest drawback with this technique is that a table must not extend beyond a page boundary. In other words, a frame cannot be split across pages.

Modifying the Table Format

With the Pick tool, click anywhere in the table. Right-click and choose one of the many options: General, Cell Color, or even Border Settings.

To add additional rows or columns, select a row or column, right-click and select Insert Rows or Insert Columns. To merge cells, select the specific table cells, right-click, and choose Merge Cells. To undo a merged (or combined) cell, select the merged cells, right-click, and choose Split Cells.

You also have the option to click on a feature that I've sort of avoided called Quick Formats. With the table selected, click the [⊞] button (or choose Format>Quick Format Roll-Up). See Figure 5.96.

You will be presented with a scrollable list of predefined formats. If you don't see a format much like the figure, select the Table in the Type field.

Choose the table format you desire and then click Apply. In addition, you can always select individual cells and reformat accordingly.

Inserting Graphics in Tables

Now that we've covered table creation, it is easy to insert graphics into a table cell. Simply place the text insertion point in a cell and anchor a graphics frame in the cell.

Using FrameMaker

In FrameMaker, the cell height is automatically resized to the height of the anchored graphics frame. The width, however, does not change. You need to resize the table cell by selecting the entire column and dragging the handle to the right of the column.

Using Corel Ventura

In Corel Ventura, you place an anchored frame on a cell's insertion point. Insert a graphics file into the frame. If the file is significantly larger than the frame (or the table cell), you have to manipulate the frame's dimensions or merge cells together to accommodate the large graphic. The frame moves with the table, as you would expect.

6 OVERRIDING THE OTHER LAYERS

NOTE The worst case I've seen is where a writer didn't use *any* paragraph tags in a publication at all.

Now that we've covered all of the basic layers, we'll discuss how to override layout definitions or change the look of certain keywords in order to improve readability or the look of the overall document. The overrides layer is used for these processes.

Some people might argue that because there are so many exceptions, the fundamental tags used in the lower levels are just a waste of time. But, keep in mind that basing your publication's design on the other three layers of objects gives you a lot of flexibility and definitely helps keep your manual properly organized.

We'll cover the objects that can be modified as an override:

- Overriding paragraph tags.
- Modifying text with character tags.
- Changing the spacing between characters.
- Creating drop caps.
- Using variables for common phrases.

REDEFINING PARAGRAPH TAGS

We will redefine a paragraph tag with two examples:

- Redefining text attributes.
- Redefining a paragraph's position on a page.

Redefining a Paragraph's Text Attributes

Let's assume that you have followed the examples in the previous chapters and have defined two paragraph tags: Body and Body Next.

NOTE   Body Next can be viewed as inheriting the tag attributes of Body.

The Body paragraph tag has been defined with 6 pt below the entire paragraph with each line having spacing of 13 pt. In addition, the font is 11 pt StoneSerif. The Body Next paragraph tag is the same, only it must be kept with the next paragraph in your document.

Let's take this paragraph of nonsense text:

> Ennius et sapines et fortis et alter Homerus, ut critici dicunt, leviter curare videtur, quo promissa cadant et somnia Pythagorea. Naevius in manibus non est et mentibus haeret paene recens?

This paragraph will be a part of your publication's fine print legal notice (this makes as much sense as most license agreements, right?) Let's modify its appearance to be 10 pt Helvetica with line spacing of 10 pt. The space below the entire paragraph is left at 6 pt.

The result should look like:

> Ennius et sapines et fortis et alter Homerus, ut critici dicunt, leviter curare videtur, quo promissa cadant et somnia Pythagorea. Naevius in manibus non est et mentibus haeret paene recens?

The goal is to redefine this specific paragraph (or paragraphs) so that its format varies slightly from how the text layer was originally styled. See Figure 6.1.

Figure 6.1
How a character override modifies a paragraph tag's settings.

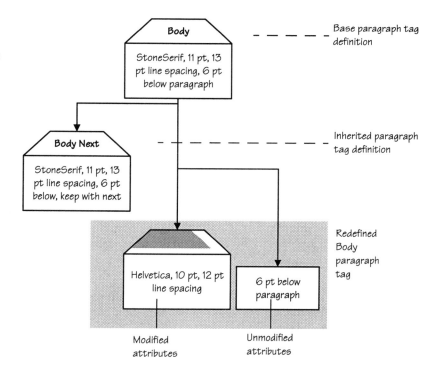

Redefining a Paragraph's Position on a Page

A common design feature is to start a specific paragraph on a new page. We'll show the easiest ways to place a paragraph (any paragraph) on a specific page boundary.

This feature is usually used when a paragraph must start either on an even or odd page to meet with style specifications.

Using FrameMaker

Overriding a Paragraph Tag

To redefine a paragraph, you must use the Paragraph Designer dialog.

1. Select the paragraph by placing the cursor anywhere in it.

2. Bring up the Paragraph Designer dialog (if it isn't displayed, press **CTRL+M**).

3. In Basic properties, change the Line Spacing (leading) to **12.0 pt** and leave the Space below alone. Click on the Apply To Selection button. See Figure 6.2.

4. In Default Font properties, change the Family to **Helvetica** and the Size to **10.0 pt**. Click on the Apply To Selection button. All done.

Notice that the status bar indicates that the paragraph is a modified Body paragraph tag by preceding the tag name with an asterisk: `Flow: A ¶: *Body`.

Removing the Overridden Paragraph Tag Anytime you wish to revert back to the original paragraph tag attributes (in this case, the Body tag), click on the paragraph from the Paragraph catalog (in this case, Body). See Figure 6.3.

Positioning a Paragraph on the Next Page

Place the cursor *anywhere* in the paragraph you wish to position at the top of the next page.

Figure 6.2
Change the paragraph tag's basic properties.

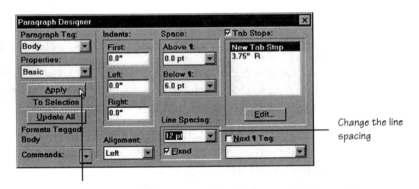

Change the line spacing

Then click here

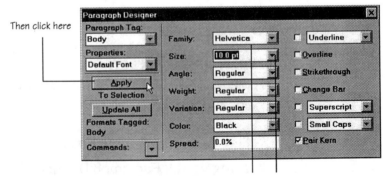

Change these two paragraph tag attributes

Figure 6.3
Remove the
paragraph's
attributes.

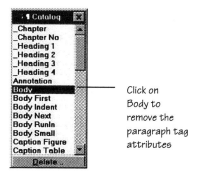

Click on
Body to
remove the
paragraph tag
attributes

There are two methods for positioning a paragraph at the top
of a page.

- Select Special>Page Break, click on Page, then Set as
  shown in Figure 6.4 (or you can use the three-character
  keyboard shortcut: **Esc** j P).

- Using the Paragraph Designer, select Top of Page from the
  Pagination properties then click on Apply To Selection.

Positioning to the Top of a Column

FrameMaker makes it as easy to move the paragraph to the
next column. Just choose Column (instead of Page) or use the
keyboard shortcut: **Esc** j C.

Figure 6.4
Alternative
methods of
advancing to the
top of the page.

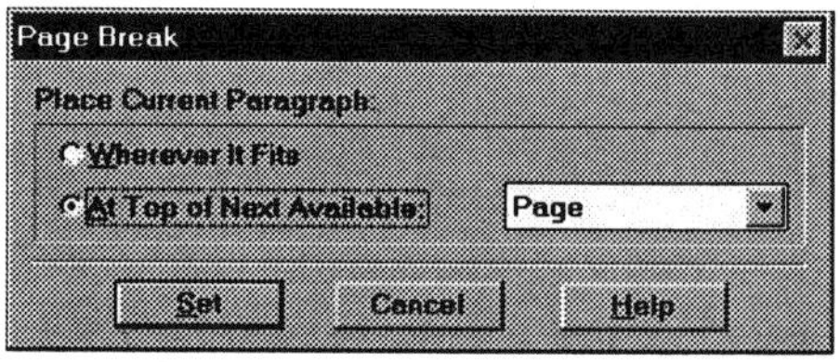

or...

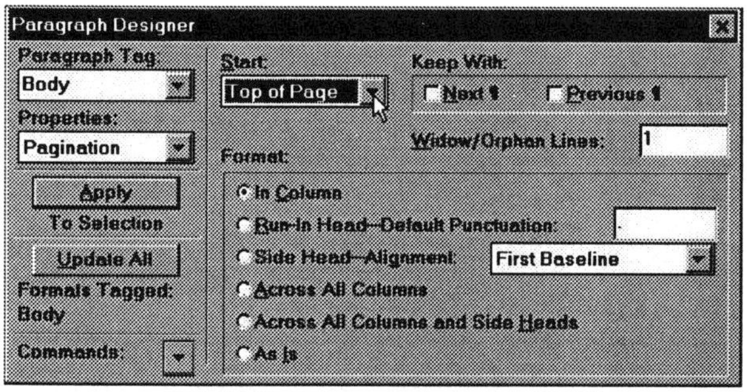

Figure 6.5
Setting a
character
attribute override.

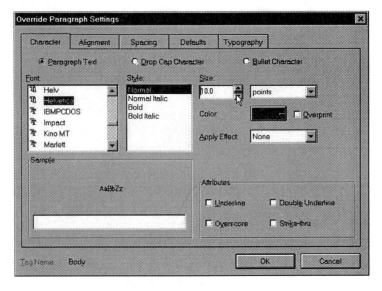

Removing the Page Break Override Place the text cursor in the paragraph that starts on the next page. Click on the Body tag in the Paragraph Catalog. See Figure 6.3.

Using Corel Ventura

Prior to version 5, you could not override an entire paragraph tag's attributes. Now, you can!

Overriding a Paragraph Tag

Make certain that you have selected the Freeform Text tool. This allows local overriding of a paragraph tag. At this point, you can use the ribbon, ruler, or the Paragraph menu command to set local formatting. You'll notice that the cursor doesn't have the little attached tag (you are now in override mode).

Click anywhere in the paragraph to place the text cursor. We'll use the Paragraph dialog method by choosing one of the following techniques:

- Type **CTRL+T** as a keyboard shortcut.

- Select Format>Paragraph menu.

- Right-click and select Format>Character.

Figure 6.6
Setting a
paragraph
spacing override.

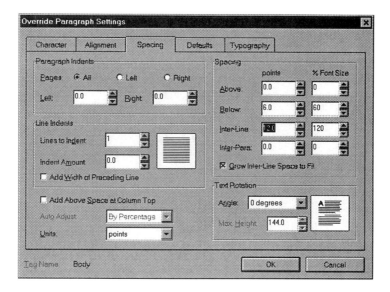

All of these techniques display the Override Paragraph Settings dialog (see Figure 6.5), where you can change the Font and Size to **Helvetica** and **10 pt**, respectively.

Click OK.

Click on the Alignment tab (Figure 6.6) and change the Units to **points** and Inter-line Spacing (in other words, leading) to **12**.

With the text cursor still in the paragraph, you'll notice that the font (family and point size) reflects the overrides, and a little tag with an X precedes the paragraph tag name (in our example, tag Body): Body Helvetica 10.

Odd—Corel Ventura's new user interface doesn't show the modified paragraph tag symbol unless you have the Freeform Text tool button selected.

Removing the Overridden Paragraph Tag   Anytime you wish to revert back to the original paragraph tag attributes (in this case, the Body tag), click on the paragraph tag name (like Body) and place the text cursor somewhere in the paragraph.

Figure 6.7
Remove a
paragraph's
overrides.

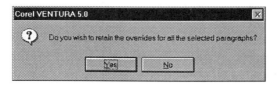

Figure 6.8
Remove overrides.

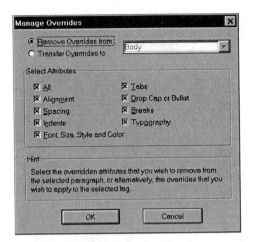

Click No when asked if you would like to preserve overrides (see Figure 6.7).

NOTE Don't forget to insert the text cursor in the paragraph.

Another method to use is the Format>Manage Overrides menu command. Select this menu (or use the keyboard shortcut **SHIFT**+**F10**) and you'll be presented the dialog in Figure 6.8.

If the Manage Overrides menu command is grayed out, it is because you do not have the Freeform Text tool button enabled and your insertion point has not selected an overridden paragraph.

Unless you would like to uncheck certain paragraph attributes (we'll leave them all checked), click OK. The paragraph returns back to its original design.

Positioning a Paragraph on the Next Page

With the overrides button still enabled (see page 248), place the cursor anywhere in the paragraph that you wish to position on the top of the next page. There are two ways to display your break choices:

- Select the Format>Breaks menu command.

- Right-click and select Breaks.

NOTE The same applies to column breaks.

Click on Page Break and you will be given a variety of options (more than the other DTP programs allow), select Before, and click OK.

Figure 6.9
Setting a page
break.

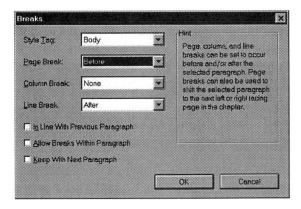

There is an alternative method for setting page breaks that you may have discovered by accident. Right-click at the insertion point and select Format>Alignment. Click on the Breaks button. There is a slight difference between setting temporary versus permanent breaks.

NOTE If, after removing a page break, the page view doesn't reflect the change, press **PAGE UP** to "refresh" the display to the previous page.

Switching between the Freeform Text tool and the Tagged Text tool may become confusing, so I offer the following explanation in an attempt to remove any mystery.

Page (and column breaks) are *temporary overrides*, if they are inserted while the Freeform Text tool is enabled.

Page (and column breaks) are *permanent attributes*, to all paragraph tags of a given name, if they are inserted while the Tagged Text tool is enabled: ▣ .

Removing the Page Break Override

Place the cursor *anywhere* in the overridden paragraph and click on the paragraph tag name (in our case, Body) to remove the break.

You will then be asked if you would like to retain overrides, as shown before in Figure 6.7. Click No and your paragraph is back to normal.

MODIFYING TEXT WITH CHARACTER TAGS

FrameMaker introduced a feature in the early 1990s that was not available in any popular DTP or word processing program. Not only did it have paragraph tags (what program didn't?), it also defined something called character tags.

Assume that you have a paragraph (with all of its attributes), but that you continually use a text feature with specific attributes. You don't want to redefine the entire paragraph—just a word or two.

Wouldn't you love to be able to select a phrase (like the keywords "character tags" above) and perhaps be able to click on a tag name that would apply both italics and boldface attributes to it?

The character tag would only change selected attributes in the character tag definition and would leave other attributes as is.

Although all DTP programs allow you to override characters (and not the entire paragraph), currently only FrameMaker and Word allow you to assign a character tag name to it.

I've defined specific character tags to create this book. Character tags, like paragraph tags, offer similar benefits to the documentation writer:

- They reduce errors.
- They ensure consistency among documents and among multiple users.

If your DTP program doesn't support character tags, I recommend that you keep a notebook handy with your definitions and at least manually make certain that you are consistent. It is definitely more work, but it should help eliminate most errors.

Standard Character Attributes

There are times when you must change the way characters look. Let's first look at the basic character attributes that are supported by the DTP applications. The table on the next page shows the character attributes supported by Corel Ventura and FrameMaker.

Character overrides apply to body flow text as well as to text in table cells.

In all DTP applications, you select the text for which you'd like to change the attribute. What you do next depends on your DTP package.

NOTE FM is FrameMaker and VP is Corel Ventura.

FM	VP	Attributes
■	■	Italics
■	■	Bold
■	■	Bold and italics
■	■	Superscript
■	■	Subscript
■	■	Forced uppercase
■	■	Forced lowercase
■		Forced small caps as used in the heading
■	■	Underline
■	■	Double underline
■	■	Overline
■	■	Strikethrough
■	■	Changing fonts
■	■	Changing font size

Using FrameMaker

In FrameMaker, you can select these attributes by selecting the Font, Size, or Style commands (on the Format menu). You can use the Character Designer dialog's options or even the character formatting buttons on the QuickAccess bar:

To remove the character attribute, select the text, then select the Format>Characters>Default Paragraph Font menu command.

Using Corel Ventura

You must first select text using the Freehand Text tool or the Tagged Text tool. You can change character attributes in two ways:

NOTE You can also right-click and select Selected Text.

- The first way is to select Format>Selected Text (or press **CTRL+SHIFT+Y**). You will have the option to change character attributes as you see fit.

- The alternative is to right-click and check any of the attributes as shown in Figure 6.10.

Figure 6.10
Set text attributes
via right-clicking.

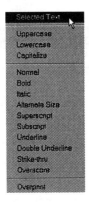

If you are not sure which attributes are currently selected, do not expect to see check marks on the popup menu or assume that the Ribbon text attributes buttons are correct. The only way that I've found to determine this is to bring up the Selected Text Attributes dialog.

Useful Character Tag Definitions

The character attributes we just discussed provide for an outstanding way to modify selected text within a paragraph. However, sometimes we need some method to attach a name to a specific combination of character attributes.

I like to divide character tags into the following categories:

- Color attributes, symbols, and bullets.
- User-interface objects.
- Programming items.
- Typographic.

To distinguish from paragraph tags, I always set character tag names in all caps.

Defining Color, Symbols, and Bullets

The table on the next page are the ones that I use.

Character Tag	Description
BULLET	A bullet character that is used normally by the LIST BULLET paragraph tag.
COLOR SPOT	Set the selected text to your spot color (leave all other attributes unchanged).
COLOR WHITE	Very important (and mostly overlooked), since it is typically used for table and thumb tab text.
DINGBAT	These interesting symbols can be used at the end of a chapter or for many other needs. This typically represents the ZAPF Dingbat font.
RUN-IN COLOR	Although not used much, if you have a run-in paragraph that also needs to be highlighted, why not use color?
SYMBOL	The character name for the SYMBOL font typically used for bullets, table notations, and other services.

NOTE Font families of the same point (pt) size may not look right together.

One word of caution. You may be switching between font families within a single paragraph. As an example for this book I use 11 pt StoneSerif (serif) and 11 pt Helvetica Neue (sans serif). If a character tag of Helvetica Neue is applied to text within a paragraph that is composed primarily of StoneSerif 11 pt text, the fonts look like they are the same height and size:

The function **afINI()** is called once every second by **main()**.

Perfect!

Another book that I designed combined 11 pt Minion with 11 pt Helvetica Neue character tags and it looked like:

The function **afINI()** is called once every second by **main()**.

Not so good! Use your eye to judge if sizes need to be adjusted when mixing fonts. My experience is that generally a sans serif font needs to be 1 to 2 points smaller than a serif font in order for them to look good together in the same paragraph.

User-Interface Objects

The table on the next page represents the character tags that I use to describe a software product's interface.

Character Tag	Description
ENTRY	Anything a user enters on the keyboard or selects from a list of choices. I like a boldface sans serif font.
ENTRY_MONO	For character mode applications (like DOS), the user's text is highlighted.
FILENAME	All filenames should be presented the same—I prefer to show all filenames in uppercase.
KEYBOARD	Used to denote keyboard keycaps. I prefer to use small caps in a sans serif font.
PROMPT	Prompts or exact text used on button controls, menus, static window text, or prompts.
PROMPT_MONO	Used for prompts and menus and generally for DOS-based, character-only display text.

Software Engineering Character Tags

I use these character tags when I'm documenting programming products:

Character Tag	Description
CLASS NAME	A C++ name used to refer to a class object.
DATADECL	Data declarations are names given to data items that are used in a software program (global or local to a function).
DATATYPE	Data types that are used to identify the "type" of data, not the data item itself.
DEFINITION	A data definition is given to the name used as a preprocessor or a compile-only data value (it doesn't actually reserve memory). I like definitions to be a bold, simple sans font.
FUNCTION NAME	The name of the function (and in the case of C and C++), including parentheses— required to distinguish functions from data declarations. I like functions to have names that are bold with a heavy font.
PARAMETER	A parameter value that is declared or used when passed to a function for processing. I like parameters to be bold, italics heavy font in a different color (or even 50% black).

Defining Typographic Character Tags

Here are the ones that I use:

Character Tag	Description
ANNOTATE	Set the text into a slightly smaller light-hearted font (like Tekton).
BOLD	Set the text to bold.
FIRST_CHAR	The first character of a paragraph if used differently than the rest of the text (like a drop cap).
ITALICS	Set the text in italics.
KEYWORD	Set the text apart from normal text (usually in a different color, bold, and italics).
RUN-IN	Bolded, sans serif font that starts a run-in paragraph.
SUPERSCRIPT	Perfect for the copyright, trademark, or registered trademark symbol.

Let's modify the paragraph we used earlier, with a couple of exceptions:

> Ennius et ***sapines*** et fortis et alter Homerus, ut critici dicunt, leviter curare videtur, quo promissa cadant et somnia Pythagorea. Naevius in manibus [non] est et mentibus haeret paene recens?

The word ***sapines*** represents the KEYWORD character tag set to the current paragraph's tag attributes of bold-italics. The word [non] is set to SUPERSCRIPT.

Maintaining Character Tags

It is a little difficult to remove a character tag and, frankly, it should be. You can reapply a paragraph tag (the same one or another one), and the character tag attributes should be maintained.

As an example, let's say your character tag just changes selected characters to AvantGarde if you change the paragraph tag to Body or to Heading 1. The other font attributes like size and color, for example, maintain the attributes of the paragraph text.

Figure 6.11
Resetting the
Character Tag to
a "maintain as is"
state.

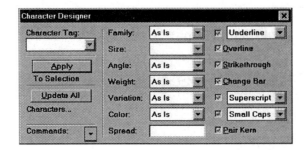

Using FrameMaker

**Defining a
Character Tag** The Character Designer is used to define, edit, and apply a
character tag.

1. If the Character Designer modeless dialog is not currently displayed, select Format>Characters>Designer (or **CTRL**+D).

2. Press **SHIFT**+**F8** to set the current character tag to a "maintain as is" state. Some of the text field items will be identified by the term As Is, while check boxes will be grayed. See Figure 6.11.

3. Click the Commands button and select New Format. Type in the character tag, uncheck Apply to Selection, and click Create (Figure 6.12).

   Make certain that Store in Catalog (the default) is checked.

4. Select **Italics, Bold,** and then click Update All. See Figure 6.13.

Congratulations! You've just defined a character tag.

Figure 6.12
Assigning a
character tag
name.

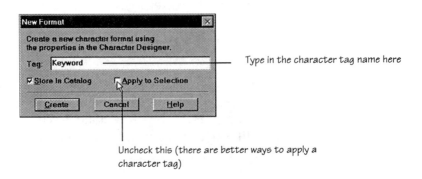

Type in the character tag name here

Uncheck this (there are better ways to apply a
character tag)

Figure 6.13
Adding attributes
to the character
tag definition.

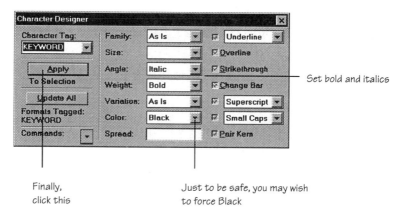

Set bold and italics

Finally,
click this

Just to be safe, you may wish
to force Black

Applying a Character Tag Make certain that you have selected the Paragraph Text tool from the Tools palette  before selecting text.

Select the text to which you'd like to apply a character tag (in this case, "sapines"). There are several ways of applying a character tag to the selected text. You can select the character tag (KEYWORD).

If the Character Tag (denoted by f Catalog) list is not displayed, click 𝑓 above the vertical scroll bar (Figure 6.14).

NOTE If you make a mistake while typing, just press **BACKSPACE**.

There is another way to do the same thing, which I actually prefer. You can type the character tag name until it is unique. First, press **F8** then the tag name until recognized on the status bar: **KEYW**: f : KEYWORD .

Figure 6.14
Applying a
character tag
from the
Character
Designer dialog
or the Character
Tag catalog.

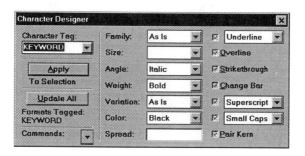

Character Tag designer

Character Tag
catalog

Of course, if you only have a single character tag that begins with K, all you have to type is: **F8 K**. Once the tag is recognized, press **ENTER**.

Removing a Character Tag Select the text previously set to a character attribute and then either:

- Click on Default ¶ Font in the f Catalog or from the Character Designer dialog.
- Use the keyboard shortcut (on the status bar) by typing **F8 D ENTER** to select Default ¶ Font.

The characters revert back to the character attributes defined in the paragraph tag. FrameMaker thinks character tags are important!

Using Corel Ventura

Hmm. The character tag concept is not yet in the product.

ADJUSTING SPACING BETWEEN CHARACTERS

Kerning is the typesetting term for subtracting space between two characters to improve both readability and appearance. For example, notice here that this almost looks like two separate groups of letters:

ToWi

But, after kerning, you can see that this is actually a single grouping of letters:

ToWi

Although not technically considered kerning, you can also "space out" characters for a special effect. Note the same letters spread evenly to 120 percent between each of the characters, a look often used for company logos:

T o W i

Using FrameMaker

To manually space characters, select the characters first, then:

- Press **ALT+LEFT ARROW** to kern 1 pt or **ALT+SHIFT+LEFT ARROW** to kern 6 pt closer (use the **RIGHT ARROW** if you wish to remove the kern). You can also hold down **ALT** while pressing on the arrow keys to get the effect you want.

- Or from the Character Designer, set Spread to a negative value and click Apply.

Removing Manual Spacing
To remove manual spacing, all you have to do is:

1. Select the text.

2. Press **ALT+HOME**.

Using Corel Ventura

To manually space characters, select either the Freehand Text tool or Tagged Text tool, the characters, then:

- Hold down both the **ALT** and the **CTRL** keys while pressing the I (to decrease the distance) or the K (to increase the spread).

- Or select Format>Selected Text menu, press **CTRL+SHIFT+Y**, or right-click) to display the Selected Text Attributes dialog. Adjust the Kerning to a positive value to decrease the distance between characters and, of course, a negative value to increase the distance (thus, spreading characters).

Finally, click OK. See Figure 6.15.

Removing Manual Spacing
Manually spaced characters can be undone by selecting the text, right-clicking, and clicking on Normal. You can also display the Text Attributes dialog and insert a Kerning value of **0**.

Figure 6.15
Set the kerning
(manual spacing)
in ems.

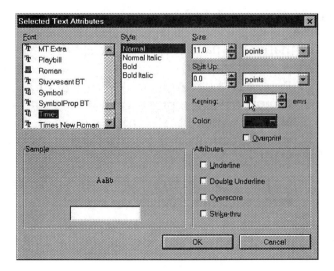

DROPPING THE FIRST CHARACTER

Referred to as "drop caps," this technique is just the thing to add pizzazz to your documentation. The following shows the first character being dropped into the paragraph:

Using FrameMaker

Starting with version 5, FrameMaker supports the ability to insert a drop cap. This is how you do it:

1. Place the insertion point at the beginning of the paragraph.

2. Insert a frame with Special>Anchored Frame. Set the Anchoring Position field to Run into Paragraph with an Alignment set to Left. You can specify gaps and frame width to your liking.

3. Click to select this frame and, from the Tools palette,

select the Text Frame tool. Drag it within the anchored frame.

4. When prompted with the Create New Text Frame dialog, accept the default field values of 1 Column and a Gap of **.25"**. Click on the Set button.

5. Type in the first character of the paragraph and reset the font and its size. You now have a drop cap.

I normally fill the anchored frame as either black, 50 percent black or a spot color.

The text frame can be set to the field values shown in Figure 6.16. The letter can be set to a Times font, 30 pt, bold character.

Figure 6.16
The anchored text frames for drop caps.

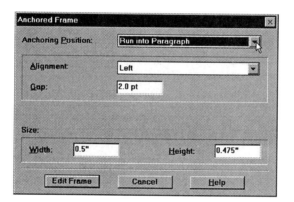

Anchored frame

Custom text frame holding the first letter

Figure 6.17
Setting the drop
cap features.

Set this button and do not forget to apply the effect

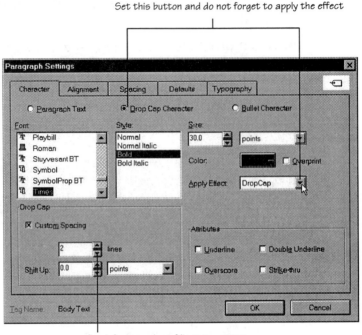

The default number of lines to reserve
may not be to your liking, so always set this

Using Corel Ventura

Nobody offers better drop cap flexibility than Corel Ventura:

1. Click in the paragraph (if you want the drop cap feature to be permanent in a paragraph tag, use the Tagged Text tool) to place the insertion point.

2. Bring up the Paragraph Settings dialog by either right-clicking Format>Character, selecting menu Format>Paragraph, or by pressing **CTRL+T**.

3. Click on the Character tab and set both the Drop Cap Character radio button and Apply Effect to **Drop Cap**.

NOTE Don't forget to set the size (Corel Ventura will not automatically do this for you).

4. Set custom spacing to 3 and set your font attributes to your heart's content. You can change the font, color, and other attributes, and assign these elements to their own paragraph tag (like Body First).

5. When you are done, click OK (or change other paragraph settings).

USING VARIABLES FOR COMMON PHRASES

Why Use Variables?

What if you use a phrase over and over again throughout your publication? For example, I use the title of this book, *A Guide to Publishing User Manuals*, throughout.

Why not assign a variable such as BookTitle to automatically insert *A Guide to Publishing User Manuals* every time? If the book title changes later, all I would have to do is change the variable's definition once, and all references to the text would automatically change.

Great feature!

Imagine all of the elements that could be placed into a variable:

- Name of the product you are documenting.
- Your company's name.
- Version number of the product you are documenting.
- Common terminology used throughout your publication.

Both Corel Ventura and FrameMaker support the concept of variables. In FrameMaker, variables are assigned to a chapter or a template chapter and can be imported into another chapter. Unfortunately for the user, there is currently no "book-wide" variable concept that can be shared among all chapters in a book. Each chapter's variables must be kept up to date by the user manually. On the positive side, FrameMaker lets you import those same variable definitions to another publication using the same import mechanism.

In Corel Ventura, variables are assigned to the book and automatically apply to all chapters of the book. Corel Ventura treats variables much like a directory of terms that can easily be inserted anywhere in the publication. In earlier versions, the user had to create a variable by first inserting a variable marker somewhere in the text. Corel Ventura has done a nice job listening to customer input in order to improve the usability of variables.

Variables That I Use

NOTE This list is just a subset of the variables I use.

It probably wouldn't surprise you that in order for me to keep the terminology straight for each of the DTP applications in this book, I created a group of user-interface variables:

Floating toolbar (a "floating" set of drawing and text tools)	Tools palette	Toolbox
Floating Para Tool (the button that represents the paragraph text tool)	Smart Selection tool	Tagged Text tool
Floating Text Tool (text tool)	Text tool	Freehand Text tool
Floating Pointer (selects objects)	Object Selection tool	Pick tool
Floating Line Tool (for creating a line normally for callouts)	Line tool	Line tool
Floating Fill Tool (for filling a drawing object or frame)	Fill pattern pop-up menu	Fill tool
Floating Frame Tool (for creating frames)	Graphics Frame tool	Frame tool
Text cursor pointer (text insertion cursor)	insertion point	insertion point
Status bar (at the bottom of a window)	Status bar	Status line
Formatting Toolbar (*usually* below the menu)	Formatting bar	Ribbon
Floating Para Tags (list box of paragraph tags)	Paragraph Catalog	Tags Roll-Up
Floating Char Tags (list box of character tags)	Character Catalog	*not applicable*

For example, to properly reference floating paragraph tools, I created the variable FrameMaker Floating Para Tool. Then, when I want to use the variable, I just insert the variable name and the DTP program inserts the variable's text.

As an example, anywhere I use FrameMaker Formatting Toolbar, the variable definition Formatting bar will be automatically substituted.

I also defined a whole group of variables that I use over and over to refer to the following text:

- Copyright, trademark, and registered trademark symbols.
- Spaces (em, en, and thin).
- Dashes (long, non-breaking).
- Company, product name, and product version.
- Typographic special characters: ellipsis, dagger, and so on.
- Keyboard equivalents (Enter key, function keys, and so on).

Great fun! But not all of the DTP programs support this feature. Let's investigate...

Using FrameMaker

Am I in Heaven or what?

FrameMaker allows variables to be kept in a chapter document file in a special list. Variables are created, edited, deleted, and inserted from a dialog that is accessed by the Special>Variable menu command.

Oops! Why aren't variables maintained in the publication for all chapters? Unfortunately, variables are not currently kept in a single variable file to be shared among all chapters in a publication. Select the publication's book file and import Variable definitions using the File>Import>Formats menu command from the chapter with the current variable definitions.

Creating and Applying a Variable Definition

Let's build the variable name BookTitle.

1. First, create a variable by selecting the Special>Variable menu.

2. When the Variable definition dialog is presented, click Create Variable button.

Figure 6.18
Define a variable.

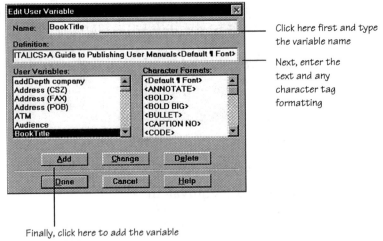

Click here first and type
the variable name

Next, enter the
text and any
character tag
formatting

Finally, click here to add the variable
to your chapter

3. The Edit User Variable dialog is then presented. Enter the name (BookTitle), the variable definition (A Guide to Publishing User Manuals), and click the Add button. See Figure 6.18.

NOTE The ability to add formatting in a variable is a spectacular feature!

If standard formatting needs to be included, you can insert character tags. I put in <ITALICS> since book titles are usually italicized. What you shouldn't forget is to restore the character tag's attributes to the normal paragraph. At the end of the variable definition, I usually append Default ¶ Font.

4. You can create other variables without exiting the dialog. We don't have anymore to add here, though, so click Done.

5. You aren't done yet. The original Variable definition dialog referenced in step 2 is redisplayed (see Figure 6.19). This dialog is used to create, edit, or to force an update of all variables (not usually necessary unless you've deleted other cross-references or variables).

NOTE If you had highlighted text in your chapter, the Insert button would display Replace instead.

6. Press the Insert button if you wish to apply the variable to the current text position in your chapter. If you don't want to insert the highlighted variable now, just click Done (or press **Esc**).

Figure 6.19
Insert a variable.

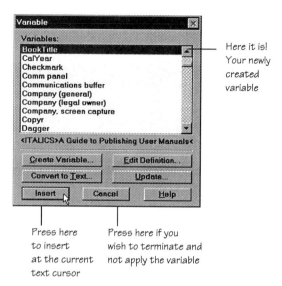

Here it is!
Your newly
created
variable

Press here
to insert
at the current
text cursor

Press here if you
wish to terminate and
not apply the variable

Like most features in FrameMaker, there is a keyboard shortcut. Type the three-key sequence **Escqv** followed by the variable name until it is recognized in the Status bar. Press **ENTER** to insert (or **Esc** to terminate).

FrameMaker keeps track of which variable you used last so that when you want to reapply a variable, the last one you used is automatically selected. This persistence feature is used throughout the many features of FrameMaker and I love it! The biggest benefit? Easy. The variable's definition is displayed immediately. You don't have to update references at a later time.

Updating the Entire Publication

In order to update the entire publication with a variable's definition, you will need to open the publication's book (mine is entitled DTP.FBK).

Click on the File>Import Formats menu command. Select the document that has the variable definitions you'll use (uncheck all except Variable Definitions) and click Import.

Using Corel Ventura

With every major upgrade of Corel Ventura, handling variables becomes easier. Before version 5, you had to insert a variable definition in the text. Good luck trying to find it!

Figure 6.20
Define a variable.

First, enter the variable name

Click to add the variable

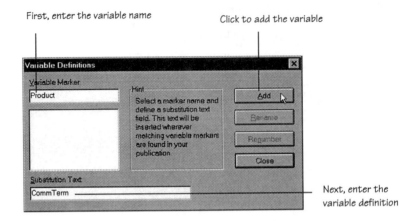

Next, enter the
variable definition

Now, like FrameMaker's implementation, variables are stored with the document's file but don't have to necessarily be inserted in the text body. Unlike FrameMaker, a variable is automatically publication-wide. This is great! With version 5 and 6 becoming more publication (or, multichapter) based, variables are visible to all chapters in a publication.

Creating a Variable

To create a variable, perform the following steps:

1. Select Edit>Define Variables to display the Variable Definitions dialog (Figure 6.20). Enter the name of the variable as **Product** in the Variable Marker field.

2. Next, enter the variable's definition **CommTerm** in the Substitution Text field. Before you commit the definition, if you wish, you can edit either of these fields.

3. Click **Add** to define the variable.

4. You can define additional variables as in the previous step or click **Close** when done.

Figure 6.21
Choose the variable name to insert.

Inserting a Variable

Let's insert a variable:

1. Make certain that you have either the Tagged Text tool or the Freehand Text tool selected. Place the insertion point at the location that you wish to place the variable.

2. Either right-click or select the Edit menu. Next, select the Insert Special Item>Variable Marker. The dialog box in Figure 6.21 is displayed. Click on your choice of variable names and choose the variable (in our case, **Product**).

   Corel Ventura allows you to enter a name that is not yet defined. Pretty neat, but a little dangerous in case you forgot which variables you plan to use.

3. Click OK and a little superscripted symbol is inserted at the insertion point: ⌐ . If you don't see this symbol, chances are you need to click on the Tabs and Returns checkbox in the View tab of the Preferences dialog under the Tools>Preferences menu.

   If you want to make certain that this is a variable reference, place the insertion point to the left of the symbol and you'll see a notation at the far right of the Status line: Reference .

   Hey! Wait a minute. How do we display the variable definition and not the variable reference symbol? There are some additional steps you must take.

4. Bring back the Variable Definitions dialog (under the Edit menu). See Figure 6.22.

5. Click Renumber (or Update, whichever is displayed in your Corel Ventura version), and you will be asked if you want to update references for the publication.

6. Click Renumber (if you click Cancel, Corel Ventura doesn't renumber the chapter, but instead terminates the request). If your publication has hundreds of pages, this may take a while.

Figure 6.22
Resolving variable
insertion markers.

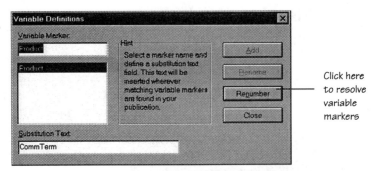

Click here
to resolve
variable
markers

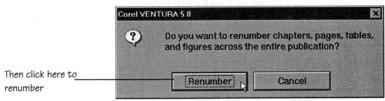

Then click here to
renumber

NOTE The vari-
able reference
symbol is still dis-
played next to the
variable's text.

The variable is properly resolved: CommTerm .

If you change the variable's definition later, you'll have to renumber the publication to show the change.

This is a real disadvantage that is a holdover from Corel Ventura's original implementation. This is frustrating because you would think that Corel Ventura would have the capability of "dereferencing" (oops, a programming term snuck in!) the variable's definition right *then and there*.

7 PUBLISHING THE BOOK

We're almost done. Now it is a simple matter of going to press. But hold on to your seats cause this stage can be more stressful than writing and illustrating the manual. We'll cover the following topics:

- Getting ready to print.

- Generating an index.

- Generating a table of contents.

- Printing.

- Archiving and updating your publication.

I'll present several situations of what can go wrong when going to press!

BUILDING YOUR PUBLICATION

Checking Your Publication

There are certain rules you should consider before going to press with your manual:

Check the spelling in your publication. If your DTP program's dictionary doesn't include words that are used frequently in your publication, add them to your DTP program's dictionary.

Chapters should always start on the right. Check that chapters start on right-hand pages (in other words, on odd numbered pages). If a chapter doesn't have an even number of pages, the document could easily get out of proper page alignment.

Validate that spot colors are correct. You can accidentally use more than one color in your publication even though you initially defined only a single spot color.

Print on a Postscript printer first. Failure to run a test print will, nine times out of ten, result in problems. What problems could occur? Some pages could be off-center, text may be clipped, text could be outside a drawing object's boundary, and fonts may appear in your document that you never intended to use.

Don't use Truetype fonts. Although Truetype is becoming a standard, don't assume that your printshop will have the proper imagesetting equipment that recognizes these fonts. You must validate that fonts used throughout your publication are those that you originally selected. A common problem is accidentally confusing Times New Roman (a standard Truetype font) with Times (the standard Type 1 font).

Unfortunately, some drawings that are to be used in on-line help graphics may have to be done in *both* formats: one version with Truetype fonts and the other with Type 1 fonts. On-line (or interactive) documentation cannot assume that users will have ATM installed on their computers.

Figure 7.1
A watermark behind
type.

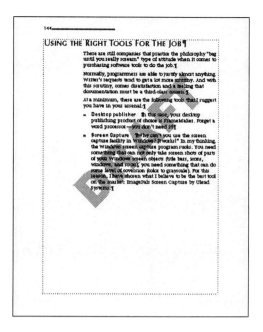

Inserting a Watermark

Before you release your draft documentation for review, you
could insert a watermark on each page. For example, we
could take one page and put the word DRAFT on it (Figure
7.1).

A watermark, regardless of the DTP program used, should
exhibit the following characteristics:

- Watermarks should be light enough (20 percent black)
  so as to not obstruct the reading of the text.

- Watermarks should be prominent enough so that they
  will show up when duplicated on a copier machine. This
  is especially true of documents marked CONFIDENTIAL.

- The watermark should be on every or every other page,
  not just on the first page of a chapter or manual.

Using FrameMaker

One of the many beauties of FrameMaker is how simple it
makes inserting a watermark.

Figure 7.2
Using the Master
page in
FrameMaker to add
a watermark.

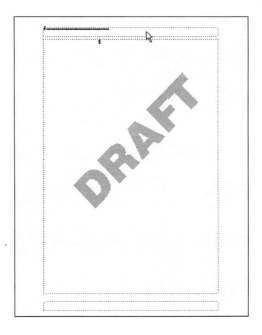

⊃ **View the master page.**
  Press View>Master Pages and select the Right master page.

⊃ **Enter your watermark.**
  Either type your text in the middle of the page using the
  Text tool, import the graphic file, or draw your object using
  FrameMaker's outstanding drawing tools.

  Don't forget to assign a tint of no greater than 20 percent
  black. You can select the tint for objects (files and drawing
  objects) with the Fill pattern pop-up menu.

⊃ **Copy it to the other master pages.**
  Select the watermark object and copy it to the clipboard
  (**CTRL+C**). Send it to the background of your text frame by
  selecting the Graphics>Send to Back menu command.

  Your master page should look like Figure 7.2. Copy the
  clipboard to your other master pages (Left, First, and so on)
  while making certain to Send to Back. If you wish to copy
  this to other chapters, you'll need to select the publication's
  book file (.FMB file extension) and then select
  File>Import>Formats and check the Page Layouts before
  clicking Import.

Figure 7.3
Set up and rotate a
watermark.

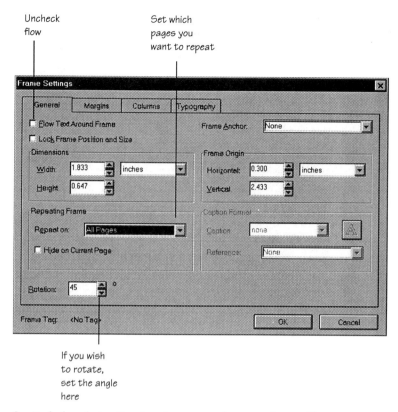

Uncheck
flow

Set which
pages you
want to repeat

If you wish
to rotate,
set the angle
here

Switch back to the body page view and you'll see your
watermark behind the body text.

Using Corel Ventura

You create a watermark much similar to a repeating frame.

1. Click the Frame tool and place on the page—this is a
   free frame (in Corel Ventura terminology). Don't worry
   if text you have displaced moves all around the frame—
   that is the default.

2. Select the Tagged Text tool in the frame and, with the
   insertion point selected, type in the text: **DRAFT**.

3. Select the text and change the text color to 20 percent
   black.

4. Select the frame and right-click to bring up the General
   tab in the Format dialog. Click the fields as shown in
   Figure 7.3 and click OK.

Figure 7.4
Add an Index
document to the
publication.

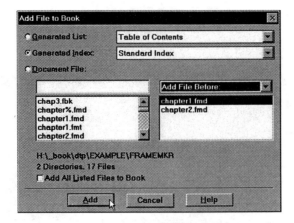

Corel Ventura uses a frame hierarchy that assumes all user-created frames cannot hide under the underlying text flow frame. So, be careful where you place the watermark since it will "ride on top" of your normal body text.

You may wish to place a watermark in the margins so that text and anchored graphics are not obstructed. In addition, you can always rotate the watermark to any angle as shown in Figure 7.3.

GENERATING AN INDEX

We've already shown how to create index entries (starting on page 143). To generate an index, follow these steps:

1. Set up the index generation formats.

2. Generate a sample index.

3. Reformat the index document to your liking.

4. Update the index before printing.

Now, let's go do it.

Figure 7.5
Setting up the index
file.

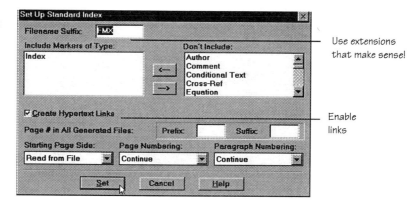

Use extensions
that make sense!

Enable
links

Using FrameMaker

Setting Up the Index Select the publication book file and highlight the first chapter (in our case CHAPTER1.FMD). Select File>Add File and, with the Add File to Book dialog displayed, click on Generated Index, Standard Index, and Add File Before. Click Add.

You will be asked to set up the index. FrameMaker shows the updated publication's index file as one of the files in the book. The + at the end of the name indicates that the file is generated.

You're not done yet. Select File>Set Up File. Change the Filename Suffix (the file extension) to **FMX** and click Set, as shown in Figure 7.5. The index file is saved in the publication's book subdirectory.

Select Files>Rearrange Files in order to move PUB.FMX to the bottom of the publication's book list.

Generating the Index Select File>Generate/Update to display the dialog in Figure 7.6. Click Update.

Figure 7.6
Generate the index.

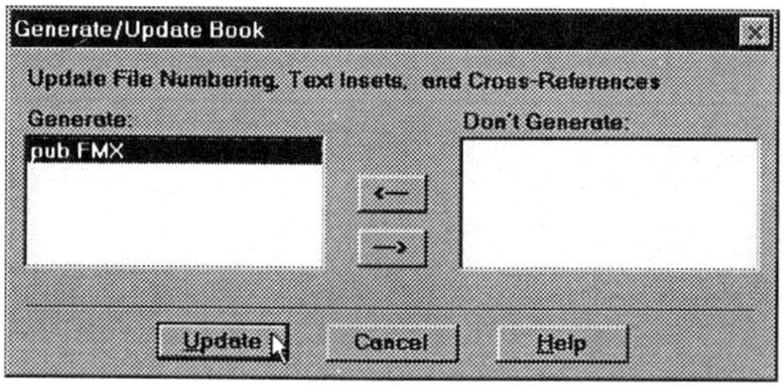

Figure 7.7
Frame's generated
index

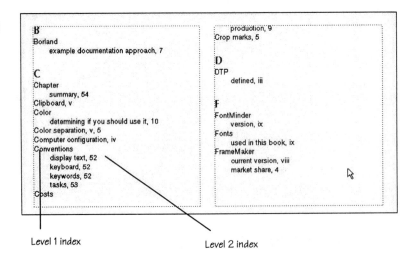

Level 1 index   Level 2 index

This same step is used when updating the index at any time (not just this *first* time).

Reformatting the Index Document Unfortunately, the index design that I like is a little more sophisticated. Indexes entries look like those shown in Figure 7.7.

The problem is that your choice of font characteristics may not match anything in this example. So, how do you change it?

Figure 7.8
Using the reference
page.

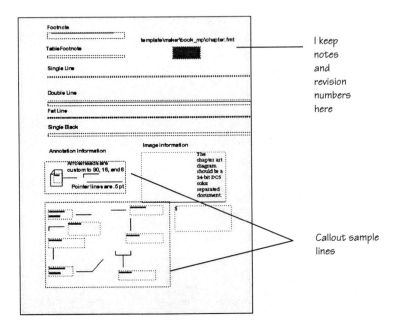

Figure 7.9
Using the index
building block.

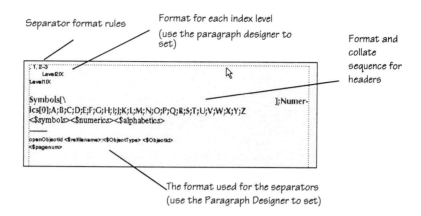

Separator format rules

Format for each index level
(use the paragraph designer to set)

Format and collate sequence for headers

The format used for the separators
(use the Paragraph Designer to set)

Index formatting instructions are defined on a special reference page. Select View>Reference Pages to view the first reference page.

The reference page I use is shown in Figure 7.8. I have defined the name of the template, the version number of the template, border lines that can be attached to paragraph styles, and callout objects composed of .5 pt lines and associated callout text.

The first time you generate an index for a publication, a special reference page (normally named IX) is generated by FrameMaker to define how index entries are formatted. Press the **PAGE DOWN** key until the reference page IX is displayed (Figure 7.9). (You'll know by looking for the name in the Status bar.)

Each of these text lines is assigned a specific paragraph tag name that you can modify if you don't like the style chosen by FrameMaker.

NOTE Index paragraph tags generated by FrameMaker all end with IX.

Although there are several index styles you can modify, the most important ones are the separator formats (paragraph style SeparatorsIX), the index level formats (paragraph styles Level1IX, Level2IX, and so on), and the group title letters (paragraph style GroupTitlesIX).

The page number format is the page format you defined in each chapter. So, if your publication has a preface that uses roman numerals, the generated page numbers will also be in roman numerals.

Figure 7.10
An index entry where
the page number
font is still too large.

*Oops! Where
did this font size
come from?*

The other styles have to do with collating sequences and other elements that you shouldn't have to care much about.

Here are the paragraph tags that you need to modify:

NOTE Do not check Leave Room for Side Heads in Flow in the Pagination properties.

GroupTitlesIX Basic: All indents to 0", space above 14 pt, line spacing fixed at 13 pt. Default Font is Optima 12 pt with the spot color (or black). Pagination: Keep with next paragraph.

I've defined three different levels (or hierarchies) of indexes—you'll probably use two at most. In FrameMaker, each level has its own paragraph tag that is generated automatically when the index file is generated.

Level1IX Basic: All indents set to 0" (except the Left which is set to .25"), Space above and below to 0 pt, line spacing 10 pt fixed, and left-justified. Default Font is Helvetica Neue (55) 8 pt. Pagination: Keep with next paragraph.

Level2IX Same as Level1IX, but set the first indent to .25", left indent to .50", and do not keep with next.

Level3IX Same as Level2IX, but set the first indent to .50" and left indent to .75".

Modify these styles to your liking, save the index file, and then regenerate the index. You may have noticed that I like to insert a comma after the index entry and before the page number (FrameMaker doesn't assume that).

When you look at the regenerated index file, you may notice that the page numbers are too large (Figure 7.10). To fix this, change the SeparatorsIX paragraph tag (the first line in Figure 7.9) font attributes then regenerate the index.

SeparatorsIX The only paragraph information that is used during the index generation process is the Default Font information. I define this tag to be the same font as the other index tags: Helvetica Neue 55 8 pt.

We have one last step to take. The index page needs to be changed to two columns.

1. In the index file, select Format>Pages>Normal Page Layout.
2. Change Columns Number field to **2**.
3. Press Set.

Adding a Title Text that doesn't use any of the generated paragraph tag names, FrameMaker leaves alone. I've added a chapter title, **Index**, using the Chapter paragraph style before the generated paragraph tags. The next time you generate an index, your title remains. This applies to body text, headings, sideheads, and so on.

Save the index file once you have it properly designed. The formats that you have saved will be maintained even for future indexes since FrameMaker searches for an existing index file in the publication's book and uses those paragraph tags or layout definitions.

Updating an Select the book file that points to each of the chapters, table
Index of contents, and index. Click on the File>Generate/Book menu command. Click Update. A dialog asking which files to regenerate is displayed (Figure 7.6).

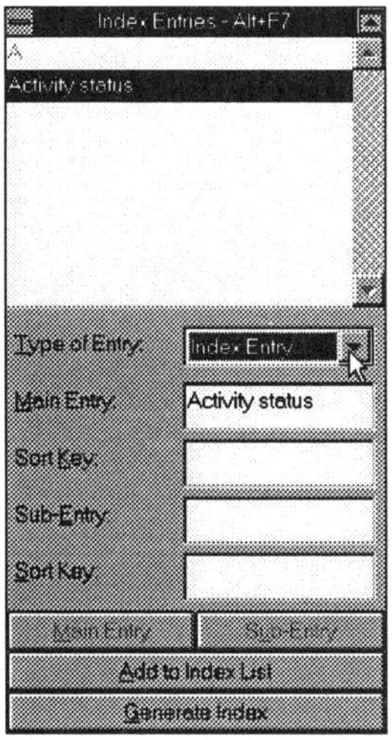

Figure 7.11
You can do
anything with
indexes with the
Index Entries Roll-Up.

Using Corel Ventura

Setting Up the Index If you haven't already been viewing index entries with the Index, press **ALT+F7** to display the Index Entries Roll-Up. See Figure 7.11.

As you build your publication, you can scroll through and see a formatted list of index entries that are currently defined in your entire publication.

Generating the Index Click the Generate Index button in the Index Entries Roll-Up (or select the Index tab from the Format>TOC & Index menu).

Figure 7.12 shows the fields you should set before generating the index. Once you select your index formats, these settings are automatically saved in the publication file. Click on Generate. You will be asked a number of questions for the generated index file. Use the default .GEN file extension and save it in a filename in your publication's PUB subdirectory (I like IDX.GEN).

Figure 7.12
Setting up and generating the index.

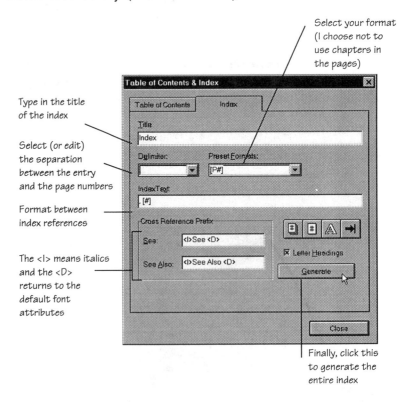

Select your format (I choose not to use chapters in the pages)

Type in the title of the index

Select (or edit) the separation between the entry and the page numbers

Format between index references

The <I> means italics and the <D> returns to the default font attributes

Finally, click this to generate the entire index

Figure 7.13
Loading the index
file.

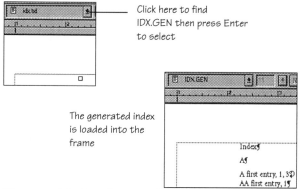

Click here to find
IDX.GEN then press Enter
to select

The generated index
is loaded into the
frame

If you wish to change the format without regenerating a
new index, click on Close.

Although you can add a generated index file to a page at the
end of an existing chapter, I recommend that you add
another chapter just for the index.

Select Layout>Add New Chapter, and Corel Ventura will
create UNTITLED.CHP. Click Layout>Save Chapter As and,
in the publication's subdirectory (PUB), rename the file as
IDX.CHP.

Using the Pick tool, click on the chapter frame. Select
File>Load Text File. Browse till you see IDX.GEN and click
on it. You could be presented with an upsetting screen that
has no text or index displayed (Figure 7.13). What do you
do now?

The trick is to use the file list pull-down. You may have
noticed that the text file IDX.TXT is selected. Corel Ventura
assumes that every chapter has a default text file with the
same filename as the chapter.

Click on the file list and select the generated index file
IDX.GEN. Press **ENTER**. Whew! Save the index file before
continuing.

Reformatting The index file, by default, assumes the same style sheet as
the Index the rest of your chapters. The first order of business,
therefore, is to save a new style sheet. Click the Save File
Sheet As menu command in the Layout menu. In your
publication's TEMPLATE subdirectory, save the style sheet
as INDEX.STY. Now, any changes you make will be reflected
in that style sheet (and not in the rest of your chapters).

Figure 7.14
Set the two-column
index page.

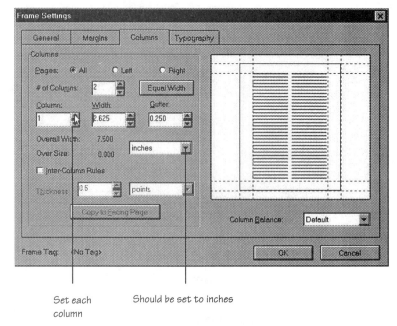

Set each
column

Should be set to inches

Let's assign the index to a two-column format. Click on the frame with the Pick tool and then right-click. From the frame menu choices, select Frame>Columns and, with the dialog shown in Figure 7.14, set the # of Columns to **2**, click the Equal Width button, and set the correct inter-column spacing (Corel Ventura uses the term Gutter).

NOTE Make sure that the measure is set to inches.

Each column can have its own gutter to the right of the column boundary. Select Column 1, make certain that the width is set to **2.625**, and set the Gutter to **.250**. Select Column 2, make certain that the width is set to **2.625** (equal widths, remember?), and the Gutter is set to **0"**. (Column 2's Gutter field may be grayed out to 0".)

When you are done, click OK.

You can now modify the three generated paragraph tags that are used for the title, letter heading, and the index entry. Unlike FrameMaker, Corel Ventura only defines one level of index paragraph tag. This single tag is used to define both main (level 1) indexes plus subentries.

View the index file with Tabs and Returns checked (enabled within the View tab of the dialog displayed by selecting the Tools>References menu).

Figure 7.15
Corel Ventura's one big paragraph index.

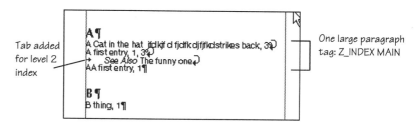

Tab added for level 2 index

One large paragraph tag: Z_INDEX MAIN

You'll see that all the entries under a single alphabetic character (A, in Figure 7.15) are one long paragraph with forced line feeds after every index entry. Second level indexes are preceded with a tab.

The paragraph tag definitions are as follows:

Z_INDEX TITLE   Character: StoneInformal Semibold 36 pt black. Alignment: Left-justified with Line Break After and Keep With Next Paragraph checked. Spacing: Paragraph indents Left and Right both set to 0", Above and Below set to 0 pt, and Inter-line to 43 pt. Defaults and Typography set to default values.

NOTE   This is sometimes set to a spot color.

Z_INDEX LTR   Character: Optima bold 12 pt, black. Alignment: Left-justified with Line Break After and Keep With Next Paragraph checked. Spacing: Paragraph indents Left and Right both set to 0", Above set to 14 pt, Below set to 0 pt, and Inter-line to 13 pt. Defaults and Typography set to default values.

Z_INDEX MAIN   Character: Helvetica Neue (55) 8 pt, black. Alignment: Left-justified with Line Break After and Keep With Next Paragraph *un*checked. Spacing: Paragraph indents Left and Right both set to 0", Tab added at .25", Above set to 0 pt, Below set to 0 pt, and Inter-line to 10 pt. Defaults and Typography set to default values.

Save your index file so that the next time Corel Ventura generates the index for you, these paragraph tag definitions remain in effect.

Updating the Index   From any chapter in the publication, you can select the Format>TOC & Index menu command. (You may also click on the Generate Index if the Index Entries Roll-Up is currently displayed.) Using Figure 7.12 as a guide, click the Generate button.

When asked if you would like to save the publication (or any other files), click OK.

After the index file (IDX.GEN) is generated, click **OK**. The index file should already be properly updated and installed in your IDX.CHP chapter file.

GENERATING A TABLE OF CONTENTS

Generating a table of contents is not much different than generating an index. You should follow these steps:

1. Set up the table of contents generation formats.

2. Generate a sample table of contents.

3. Reformat the table of contents document to your liking.

4. Update the table of contents before printing.

Using FrameMaker

Setting Up the Table of Contents Select the publication book file and highlight the first chapter (in our case CHAPTER1.FMD). Select File>Add File and, with the Add File to Book dialog displayed (Figure 7.16), click on Generated Index, Standard Index, and Add File Before. Click Add.

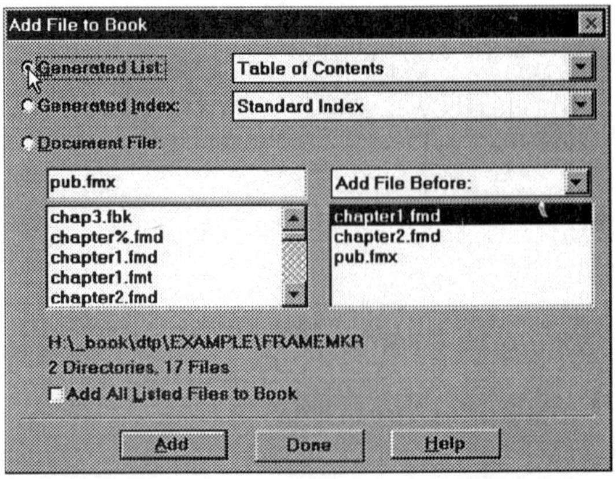

Figure 7.16
Creating a table of contents file in your publication.

Figure 7.17
Selecting the
paragraph tags to
be used in the table
of contents.

These paragraph
tags will
be used to
generate a table
of contents

First, type
in extension

Highlight paragraph tag and
move to include (or not include)

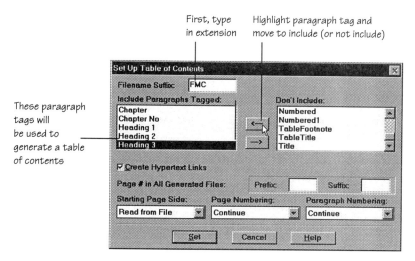

Next, you'll be asked to set up the table of contents file itself (Figure 7.17). Enter a better filename suffix than IX (I like **FMC**) and then click on the paragraphs you wish to include in the order of hierarchy.

I used four levels of headings in this book. You may choose to use the fourth (or fifth) level as a descriptor that will not be included in the table of contents.

The publication's book file now has the generated table of contents file (the + signifies that the file is generated). See Figure 7.18. Save the book file.

Generating a Table of Contents Select the book file that points to each of the chapters, table of contents, and index. Click the File>Generate/Book menu command.

A dialog asking which files to regenerate is displayed (Figure 7.19).

FrameMaker assumes that the generated files (table of contents and index) are to be processed. Click Update.

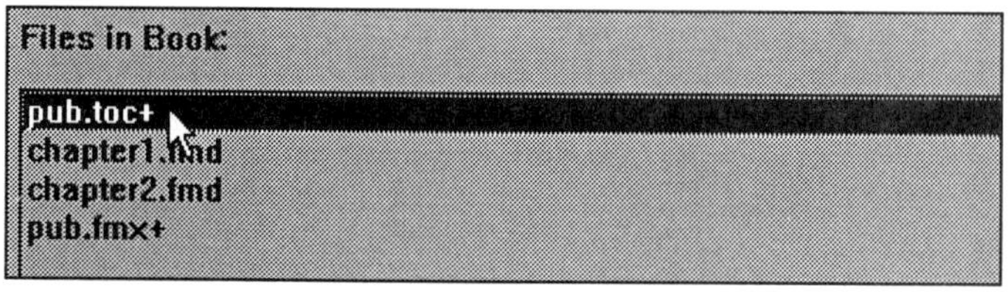

Figure 7.18
Publication now
includes the table of
contents.

Files in Book:

pub.toc+
chapter1.fmd
chapter2.fmd
pub.fmx+

Figure 7.19
Generating the
table of contents.

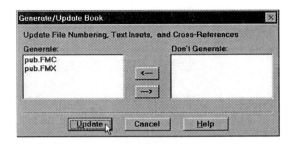

Reformatting the Table of Contents

Unfortunately, FrameMaker doesn't know how to apply the look that we want automatically. See Figure 7.20.

Table of contents paragraph tags generated by FrameMaker all end with TOC. In fact, the paragraph tag names that you included are used as part of the name (Figure 7.17).

Here are the paragraph tags that you'll need to modify:

NOTE Check Leave Room for Side Heads in Flow in the Pagination properties.

Chapter NoTOC   Basic: All indents to 0", space above 13 pt, below 0 pt, line spacing fixed at 0 pt. Default Font is StoneInformal 14 pt with spot color (or black). Pagination: Keep With Next paragraph and Side Head-Alignment at First Baseline. This normally is set to the paragraph tag used for the chapter number (paragraph tag Chapter No).

NOTE This is typically set to a spot color if you are using one.

ChapterTOC   Basic: All indents to 0", space above and below set to 0 pt, line spacing fixed at 17 pt, right tab set to 4.25" with no leader. Default font set to Optima Bold 14 pt. Pagination: Keep With Next paragraph, and Format set to Normal. This is the Chapter paragraph tag.

Heading 1TOC   Basic: All indents to 0", space above and below set to 0 pt, line spacing fixed at 12 pt, right tab set to 4.25" with ... leader (Figure 7.21). Default font set to Optima 10 pt. Pagination: Uncheck Keep With Next paragraph, and Format set to Normal. This is used for Heading 1.

Heading 2TOC   Same as Heading 1TOC, but set the first indent to .25" and the left to .50". This is used for Heading 2.

Heading 3TOC   Same as Heading 2TOC, but set the first indent to .50" and the left to .75". This is used for Heading 3.

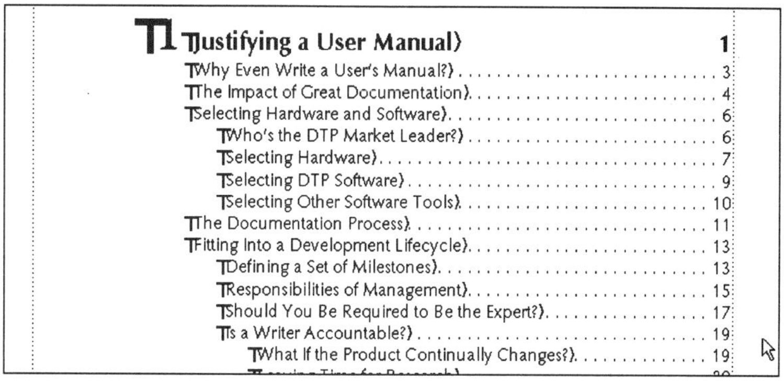

Figure 7.20
The generated table
of contents.

The first time you generate a table of contents for a publication, a special reference page (normally named TOC) is generated by FrameMaker to define how the table of contents is to be formatted.

Press the **PAGE DOWN** key until the reference page TOC is displayed (Figure 7.22). You'll know by looking for the name in the Status bar.

You can update the format by replacing the space with a tab between <$paratext> and <$pagenum> as I did. FrameMaker assumes that each generated table of contents entry and its page number are separated with a space.

The page number format is the one you defined in each chapter. So, if your publication has a preface that uses roman numerals, the generated page numbers will also display roman numerals.

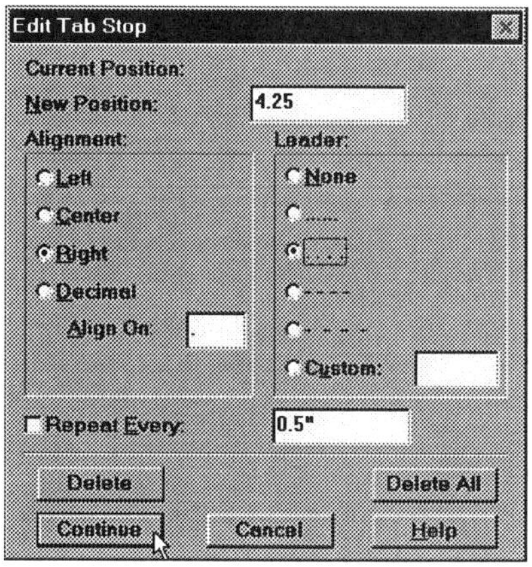

Figure 7.21
Leader used for tabs
in table of contents.

Figure 7.22
The TOC reference
page.

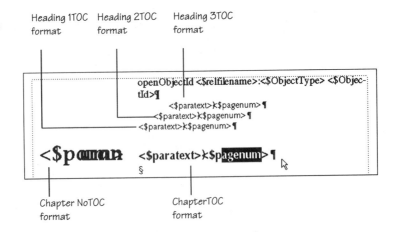

Heading 1TOC format

Heading 2TOC format

Heading 3TOC format

openObjectId <$relfilename>:<$ObjectType> <$Objec-tId>¶

<$paratext>\<$pagenum>¶

<$paratext>\<$pagenum>¶

<$paratext>\<$pagenum>¶

<$pagenum>

<$paratext>\<$pagenum>¶

§

Chapter NoTOC format

ChapterTOC format

Adding a Title FrameMaker does not modify any text not assigned to one of the generated paragraph tag names. The tag names may look odd but they are simply your tag names plus TOC. I've added a chapter title **Table of Contents**, using the Chapter paragraph style before the generated paragraph tags. The next time you generate an index or table of contents, your title remains. This applies to body text, headings, sideheads, and so on.

Once you have set the format properly, save the table of contents file.

Updating the Table of Contents Select the book file that points to each of the chapters, table of contents, and index. Click on File>Generate/Book menu command. Click Update.

Using Corel Ventura

Generating the Table of Contents From any chapter in a publication, you can generate the table of contents either by selecting Format>TOC & Index or by clicking on Generate Index from the Index Entries Roll-Up. Select the Table of Contents tab (see Figure 7.23). We'll select five levels, the title (Table Of Contents), and we'll set each level.

Click on Level until the 1 appears. Select the reference tag Chapter No, and the Table of Contents Text field is automatically displayed as the reference tag surrounded by brackets (such as [*Chapter No]).

Figure 7.23
Configure a table of
contents.

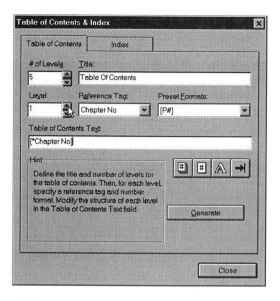

This means that when the table of contents is generated,
every time the tag Chapter No is encountered, a level 1 TOC
entry is formatted with the attributes of that tag. We have
defined it so that there is no page number generated,
because our level 1 tag is actually the chapter number.

Click on each tab level in order to select the format for each
level. Our second level is shown in Figure 7.24.

Once you select the level and the Reference Tag fields, place
the cursor in the Table of Contents Text field. With the aid
of the insert format buttons to the right, you can construct
the format for the generated text. In this case, we've
followed the assumed text contents of paragraph tag
Chapter with a tab and the page number.

Figure 7.24
Setting another level
table of contents
format.

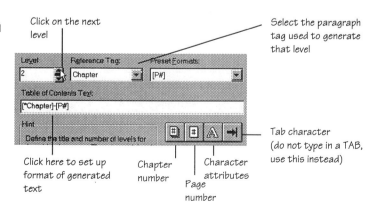

Click on the next level

Select the paragraph tag used to generate that level

Tab character
(do not type in a TAB,
use this instead)

Click here to set up
format of generated
text

Chapter number

Page number

Character attributes

This same format will be used for levels 3, 4, and 5. Level 3 will use paragraph tag Heading 1, Level 4 will use Heading 2, and level 5 will use Heading 3. Heading 4, in our case, will not be used in the table of contents generation (although you could include it if you increased the number of levels to 6).

Click the Generate button (depending on the size of your manual, this could take a while). Next, click on Close to return to your document.

Select the Add New Chapter menu command (in the Layout menu) and click on the underlying page frame so that the whole document page has handles.

Select the TOC.GEN from the File>Load Text menu and you have created the table of contents file. Although you could have added the table of contents to an existing chapter, it always makes sense to segment your publication into distinct publication files.

Before going further, let's save two important files. First save the style sheet as a new one using Layout>Save Style Sheet to file TOC.STY in your TEMPLATE subdirectory.

Finally, save the generated file as a chapter in your publication as file TOC.CHP in your PUB subdirectory with the Layout>Save Chapter As menu command.

Reformatting the Table of Contents You have generated the file, so now it should be reformatted and the associated style sheet with this reformatting information saved.

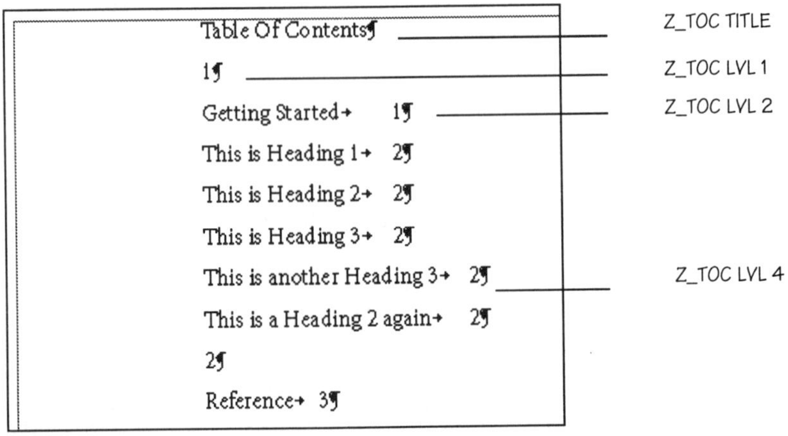

Figure 7.25
The generated table of contents file (paragraph tags shown).

Table Of Contents¶	Z_TOC TITLE
1¶	Z_TOC LVL 1
Getting Started→ 1¶	Z_TOC LVL 2
This is Heading 1→ 2¶	
This is Heading 2→ 2¶	
This is Heading 3→ 2¶	
This is another Heading 3→ 2¶	Z_TOC LVL 4
This is a Heading 2 again→ 2¶	
2¶	
Reference→ 3¶	

Look at a portion of our sample generated table of contents document (Figure 7.25), and you'll see that each level of text includes the information that you originally set up along with a unique paragraph tag.

The paragraph tag information for each of these generated items is detailed here:

Z_TOC TITLE Character: StoneInformal Semibold 36 pt black. Alignment: Left-justified with Line Break After and Keep With Next Paragraph checked. Spacing: Paragraph indents Left set to 1.25" and Right set to 0", Above and Below set to 0 pt, and Inter-line to 43 pt. Defaults and Typography set to default values.

NOTE If you wish to use spot color, the Z_TOC LVL 1 entry should be set to it.

Z_TOC LVL 1 Character: StoneInformal Semibold 24 pt, black. Alignment: Left-justified with Line Break Before, In Line With Previous Paragraph, and Keep With Next Paragraph checked. Spacing: Paragraph indents Left set to 0", Right set to 0", Above set to 13 pt, and Inter-line, Inter-Para, Below *must* be set to 0 pt. Defaults and Typography set to default values. This paragraph is used exclusively for the chapter number.

Z_TOC LVL 2 Character: Optima Bold 14 pt, black. Alignment: Left-justified with Line Break After and Keep With Next Paragraph unchecked. In addition, the *first* tab is set (delete all of the others) to right-justified 5.5". Spacing: Paragraph Indents Left set to 1.50", Right set to 0", Lines to Indent to 1, and Indent Amount to -0.250", Above set to 0 pt, and Inter-line, Inter-Para, set to 0 pt, and Below set to 17 pt. Defaults and Typography set to default values. This paragraph is used exclusively for the chapter name.

Z_TOC LVL 3 Character: Optima 10 pt, black. Alignment: Left-justified with Line Break After and Keep With Next Paragraph unchecked. In addition, the *first* tab is set (delete all of the others) to right-justified 5.5". Spacing: Paragraph Indents Left set to 1.50", Right set to 0", Lines to Indent to 1, and Indent Amount to -0.250", Above and Below set to 0 pt, and Inter-line, Inter-Para set to 0 pt, and Below set to 12 pt. Defaults and Typography set to default values. This paragraph is used exclusively for the first level heading (the Heading 1 paragraph tag).

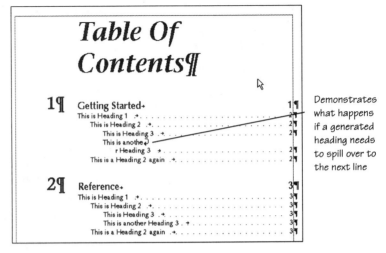

Z_TOC LVL 4 Same as Z_TOC LVL 3, but set the Paragraph Indents Left to 1.75". This is used for Heading 2.

Z_TOC LVL 5 Same as Z_TOC LVL 3, but set the Paragraph Indents Left to 2.0". This is used for Heading 3.

After you've set the paragraph tags of the generated table of contents file (TOC.CHP), the document should look something like Figure 7.26. Save the table of contents chapter with **CTRL+S**. You should not have to change the format later unless you don't like your paragraph tag definitions.

Updating the Table of Contents You must generate table of contents and indexes separately with Corel Ventura. To generate a table of contents, select Format>TOC & Index (or click on Generate Index from the Index Entries Roll-Up).

Click on the TOC tab and then Generate. Depending on the size of your publication, this may take a while. The TOC.CHP document is automatically updated.

Click on Close when done.

If you have added any text to the file and applied different paragraph tags to it, they are lost forever. This also applies to changing the formatting of text. Corel Ventura "nukes" the entire text file and replaces it with the regenerated table of contents entries.

Figure 7.27
Generating a table of contents with a floating frame header.

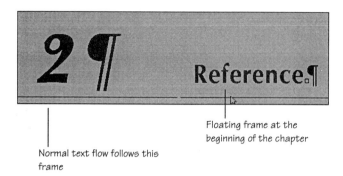

Floating frame at the beginning of the chapter

Normal text flow follows this frame

One final note—To see what happens to those chapters to which you have added a text frame at the beginning, filled with a background color, or inserted a heading as part of your generated table of contents, look at Figure 7.27. This shows an example frame that includes both the chapter number and the chapter title.

Corel Ventura does a great job of adding headings in separate frames into your generated table of contents document file. Unfortunately, it adds these references at the end of the list. So, the chapter number and chapter title would follow all of the headings in the chapter. You'd have to generate the table of contents and then edit the TOC.CHP text so that the chapter information would precede the headers. It's not a big deal, but it is time-consuming.

PRINTING THE PUBLICATION

There are several things that you should consider when you print:

- Will you use spot color?
- Should you generate comprehensive instructions?
- Which printshop will you use?
- How can you best monitor the printing process?

You should plan print sample runs on your own in-house laser printers with the goal to produce a file that is so complete that it can be used by your printshop without you having to explain your imaging, drawing, or DTP programs.

Once the file prints in house, you can deliver it to your printshop with all of the registration marks, text, fonts, graphics, and layout information required to create the film directly from the shop's imagesetting equipment.

This film is used as a master for subsequent printing of the final document (including spot color "runs") as many times as you wish.

Determining Color Use

I mentioned spot color briefly in Chapter 5. Spot color is interesting because it can be used as a highlight for documentation at key points, such as:

- Annotations in figures.
- Table backgrounds.
- Sideheads.
- Headings.
- Headers and footers.

Spot colors are usually primary colors: red, green, or blue. In fact, with all DTP products, black is treated as a spot color. Spot colors cannot be mixed with other spot colors, but you can usually define a spot color and black of varying tints and actually make two colors appear like many more colors.

NOTE The more passes a printer has to perform on your document, the more expensive it will be.

A two-color print job makes two passes on a page; 20 percent black, 50 percent black, and black all print in one pass since the depth of the color varies, but the color doesn't. The same is true with another spot color (like red).

For manuals, the use of more than two colors is usually a waste of money unless the product you are documenting has strong color content. For example, trying to document a graphics editor (like Adobe Systems Incorporated's Photoshop) without color leaves a lot to the imagination. Explaining the difference between 16, 256, and true color (16.7 million colors) without some color presentation is next to impossible.

Designing your manual with spot color is smart, especially if your DTP application allows you to optionally print colors as black (FrameMaker does). If you plan on using your publication as the source of on-line documentation, then color can be a real advantage to the user.

What about cost? If you plan it right and print enough copies to bring the per-book price down, one additional spot color (over black) may not be much of a cost premium; for example, printing a 300-page manual with two colors (black and one spot color) on high-quality paper with a four-color cover can cost as little as $6.50 for 1,000 books.

It doesn't have to cost a fortune!

Supplying only documentation with no on-line help will make your product look a outdated; on the other hand, providing just on-line help with no corresponding paper documentation makes your product look incomplete.

Today, users expect products to have context-sensitive help and paper documentation that a user can search through. Your manual should be able to be used for both paper and interactive material available from the program. If printed, however, there is some concern whether you should consider fast xerography, high-speed disk-to-paper printing (Docutech), or standard film printing.

Note that delivering documentation on an aggressive printing schedule while maintaining quality can sometimes be at odds, as shown in this chart:

	Quality	Time to print
Least favorite solution	Xerography	Film
	Docutech	Docutech
Best solution	Film	Xerography

There is always the cost to consider, too. If you intend only to print as needed, the Xerography method is the least costly investment. If you wish to manage your inventory better and print in larger quantities less often, going to film doesn't have to cost any more than the xerography or Docutech.

Printing a Sample

Follow the examples in the next sections based on the DTP program that you use. It is a good idea to print a small chapter to a file to give to your printshop in advance of release of your final product to make certain that the fonts, graphics, and target page size are all compatible.

Using FrameMaker

Let's assume that you've saved the publication and all of its files. Follow these steps to print:

1. Select the printer.

2. Set up the print options.

3. Print to a laser printer to review.

4. Print to a file.

Selecting the Printer

Although many of us use an HP LaserJet printer, when you go to print, you'll need to select a Postscript driver that your printshop recommends. The shop that I use recommends either the Agfa 9000 Postscript or the Linotronic 630 driver since their output imaging resolution closely matches the printshop's own equipment. By the way, most Postscript drivers are really the same—only some attributes are different (such as resolution, page handling, or page size). See Figure 7.28.

Figure 7.28
Selecting the printer.

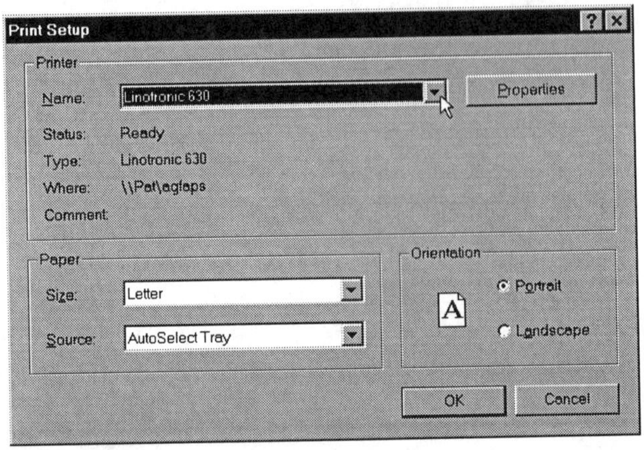

Figure 7.29
Setting printer
properties.

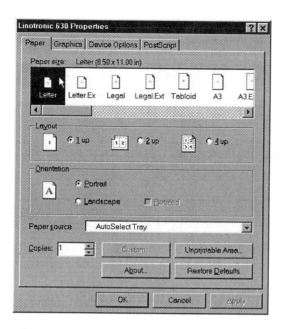

NOTE Don't forget
to ask your printshop
about paper size in
advance!

The **Paper Size** obviously is where you select the size paper that you'll use. Although you can select a size that is supported with your local laser printer, when you go to final printing, you'll need to use the size that your printshop recommends. As an example, select **Letter Extra** 9.5"x12" so that there is room for registration marks.

The Graphics tab presents resolution and halftoning options that you need to agree on with your printshop. Normally, you would choose 2438 dpi with a screen frequency of 120 and screen angle of 45. Click OK.

Set Up Your Printing Option

Make certain that all of the chapters are in the right book order (Figure 7.30). I like to place the table of contents and index generated files at the beginning and end, respectively.

Notice that I name the title and preface chapters a little differently than the body chapters. They have an underscore preceding their names because they use slightly different templates than the rest of the chapters.

You can click on File>Rearrange Files to move chapter files within a publication (or even to delete the publication's pointer to a chapter). See Figure 7.31.

Figure 7.30
Verifying that the files in the book are in the correct order.

Although it is not necessary for chapter numbers to precede each chapter name, doing so makes it easier to remember the chapter order. Earlier, we created a publication with the names CHAPTER1.FMD and CHAPTER2.FMD. This works fine as an example, but in real practice, FrameMaker replaces the eighth character in a filename with an autosaved special character (%) in case of a system crash. This save file can be loaded preserving your latest changes.

Select File>Print. You will be presented with a dialog with a list of the files in your document. Click on the document and then, with the appropriate arrow button, select which files you wish to print. See Figure 7.32.

FrameMaker keeps track of which files you printed, and the next time you print, the last list is maintained with your publication. Pretty neat.

Figure 7.31
Arrange chapters within a publication.

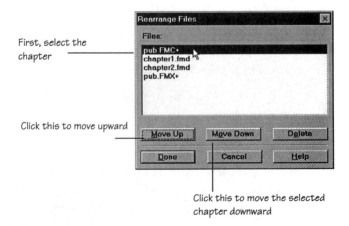

First, select the chapter

Click this to move upward

Click this to move the selected chapter downward

Figure 7.32
Specify which documents you wish to print.

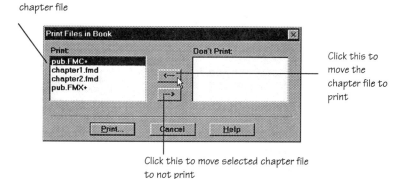

First, click to select the chapter file

Click this to move the chapter file to print

Click this to move selected chapter file to not print

Once you click Print, you'll be asked whether you wish to print all of the pages or just a range of pages (among other things). See Figure 7.33. Always check Registration Marks.

To print the document with any spot colors set to black, click on Spot Color As Black/White and click the Print button.

If you don't use spot color, simply skip this part and go to "Printing the Final Publication". Otherwise, if you wish to print one page per color, click on the Set Up Separations button and you'll be presented with yet another dialog.

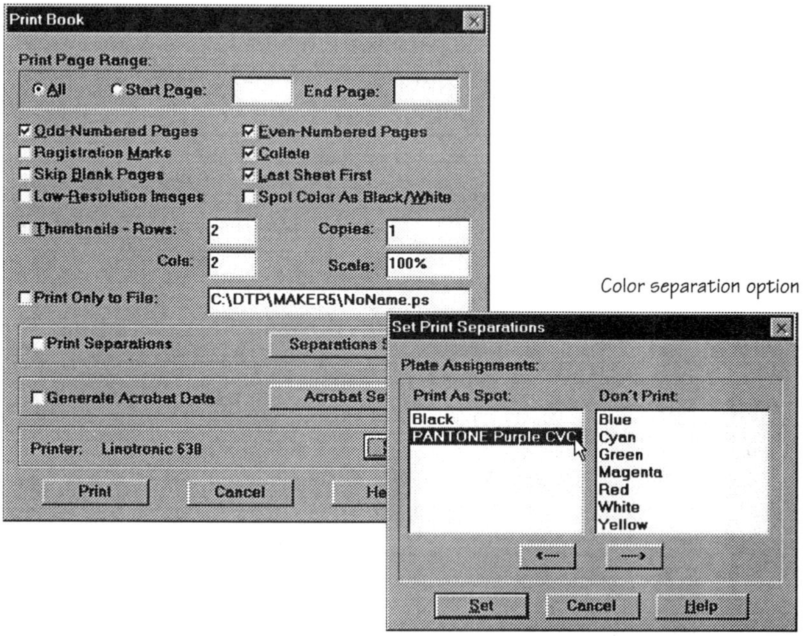

Figure 7.33
Printing the book with separations.

Color separation option

Figure 7.34
Creating a view-only document.

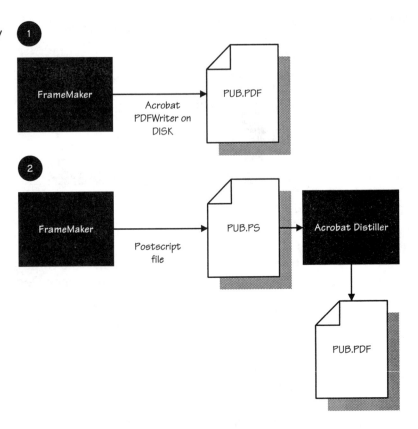

FrameMaker has a print option for the output of Acrobat files. Although you could always save a document to be viewed with FrameReader, FrameMaker now supports the ability to export a file to be read by Adobe Acrobat Reader. This is exactly what you can use to place your manuals on a CD.

NOTE You can distribute Acrobat Reader now without royalty fees.

Acrobat only displays .PDF (Portable Document Format) files created with either the Adobe Exchange or the Adobe Distiller package (Figure 7.34). You have two choices:

- Output a Postscript file to the device called **Acrobat PDF Writer**. This driver is available once you install Adobe Exchange. This driver will allow output files to be written in PDF format.

- If you have purchased Distiller, output a Postscript file. Using Distiller, convert the .PS (Postscript) file to a .PDF file.

Figure 7.35
Choosing the
hierarchy for the
Acrobat output file.

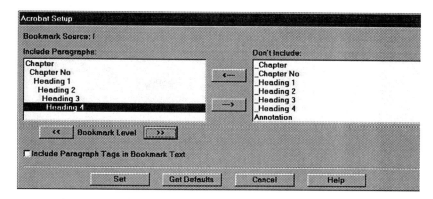

The advantages of the Distiller approach are:

- Distiller will do a much better job translating to a .PDF file if the document has EPS objects, complicated blends, and gradient artwork.

- You have the ability to convert any Postscript file so that it can be viewed.

- You have the ability to convert high-resolution graphics images.

- You have the facility to automatically construct bookmarks so that a user can traverse through a .PDF file randomly like a hypertext link. This feature is really an important one and Figure 7.35 shows how you construct a hierarchy for subsequent Acrobat access.

In any case, print with Registration Marks and Print Separations unchecked.

Printing the Final Publication

If you haven't displayed the print dialog yet, select the File>Print menu command. Click Print.

After the publication has printed, verify that each chapter and page numbering are correct. Also, verify that chapters start on odd-numbered page.

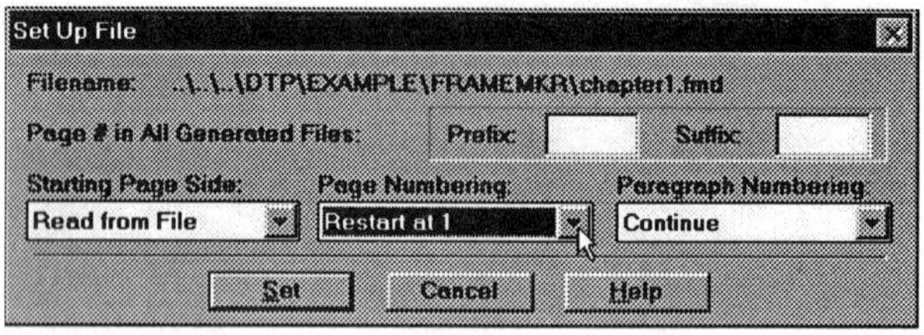

Figure 7.36
Setting page
numbering for a
specific chapter.

If a chapter restarts the page count, go back to your publication file, select the chapter, and click on File>Set Up File (Figure 7.36).

Make certain that the Starting Page Side is set to **Read from File** and that Page Numbering is set to **Continue** (the same with Paragraph Numbering). If you wish to force a chapter to start the page numbering as in Chapter 1, set **Page Numbering** to **Restart at 1** for that particular chapter file.

Once you have examined your laser print copies and you are satisfied, print the output to a file.

With the Print Setup menu command, select the Postscript printer that your printshop recommends. With the publication book file opened, click File>Print (Figure 7.37). Click on Print Only To File and enter a file name with a .PRN file extension. Click Print. Unless you use a fully qualified filename (like C:\OUTPUT\DTP.PRN), this file will be automatically printed to FrameMaker's FILTERS subdirectory (of all places).

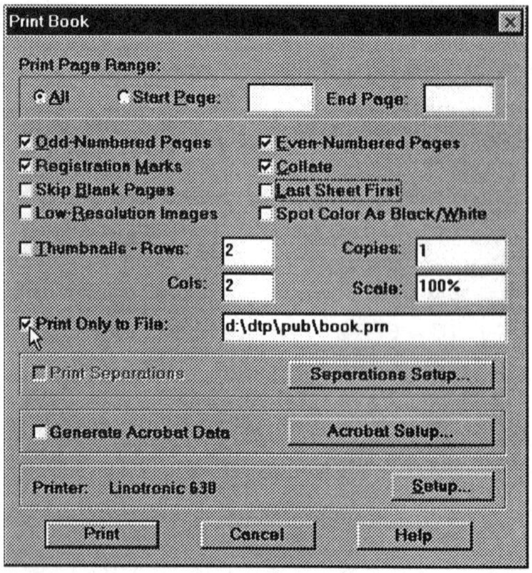

Figure 7.37
Printing your
publication for the
printshop.

Figure 7.38
Corel Ventura's print dialog.

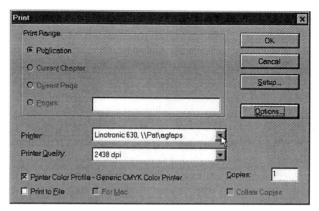

Using Corel Ventura

Selecting the Printer

Rather than just use the setup in the File>Print Setup menu, you can choose to set up the printer while you output the publication. You can combine the steps by clicking on File>Print Publication (Figure 7.38). Click the Setup button and select the printer device driver that your printshop recommends.

A printshop I use here in Texas prefers the Agfa 9000 imagesetter driver (1200 dpi) with a paper size of Letter Extra 9.5"x12". Don't forget to select a paper size that will hold the registration marks around your publication's target page size (in our case, 7.5"x9.25"). And, by all means, don't forget to try a practice mini-manual early in manual development.

Click OK when you have configured the printer device driver correctly.

Setup Printing Options

Make certain that all of the chapters are in the right book order.

Although the generated files (index and table of contents) don't need to be in a specific order, I like prefixing the chapters with the table of contents and ending the list with the index.

Figure 7.39
Selecting the print
options.

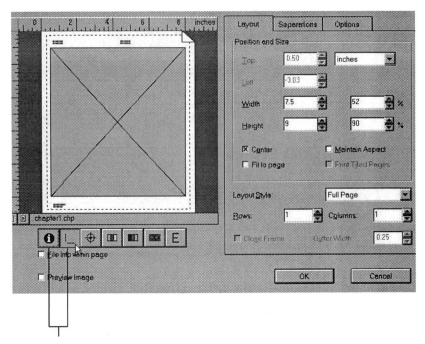

Enable these two buttons

The steps necessary to adjust the order of chapters are:

1. If you haven't already, close the Print dialog. Click File>Publications Manager and double-click on the publications filename (for example, DTP.PUB).

2. Select the chapter and drag up or down until you have the order desired. Close the Publications Manager dialog.

3. Select Format>Renumber Publication to readjust all figure, table, and page numbering information across the entire publication.

NOTE You can print just a chapter or a range of pages with the File>Print menu command.

If you haven't already done so, select File>Print Publication to display the Print dialog (Figure 7.38). Click the Options button to bring up the sophisticated printer options and click on the Layout tab.

Corel Corporation did an amazing thing by integrating the same print software already provided by CorelDRAW. So many of the layout, preview, and separation features of a great drawing program are accessible to your DTP program!

Figure 7.40
Setting the color
separations.

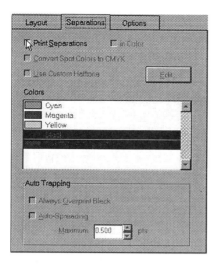

NOTE Your print-
shop may not want
the target page cen-
tered.

Depending on your requirements, check Center and make
certain that the Maintain Aspect is checked.

Do not check File info within page. Also, make certain that
Preview Image is checked and that you have enabled
registration marks and the page information buttons. This
places both the registration marks on the paper (and,
ultimately, on the film material) and indicates the color
(black or spot color) outside the target page boundaries.

Click on the Separations tab (Figure 7.40), check Print
Separations, and click on the colors you wish to print
(including, in this case, black and our one spot color
purple). If you have designed the publication to print in
black and at least one spot color, there is currently no way
to convert all spot colors to black in case you only wish to
print in black (FrameMaker has this feature).

Click OK, and with everything set, click OK in the Print
dialog. Once you print the document, inspect it for
accuracy before creating the final publication print.

Once you select OK in the Options dialog, Corel Ventura
maintains your choices so that you don't have to reset them
all the next time you decide to print.

Printing the Final Publication

Check that all chapters start on odd-numbered pages and

that the page numbers are correct. If not, you must go to the individual chapters and change the Numbering tab fields in the Layout>Chapter Settings menu.

NOTE Don't forget to select the correct Page Size by clicking on Setup.

Select the File>Print Publication menu command and select the correct Postscript printer and resolution that your printshop recommends. Check the Print to File box and you will be asked for the filename and the pathname—I'd recommend using a .PRN file extension.

Providing Specifications to the Printshop

Be smart and tell your printshop what needs to be done in writing as shown in Figure 7.41. The specification should hold all necessary information so that a printshop needs to successfully produce blue lines (sample master produced by the printshop from final film).

Figure 7.41
Printer specifications.

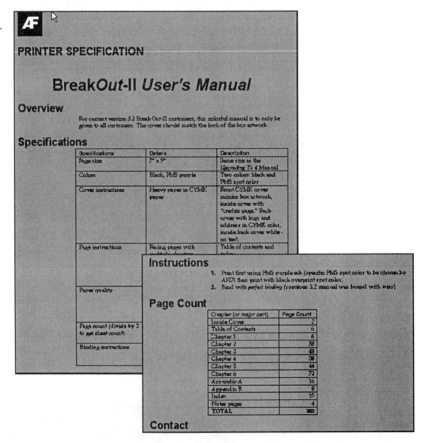

These are the items to include:

Overview   Brief summary of what the document is. A brief description will help to distinguish *your* document from all of the others submitted from other companies.

Print specifications   Specifying the paper size, weight, quantity, recycled information, header and gutter margins, page count, binding, and spot color will eliminate the need for a printshop's guessing what you really want.

Instructions   Specify the files you have provided and how to print spot colors (which spot color prints first).

Page count   I can't tell you how many times I've seen folks present documents in which several pages have been accidentally deleted. The printshop cannot be expected to know if pages are missing (even if there are missing page numbers). Make certain that you have provided exact page counts per chapter so that the printshop can validate prior to final printing (including blank sheets). Also, ask your printshop if the number of pages needs to be in groups of, say, 2, 4, or even 16.

Contact   Last, but not least, give your name, address, phone number, and fax number in case of trouble. Why fax number? Because if the work is done late at night and your company doesn't have an answering system, a fax may be the only way that the printshop can deliver (usually negative) feedback.

Managing the Print Process

Once you have printed to a Postscript print file, you will need to deliver it to your printer. Typically, this file is huge since it includes all the fonts and graphics used in your publication.

This file can then be compressed (using PKZIP or something equivalent) and backed up to diskettes, modemed (not recommended), or saved to a tape.

The Blue Line

At that point, your printshop will return to you the blue lines, which are sample masters printed with color separations combined onto one sheet (you can tell the difference since black will be pure black and spot colors will appear as a tint of the black). These blue lines are printed on a special paper that is produced from the real plates on the printshop's press. This paper usually loses its image with exposure to light.

You can make any minor corrections on the blue lines and return it to the printshop for final printing. Although it may cost you money, the best approach is to make modifications yourself—you should always have the master publication files that represent the final print job. Otherwise, it is easy to forget those late changes when you have to perform reprints or if you change printshops.

Managing Quality

A big lesson I've learned is to not depend on the printshop to make corrections and adjustments. You are relinquishing control of the process and placing unfair responsibility on the printshop to know what should be changed.

Most good printshops know how to provide check points at which the customer signs off on every step.

Make certain that you have a clause in the contract that provides for inferior print manuals to be returned at no cost. Don't pay until you verify that the quality is superior. Most printshops make you pay if they accidentally print too much *quantity*—you should have the same protection based on their *quality*.

BACKING UP A PUBLICATION

Using FrameMaker

By using subdirectory-relative file linking, the way that you move a FrameMaker publication to another location is to simply use the Windows File Manager (or Explorer). I have actually created a publication (DTP.FMB) including all templates, artwork, and generated files on one computer system under a directory like D:_BOOK\DTP under

Windows for Workgroups.

Figure 7.42
Backing up a
publication using the
Publication
Manager.

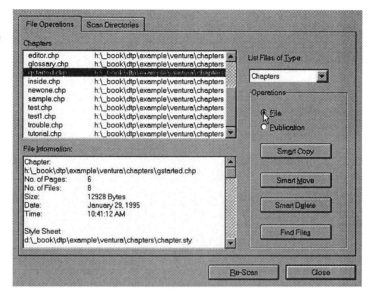

This computer's entire drive could be accessed by another computer as drive P using Windows 95. I started FrameMaker on this computer and opened the publication as D:_BOOK\DTP\DTP.FMB—and, surprisingly, the entire publication was accessible without a single change! This includes all drawings and screen shots.

This means that you can archive an entire publication by copying all of the files under a publication's directory onto a network server and use network backup facilities to handle the rest. If the publication is restored, it does not have to be restored under the same drive or with the same directory in which it was originally created.

Using Corel Ventura

Corel Ventura provides a mechanism to move a publication, although it does require some work. With any of the chapters open in your publication, select File>Publication Manager. The dialog looks like that shown in Figure 7.42 once you click on the File button (Publication is originally selected by Corel Ventura).

Click on **Smart Copy** and you will be presented with an outstanding mechanism to save your publication based on the type of file types.

Figure 7.43
Performing a Smart Copy.

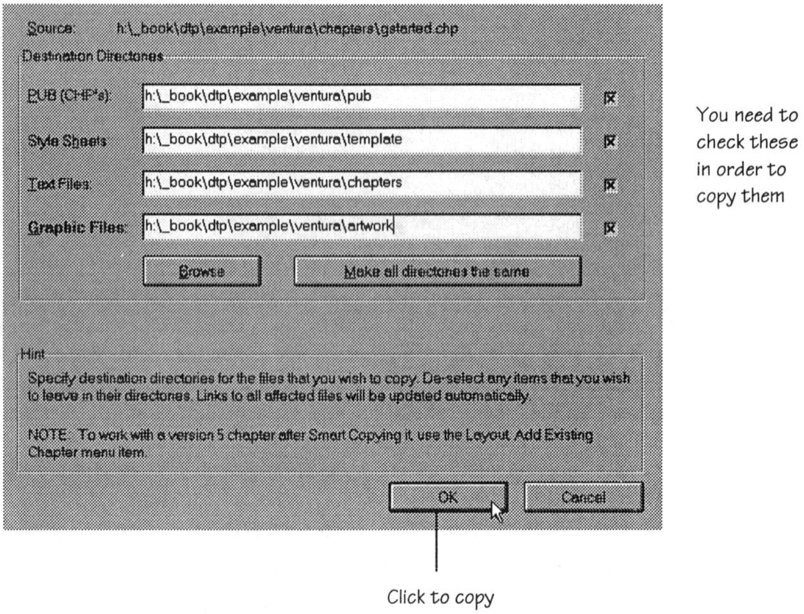

You need to check these in order to copy them

Click to copy

Although Corel Ventura's view of how files should be segmented (publication, chapters, style sheets, text files, and graphic files) is slightly different than our subdirectory segmentation presented throughout this book, the concept of dedicating certain subdirectories for certain information is very similar.

NOTE The same instructions apply if you wish to perform a Smart Move.

Set up the subdirectories and click OK to copy. I've made the subdirectories the same except for the final subdirectory, which I changed to PUB, TEMPLATE, CHAPTER, and then ARTWORK.

Backing Up with Tape Backup Units

The Microsoft Backup utilities are fairly cumbersome to use (if not darn confusing) although this has been greatly improved in Windows 95. If you are not taking advantage of network backup services, then purchase a parallel tape backup unit (such as the HP CMS Trakker 250 or Trakker 350). It is relatively inexpensive, widely used, and tapes are readily available.

I prefer the parallel port version (other than the internal version installed in your computer system). I have convinced several printshops to invest in them, also.

What about Graphic Files?

You've moved your publication and the DTP programs can access everything. Great! Did you forget that your cataloging programs (such as Ulead Systems' Album) has pointers to complete filename and pathname information. In other words, even though the catalog files themselves moved with your publication, the information about each file still assumes that the files are located in the original subdirectories!

All you have to do is relink all file references (Album menu command Thumbnail>Relink) once you move or restore your publication from backup media.

THE FUTURE OF INTERACTIVE PUBLICATIONS

In the February 13, 1995 issue of *PC Week*, an interesting headline was presented on page 8:

"Frame, Corel Move to Bring Desktop Publishing On-Line"

Further inspection of the article revealed that both companies have embedded SGML (Standard Generalized Markup Language) and HTML (Hypertext Markup Language) document output technology as standard output "filter converters."

NOTE FrameMaker already provides a proprietary viewer called FrameViewer.

Although HTML is basically a subset of the ever-languishing SGML standard that has been around in some form for years, the significance of this announcement lies in what it means for the future of electronic books.

HTML is the formatting language that incorporates hypertext and graphics information in a more structural technique not unlike the Postscript page layout language. HTML is the basis for on-line documentation used in on-line documents distributed on the Internet. It allows you to hop between topics rather than having to look at information one page at a time (for an entire publication, that could take forever).

HTML is so flexible and offers such great platform-independent text and graphics presentation capabilities that software application framework toolsmith vendors are starting to use it for their on-line help assistance technology. Inmark Development Corporation's outstanding zApp application framework's entire context-sensitive help system is based on HTML files (which can now be generated from both Corel Ventura and FrameMaker).

The next great frontier will place publications on-line in ways that allow the documents to be viewed using viewer software programs on most any operating system platform independent of that platform's font rendering technology (like ATM, TrueType, or even Bitstream's SPEEDO). Adobe's Acrobat is an example of such a viewer that reads Adobe's Portable Document Format (PDF) files generated by both Corel Ventura and FrameMaker.

It appears that both software vendors (Corel and Adobe) are driving fast to become the standard DTP program to produce both documentation on-line and on paper in most formats: PDF, HTML, and SGML. Viewers will be given away for free. I foresee the day when schools will replace books with CDs.

I also see the day when CD books include full-motion video and animation to make learning much more interesting than current book techniques. The opportunity to view and to ultimately purchase publications over on-line services such as the Internet is becoming a possibility in the near future.

In Closing

Thank you so much for *reading* this manual! I hope this helps you *write* spectacular manuals.

APPENDIX

Windows-Windows everywhere. Well, we've finally migrated from proprietary user interfaces and standards to comprehensive DTP offerings offered on Windows.

I've mentioned several products in this book and this appendix should serve as a resource to help you find them.

References to these products fall into the following categories:

- DTP Applications.
- Graphics Software Applications.
- Plug-In Applications.
- Font Suppliers.
- Magazines and Periodicals.
- Books.
- Hardware.

DTP APPLICATION PROGRAMS

RoboHelp
Blue Sky Software
1.619.459.6365

Although this isn't a DTP product, RoboHelp can provide many innovative ways to integrate documents, graphics, and multimedia into an application. So, if your fellow programmers need to create some interesting on-line help (either exported from your DTP program or created from scratch), RoboHelp is the ticket!

Corel Ventura
Corel Corporation
1.613.728.8200

Not only has Corel Corporation done a great job renovating Corel Ventura, it has an assortment of outstanding graphics products including CorelDRAW. We'll no doubt see more innovative integration of DTP and graphics technology in the future from this powerhouse company.

FrameMaker
Frame Technology Corporation
1.408.975.6000

The great thing about this program is that it executes on multiple platforms (Mac and Unix, too!). Interactive CD-based technology provider? This company really has a great plan. By the time you buy this book, Frame should be a part of Adobe.

GRAPHICS SOFTWARE PROGRAMS

Fauve Matisse and xRes
Fauve Software, Incorporated
1.415.543.7178 (1.800.898-ARTS)

This product has really taken off from the feature set released with version 1. It is easier to use than Painter and now with color separation support and lightning speed, this product is a winner.

This product could be called something like "Fractal Painter on Steroid." I can't say enough about the power of xRes. Since version 1, Fauve has definitely improved the product by focusing on advanced painting techniques coupled with all sorts of gradient fill effects that match some of the sophisticated drawing products.

ImagePals
Ulead Systems Incorporated
1.310.523.9393

This is the surprise software package of the decade. This unknown company was originally responsible for PhotoStyler and now it has added to its innovative creations with the latest release of a multimedia authoring tools: MediaStudio (which includes all of ImagePals functionality).

All screen shots in this book were taken with ImagePals' screen capture program, and all graphics (including Visio drawings) were archived using ImagePals' album program.

Painter
Fractal Design Corporation
1.408.688.8800 (1.800.297.2665)

Although very complicated to learn, there is virtually no artistic effect you can't produce using this product. The future of electronic art (and now with integrated multimedia support) is here with this outstanding product. With version 3.1 of Painter, you are able to convert layered artwork with Photoshop.

Photoshop
Adobe Systems Corporation
1.800.521.1976

This is the premier image editing program. I can't say enough about this outstanding product. Now that it has multiobject layering, it is just about perfect. The learning curve is tough, though. I particularly like the way that Photoshop and Painter products complement each other. (Should Adobe purchase Fractal? Hmm.)

Picture Publisher
Micrografx, Incorporated
1.800.289.6075

I've been working with the Windows 95 version of Picture Publisher and what strikes me most is the blazing speed. This product has always provided striking features and is highly regarded as a Photoshop competitor while being the first out specifically with Windows 95 support.

Visio
Shapeware Corporation
1.206.521.4500

If you haven't heard of it, then you haven't read this book carefully. Visio was invented by the man who brought you PageMaker. The drawings in this book were all done with Visio. If they added gradient color and the ability to color separate, then this product would be complete.

Along with ImagePals, Visio is a required tool for all writers.

PLUG-IN GRAPHIC PROGRAMS

Adobe Classic Art (series 1, 2, and 3)
Adobe Systems Corporation
1.800.521.1976

This series has become the standard set of high-quality plug-ins for all image editor programs.

The Black Box
Alien Skin Software
1.919.832.4124

This unusual and spectacular package includes a handful of useful plug-in filters that provide visual methods to include common features like drop shadows and embossing. In making the filters powerful, however, the technology has to be tuned for specific image editing programs. Thus, these magic filters work only on a select set of imaging applications.

Check with Alien Skin for its current list of supported products. At the time of this writing, the filters currently support Photoshop and Picture Publisher.

Kai's Power Tools and KPT Convolver
HSC Software Corporation
1.805.566.6200 (1.800.472.9025)

Named and created after HSC's legendary programmer/
designer, Kai Krause, these filters are spectacular and fun to
use. With the release of Convolver, you are visually rewarded
with new feature options as you get better at using the tool.

MAJOR FONT SUPPLIERS

Adobe Type On Call
Adobe Systems Incorporated
1.800.521.1976

NOTE Adobe
was one of the first
to supply fonts on
CD.

The only problem with Adobe's fonts are that they are still
distributed only in Type 1 format. Adobe should start
recognizing itself as the leading font maker and supply its
spectacular fonts for Truetype. Please?

Bitstream Fonts
Bitstream Incorporated
1.617.497.6222 (1.800.522.FONT)

Bitstream has always been my favorite font supplier. Years
ago when its Speedo font scaling technology could have
rivaled Adobe's ATM, they were on the brink of high growth.
I still prefer the wonderful Charter font. I would like to see
Bitstream become a real force in the font market. Bitstream
provides fonts on CD and with CorelDRAW.

ImageClub Fonts
Image Club Graphics Incorporated
1.800.661.9410 (1.800.387.9193)

These folks are great to deal with when you need something
overnight. Their clip art and fonts are first rate. ImageClub is
now part of Adobe.

Monotype Fonts
Monotype Typography Incorporated
1.312.855.9475 (1.800.MONOTYP)

Monotype has successfully transitioned from a font foundry
to an electronic font supplier. Monotype does an excellent

job of providing both Truetype and Type 1 font packages. It also supplies fonts on CD.

Don't forget that Corel Corporation has done an incredible service to its customers by incorporating a huge amount of fonts in its products. Most, but not all, of these fonts are name-brand, quality fonts.

SUPPORTING PERIODICALS

Corel Magazine
Omray Incorporated
1.800.856.0062

If you use CorelDRAW or Corel Ventura, you can't get along without this monthly magazine. Its design hints are just stupendous.

NADTP Journal
National Association of Desktop Publishers, Incorporated
1.617.380.3563

A professional organization involved in all aspects of the DTP world, it offers magazine, book, and product discounts.

Publish Magazine
Integrated Media, Incorporated
1.800.685.3435

Publish is a superb magazine. I once cancelled my subscription but found that after two months I suffered withdrawals and quickly resubscribed. I haven't been sorry since.

BOOKS

Bonura, Larry S. *The Art of Indexing.* New York, NY: John Wiley & Sons, Inc., 1994.

A book devoted to indexing publications that thoroughly covers everything you ever wanted to know about indexing, but were afraid to ask.

Burke, Chris. *Designing Business Documents.* Chicago, IL: Monotype Typography, Inc., 1992.

In less than 40 pages, you'll get page design and font metric fundamentals. An absolutely incredible book.

Gosney, Michael, John Odam, and Jim Benson. *The Gray Book.* Chapel Hill, NC: Ventana Press, 1990.

Looking for ideas for chapter art or your manual's cover? This book is the place to look. It is probably one of the best-selling of all graphics design books. You can truly learn a lot from this book.

Hackos, JoAnn T. *Managing Your Documentation Projects.* New York, NY: John Wiley & Sons, Inc., 1994.

If you are a new documentation manager or just need help understanding the documentation process, this book is for you. What I like most about it is that it is based on years of "hard knocks" experience. It makes a nice Christmas gift for your boss.

Parker, Roger C. *Looking Good in Print.* Chapel Hill, NC: Ventana Press, 1990.

This book is a great introduction to DTP layout and page design styles for newspapers, magazines, and brochures.

Whitaker, Ken. *Managing Software Maniacs.* New York, NY: John Wiley & Sons, Inc., 1994.

Yep, I wrote another book. If you want to help your organization treat documentation as a true development partner, read this book. There is also lots of helpful information on how to handle team and performance issues.

Miscellaneous Hardware

MiniTouch Keyboard
SIIG, Inc.
c/o Central Computer Systems, Inc.
1.408.241.0185

I can't say enough about this keyboard. It is two-thirds the size of a normal keyboard, its tactile feedback is great, and, if you don't have a lot of space on your desk, this keyboard is the answer.

Scanjet 3C
Hewlett-Packard
1.800.752.0900

I purchased the earlier model, IICX, and enjoyed extraordinary results, and now they have introduced model 3C. The HP color scanners provide superb quality results and are very easy to install.

Trakker
Colorado Memory Systems, Division of HP
1.800.752.0900

Desktop publishing jobs take many MB of space, sometimes in excess of 100 megabytes to include all of the images, drawings, and text. In fact, this book takes about 100MB. In order to back up a project, tape units work the best. The Trakker is one of the most cost-effective and widely recognized tape unit around. You can purchase the portable model that uses a standard parallel printer port interface so that you can hand off the unit to other writers. It can even back up files on a network.

INDEX

Symbols

.$HP file extension, 93
.CHP file extension, 70, 93
.FMB file extension, 65, 86, 276
.FMD file extension, 64, 85, 86
.FMT file extension, 65, 87
.GEN file extension, 284
.PDF file extension, 316
.PRN file extension, 310
.PS file extension, 304
.PUB file extension, 70
.STY file extension, 70
.TIF file extension, 166, 197
.WMF file extension, 161, 162

A

Acrobat, xvi, 304, 316
Active tense, 128
Adobe Acrobat *See* Acrobat
Adobe Distiller, 304
Adobe Exchange, 304
Adobe Systems Corporation, 320
Adobe Systems Incorporated, 44, 321
Adobe Type Manager (ATM), 44, 97, 274
Agfa 9000 imagesetter, 300, 307
Album, 157, 165, 315
Alien Skin Software, 8, 320
Annotation:
    paragraph tag, 120
Ares Software Corporation, 8
Artwork. *See* Graphics
AvantGarde, 100, 257

B

Backing up:
    in case of emergency, 66
    template files, 34

Backup files, 66, 314–315
Binding:
    as copy protection, 38
    for training material, 36
    paperback, 37
    perfect, 36, 57
    plastic comb, 36
    printshops and, 35–38, 311
    spiral, 37
    three-ring, 37
    types of, 35
    wiro, 37
Bitstream Incorporated, 321
The Black Box:
    current version, 8
    purchasing, 320
Blue Line, 311
Blue line, 10, 310
Blue Sky Software, 318
BMP, 166
Body page:
    switching to, 77
Body text:
    paragraph tag, 116
Books:
    purchasing DTP, 322
Borders and symbols:
    viewing, 68
Borland:
    example documentation, 48
Breaking on a page boundary, 134
Bulleted list, 124, 126, 127

C

Capitalizing:
    in headings, 132
Caption:
    bad design examples, 179
    figure, 121

good design examples, 181
CD, 3, 6, 57, 58, 304, 316
Change, handling of, 16
Chapter tab:
    creating, 75, 81
    located on odd pages, 71
    overview, 141
Chapter:
    adding to publication, 65, 70, 85
    choosing fonts, 100
    creating, 62
    deriving paragraph styles, 100
    end of symbol, 121
    number, 71, 139
    saving, 65
    settings, 82
    starting on even numbered pages, 274
Character tag:
    applying, 259
    color, symbols, and bullets, 254
    defining, 251, 258
    maintaining, 257
    removing a, 260
    software engineering, 256
    typographic, 257
    user-interface, 255
Charter, 321
Classic Art filters, 320
Clipboard, xvi, 85
CMYK, 197
COGS, 3, 56, 58
Color:
    determining if you should use it, 298
    in headings, 132
    in text. *See* Text
    separation, xvi, 5, 309
    See also Spot color
Columns:
    indexes, 147
    viewing the number, 87, 88
Conflicts in opinion:
    resolving, 17
Copy protecting with documentation, 38
Corel Corporation, 7, 318
Corel magazine, 25, 322
Corel Mosaic, 177
Corel Ventura:
    adding attributes to a frame, 194
    adding chapters, 70
    anchoring a frame, 191, 195
    assigning a frame tag, 195
    creating a publication, 66
    creating the footer, 79
    creating the header, 78

current version, 7
deriving paragraph styles, 100
disabling headers or footers, 78
drop cap, 264
Frame tool, 82
Freehand Text tool, 82
headings paragraph tag, 139
index generation, 284
Indexing, 151
inserting graphics in a line, 195
keeping paragraph with figure, 190
kerning, 261
knowledge of, 25
lists and run-ins, 126
moving a publication, 312, 313
pagination, 134
paragraph borders, 133
paragraph rules, 133
paragraph tag, 109, 119
placing repeated graphics, 174
pre-Corel (Xerox), 48
printing publication, 307–310
purchasing, 318
referencing a marker, 193
refreshing the screen, 195
removing a graphics frame, 195
setting margins, 67
snap to guides, 91
special paragraph tag, 122
style sheet, 116
table of contents generation, 292
text attribute codes in, 81
typographic symbols, 93
variables, 269
viewing facing pages, 77
watermarks, 277
CorelDRAW, 24, 25, 308, 318
Cost of Goods. *See* COGS
Courier, 50
Courier New, 50
Creating a publication, 65
Cross-references:
    inserting, 145
    overview, 143
    to a publication title, 144
Customer support:
    approving documentation, 39
    as the "real" customer, 2, 13, 53
    organization with, 13
    reviewing documentation, 15
Customer:
    getting feedback, 11
    knowing your, 22, 29
CYMK color model, 76, 165, 222

D

Dash:
    em, 49
    en, 49, 146
    non-breaking, 49, 146
DCS, 166
Development decisions:
    prioritizing, 18
Development goal, 14
Directories:
    to hold graphics, 157
Display:
    refresh the, 93
    refreshing, 91
Documentation:
    team forming, 11
Docutech printing, 299
DPI, 6
Drawing tools:
    using the DTP, 163
Drop caps, 262
DTP:
    books, 322
    defined, xv

E

Electronic book, xvi, 304, 315
Encapsulated Postscript, 161
Engineering:
    organization with, 13
    reviewing documentation, 15, 21, 22
EPS, 166, 170

F

Facing Pages:
    viewing, 73, 77
Fauve Matisse and xRes:
    purchasing, 318
Features needed for manual creation, 8
Figure:
    caption, 122, 123
    keeping with paragraph, 181
    numbering, 121, 186
Filename, 53
Filename extension, 53
Files:
    conventions used, 160
    in a publication, 34
    multiple per chapter, 34
    rearranging, 86, 89
    relative reference within document, 190
Film (imagesetter), 298
Film printing, 299

Font:
    angle, 96
    availability of high-quality, 6
    family, 96
    mixing during the final print, 274
    mixing families in the same paragraph, 255
    sans serif, 71
    used in this book, xix
    weight, 96
    See Also Truetype or Type 1
FontMinder:
    current version, 8
    overview, 24
Footer:
    different from headings, 134
    in page layout level, 42, 43
    paragraph tag, 141
Fractal Design Corporation, 319
Frame Technology Corporation, 7, 318
Frame:
    in page layout level, 43
    inserting an anchored, 195
    repeated, 72
    text around, 81
    tool, 82
FrameMaker:
    adding attributes to a frame, 190
    adding chapters, 86
    anchored frame, 189
    book, 65
    character tag, 258
    choosing, 24
    creating a chapter, 62
    creating a publication, 65
    creating the footer, 74
    creating the header, 73
    current version, 7
    dash and space support, 49
    deriving paragraph styles, 100
    drop cap, 262
    headings paragraph tag, 137
    importing formats, 87
    index generation, 279
    Indexing, 148
    kerning, 261
    lists and run-ins, 125
    manual, 129
    multiple graphic files in one frame, 190
    overriding a paragraph tag, 245
    paragraph designer, 102
    paragraph tag, 102, 118
    Pick tool using, 69
    placing repeated graphics, 171
    printing publication, 300–306
    purchasing, 318
    reference page, 85, 100

referencing a marker, 188
removing a graphics frame, 186
saving a chapter, 64
setting margins, 62
setting number counters, 107
setting the text flow, 63
sidehead creation, 62
Smart quotes, 64, 90
Smart spaces, 64, 90
snap to guides, 89
special paragraph tag, 121
spot color, 299
Status bar, 75
table of contents generation, 288
to top of a column, 247
to top of a page, 246
typographic symbols, 90
User Manual, 48
variables, 267
viewing color plates, 218
viewing facing pages, 73
watermarks, 275
FrameReader, xvi, 304
FrameViewer, xvi
Freehand Text tool, 82
Futura, 129

G

Generate a list, 65
Graphics Frame tool, 75
Graphics:
anchoring, 179
as repeatable objects, 171
CGM, 161
defined as an object, 45
EPS, 161
organizing, 156
scaling, 171, 175
WMF, 161
wrong method to insert, 170
Grayscale:
color model, 169
conversion, 24

H

Hardware:
purchasing, 323
selecting, 6
Header:
choosing fonts, 100
creating, 73, 78
different from headings, 134
in page layout level, 42, 43
running, 43, 74, 79

Headings:
assigning styles, 99
choosing fonts, 100
color and capitalization, 132
examples of great, 128
keeping with next paragraph, 134
paginating, 134
paragraph tag, 129
rules, 133
subheadings, 131
using spot color, 133
Help:
context-sensitive, 57, 299
Helvetica, 44, 129, 140, 244, 249
Helvetica Inserat, 129, 147
Helvetica Neue, 50, 126, 255, 282
Hierarchy. *See* Object layers
Home office benefits, xvi
HP CMS Trakker, 314
HP LaserJet, 300
HSC Software Corporation, 321
HTML, 315
Hyphenation:
enabling, 50
using, 50

I

Image Club Graphics Incorporated, 321
ImagePals:
Album, 24
current version, 8
Image Editor, 24
purchasing, 319
Screen Capture, 24, 45
Index:
creating an entry, 145, 148, 151
generating, 33, 145, 278
group titles, 147
prime entry, 146
rules for, 143
use of reference page, 85
using See, 146
using See also, 146
when to write, 147
Insertion point, 68
Integrated Media, Incorporated, 322
Integration:
with other applications, xvi
Internet, 316
Italics, 144

J

JPEG, 166

K

Kai Power Tools, 321
Keeping:
    with next paragraph, 134, 181
Kerning, 96, 260
Keyboard:
    representing keys, 50, 51
Keycaps, 51
Keywords, 49
Knockouts, 225
KPT Convolver, 321

L

Layer:
    graphics and table, 45
    overrides, 46
    page layout, 42
    paragraph, 43
Letter Gothic, 50
Linotronic 630 imagesetter, 300
Localizing documentation, 20
LZW compressed images, 169

M

Management:
    role of, 12, 27
Manual:
    benefits of writing, 2
    creation, 10
    importance, 4
    including the revision number, 27
Margins:
    setting, 62, 67
    viewing the number, 87, 88
Marketing:
    approving documentation, 39
    documentation reporting into, 12
    organization, 14
    reviewing documentation, 22
    role, 22, 56
Masks, 198
Master page:
    defined, 41, 59
    switching, 73
Menu command:
    documenting, 50
    taking a screen capture, 52
    using a table to show, 52
Micrografx, Incorporated, 319
Microsoft:
    manual (quality of), 146
Milestone:
    alpha, 11
    beta, 12
    concept, 11, 20
    post mortem, 12
    proposal, 11
    release, 12
    specification, 11
Mirrored headers and footers, 72, 78
Monospaced text, 50, 119
Monotype fonts, 321
Monotype Typography Incorporated, 321
Mosaic, 174, 177

N

NADTP Journal:
    subscribing, 322
National Association of Desktop Publishers, Incorporated, 322
Network, xvi, 6, 313
Numbered lists, 125
Numbering. *See* Paragraph tag
Numbering:
    automatic, 127

O

Object layers, 40
Object Linking and Embedding. *See* OLE
Object Selection tool, 63, 185
Object-oriented document design, xix
OLE, xvi, 165, 170
OLE, pitfalls of, 162
Omray Incorporated, 322
On-line help. *See* Help
Optima, 139, 147
Outline:
    deriving from table of contents, 39
    sample, 40
Out-of-Context terms, 49
Overprint:
    graphics, 216
    text and table text, 236

P

Packaging:
    designing the, 22
    documentation impact, 2
    optional manuals, 3
Page count:
    determining, 58
    estimating, 39, 311
    impact on customers, 23
    making even for chapter, 61
    making it even, 64
    perception, 58

Page layout:
     appendix, 34
     attributes, 60
     break, 134
     deleting, 87
     double-sided, 61, 87
     layer, 42
     overview, 33
     preface, 34
     repeated objects, 43
     setting, 62, 67
     verifying, 87
Page numbers:
     creating, 75
     in page layout level, 43
     in the footer, 75, 80
     restarting, 86
     setting the first in a chapter, 64
     setting the format, 64, 69, 86
Page size:
     determining, 22, 56, 57
     determining best, 38
     setting, 62, 67
     typical, 37
Painter:
     purchasing, 319
Palatino, 46, 129
Pantone color model, 76, 81, 223
Paper:
     as the medium, 2
     thickness and quality, 23
Paperbacks. *See* Binding
Paragraph style. *See* Paragraph tag
Paragraph tag:
     basing one on another, 99
     body text, 116
     creating from an existing paragraph, 107
     defined, 44
     headings, 135
     keeping with figure, 183
     lists and run-ins, 124
     redefining attributes, 244
     removing, 109, 115
     sample names, 44
     special, 120
PCX, 166
Photoshop:
     creating a shadow using, 197
     creating bitmap images, 45
     current version, 8
     example of a color manual, 298
     for imaging, 24
     purchasing, 319

Pick tool, 81
Picture Publisher, 319
Placement of object, 89
Positioning the paragraph on a page, 245
Postscript:
     doing a sample print, 274
     for printing the publication, 315
     print file, 26
     printing, 215, 300
     supported by printshop, 44
Prepress, xvi, 57
Printers:
     different results, 220
Printing:
     methods, 299
     overview, 10
     spot color, 298
     the publication, 305
Printshop:
     binding, 36
     problems encountered, 26, 27
     quality, 312
     submitting final proofs, 34
     supporting TrueType, 44
     supporting Type 1, 44
     testing for PC literacy, 25
     watching costs, 134
Process:
     documentation, 9
Product development process. *See* Milestone
Product management. *See* Marketing
Production:
     defined, 57
Programmer code:
     documenting, 52
Programmer reference manuals, 48, 131
Promotional material, xvii
Publication:
     adding chapter, 85
     backing up, 312
     creating, 66
     managing, 84
     notes, 85, 88
     opening, 70
     printing, 297
     saving, 65, 70
Publish magazine:
     subscribing, 322

Q

Quality assurance:
     organization with, 13
     reviewing documentation, 15, 22

QuickAccess bar, 253
Quotes:
    curly, 90, 92

R

Ragged right alignment, 50
RAM requirements, 7, 78
Reference approach:
    benefits, 48
    using, 47
    Xerox Ventura example, 48
Reference marker:
    consistency of placement, 144
    creating, 148, 152
    inserting, 145
Reference page:
    overview, 85
    See Also FrameMaker
References:
    updating all, 149, 153
Registration marks, 5
Revision number. *See* Documentation revision number
RoboHelp, 318
Rotation, 75
Rules:
    guidelines, 134
    in headings, 133
    in paragraph, 133
Run-in paragraph, 125, 126
Running header. *See* Header

S

Sales:
    approving documentation, 39
    impact of documentation, 3
    organization, 14
Sans serif:
    defined, 100
    used in headings, 129
Saving:
    automatic, 90, 93
    chapter, 64, 69
    publication, 65, 69
Screen capture:
    auto-numbering, 167
    fundamentals, xvii
    using, 167
See (and See Also). *See* Index
Selecting a DTP program, 8
Serif:
    defined, 100
    used in body text, 129

SGML, 315
Shadows:
    adding to a graphic, 196
    why use them, 169
Shapeware Corporation, 8, 320
Sidehead:
    creating, 62
    in page design, 38
    in page layout layer, 42
    leaving room, 131
    paragraph tag, 138, 140
    part of guideline, xvii
    using for notes, 51
Smart Selection tool, 62, 75, 87
Snap to guides, 89, 91
Software recommendation, 24
Software:
    selecting, 7
Space:
    em, 49, 126
    en, 49
    thin, 49
Spacing:
    between characters, 261
Specifications:
    to the printshop, 310
Spell checking, 274
Spot color, 22, 56, 71, 76, 80, 83, 126, 131, 274, 298, 311
StoneSerif, 100, 122, 244, 255
Storyboards:
    overview, 39
Style sheet:
    creating, 70
    overview, 35
    saving, 116
Style:
    benefits, 31
    impact of DTP, 32
    overview, 31
Subheadings. *See* Headings
Survey:
    NADTP platform, 5
    Publish magazine hardware, 7
System crash:
    handling, 66

T

Tab stops, 75
Table numbering, xvii
Table of contents:
    generating, 33, 288
    use of reference page, 85
    using headings to generate, 130

Table:
    caption, 121, 122, 123
    choosing fonts for, 100
    numbering, 122
Tag. *See* Paragraph or Character tag
Task approach:
    benefits, 48
    FrameMaker example, 48
    using, 47
Task:
    creating, 51
    paragraph tag, 138, 140
Team:
    agreeing to documentation, 39
    meetings, 17
Technical publications. *See* Documentation
Technical support. *See* Customer support
Tekton, 51, 122, 138, 140, 185, 257
Template:
    defined, 34
    persistence, 35
    saving, 87
    updating the publication, 87
Text flow:
    defined in FrameMaker, 63
    defined in page layout level, 42
Text Frame tool, 75
Text:
    attributes, 96
    color, 96
    size, 96
TextPlus:
    used for graphics, 45
Thumbnail:
    of graphic, 158
TIFF, 166, 169, 170
Times, 96, 100, 129, 139, 263
Times New Roman, 274
Times Roman, 44
Title:
    paragraph tag, 138, 140
Top ten guidelines, 26
Translating manuals. *See* Localizing documentation
TrueType:
    printshops and, 44
    provided by Windows, 44
    used in final printing, 156, 274
Type 1:
    printshops and, 44
    purchasing, 321
    used in final printing, 156, 274
    when to use, 97

Type On Call, 321
Typesetting:
    overview, 10
Typographic symbols:
    typing, 90
    typing in, 93

U
Ulead Systems, Incorporated, 8, 319
Unresolved references, 150, 154
User interface, 4, 57
Utopia, 99

V
Variable:
    using in header, 73
Ventura. *See* Corel Ventura
Visio:
    current version, 8
    drawing in manuals, 24
    for basic drawing, 162
    overview, 163
    purchasing, 320
    used for graphics, 45

W
Watermark:
    inserting, 275
White space, 57
Windows Metafile, 161
Windows:
    DTP market, 4
    Windows 95, xix, 5
WMF, 166, 221
Word processing:
    using with DTP, xvii, 24, 27, 59
WordPad:
    keeping track of styles, 100
    using for notes, 88
Writer:
    accountability, 16, 27
    contracting, 20
    equal status, xviii, 14
    handling of changes, 16
    understanding of product being documenting, 14

Z
Zapf Dingbat, 46, 122, 123, 126, 140
zApp application framework:
    use of HTML, 316